Jan Sokol

Thinking about Ordinary Things
A Short Invitation to Philosophy

CHARLES UNIVERSITY
KAROLINUM PRESS 2017

CATALOGUING-IN-PUBLICATION – NATIONAL LIBRARY OF THE CZECH
REPUBLIC

Sokol, Jan
Thinking about ordinary things : a short invitation to philosophy / Jan Sokol. – 1st
English ed. – Prague : Karolinum Press, 2013
Published by: Charles University
ISBN 978-80-246-2229-3

101 * 101.8
– philosophy
– philosophical thought
– lectures

100 – Philosophy [5]

Contents

Introduction   7

1. Philosophy: between Science, Art and Myth   11

2. How We See and Hear   19

3. Perception and Attention   25

4. Things, Words and Names   28

5. Language and Thought   36

6. Man in the World   44

7. Holiday and Everyday, Myth and Logos   52

8. You and I   59

9. Action and Freedom   64

10. Play   70

11. Language as Play   75

12. Time   80

13. Science and Knowledge   88

14. Truth   101

15. Scale and Ratio   108

16. Likeness and Imitation   115

17. Life   122

18. Nature   129

19. Necessity and Chance   135

20. Technique and Technology   140

21. Society, Institutions and State   148

22. Values and Money   157

23. Custom and Society   167

24. Morality and Ethics   173

25. Law   181

26. Text and Interpretation   188

27. The City   194

28. History 200
29. What Happens in History? 210
30. Civilisation, Culture, and Religion 218
31. Tolerance and Pluralism 226
32. Man and the World 233

Introduction

For the study of philosophy is not that we may know what
men have thought, but what the truth of things is.[*]

This book is based on a series of lectures for an Introduction to
Philosophy course, primarily aimed at students of other subjects which
share some common ground with philosophy. But it can serve equally as
an introduction to the colourful world of philosophy for students and
teachers of that subject, as well as for the general reader.

Like many other subjects, philosophy today is a multifaceted and
diffuse subject. No one person can possibly read all the journals
and publications that exist and as a result philosophical discussion has
broken off into various schools and circles, becoming more opaque, and
harder to teach, in the process. For that reason, I have sought to avoid
the traditional 'history of philosophy' approach, preferring to come
at this introduction to philosophical problems from a different angle.
Although I am sure that the history of philosophy will continue to occupy
a fundamental place in the teaching of philosophy *per se*, I believe it does
not serve especially well as a method of introducing the subject to the
student of today. I will try to explain why this is.

The history of philosophy represents a tremendous amount of
valuable positive knowledge, which can be taught, interpreted and
examined. But this can lead the beginner to suppose, falsely, that
philosophy is, like other sciences, basically a volume of knowledge. As
the botanist is concerned with plants, the philosopher is concerned with
philosophers, the development of their thought and their disputes
with each other. If, in the exposition of the enormous bulk of the

---

[*]   Thomas Aquinas, *De Coelo, Commentarius*, 1.22.

historical material, no place remains for the opinions and convictions of at least some philosophers, the whole point of philosophical research and discussion will be lost. All that will be left is a list of names, biographical data and wise sayings ('You can't step into the same river twice', 'Know thyself', 'I think therefore I am', 'God is dead') which may serve well as rhetorical flourishes, but which have no value as a tool to help us think critically about life and the world. In this way, philosophy could easily become a closed discipline for experts who have learned it all and who simply carry on their investigations along these closed lines. But then why would we bother students of other subjects with it?

Encouraged by some positive recent developments, I have attempted an introduction to philosophical thought which is based on philosophical topics and themes. Its method is a sort of phenomenology, by which I mean a close-up analysis of our experience, but as far as possible expressed in plain language, without resorting to jargon. Let me nail my colours to the mast straight away: I named the Czech version of this book *Malá filosofie člověka*, which would translate as *A Short Philosophy of Man*. As we shall see, it does not deal solely with man or woman *per se*, but human experience, actions, knowledge and thought are the starting point. As opposed, for example, to the philosophy of science or the philosophy of language, our focus here is on humans as physical beings in the world, as historical, social and moral persons.

In this way, we shall be able to point to the relations between philosophy and other branches of human intellectual effort – mainly science, but also art, technology, law and religion. The goal which I have followed throughout is to show the omnipresence of philosophical questions and to encourage students of other subjects to *think philosophically*. For this reason I make only limited reference of such classic philosophical themes as being and consciousness, or spirit and matter. I hope that I have not lost sight of the heart of these themes in my lectures; it is just that they may appear under different headings. On the other hand, I have been bold enough to include several excursions into the realms of other subjects, such as linguistics, history, sociology and law; although naturally my work in these areas is that of a mere dilettante.

After many years of teaching, it has became clear to me that the danger of a relatively accessible text is that it can be read without a great deal of thought, so that the content of the book flows over the reader like water. For this reason I have included several questions at the end of each chapter. They relate to the preceding content, but the reader cannot find the answer in the text alone – he has to think for himself.

I need hardly add that I will be sincerely grateful for any criticism. That the book continues to need it after six Czech editions is not in doubt. On the contrary, to the extent that the book has any value, this is largely down to the contributions of others – most of all Zdeněk Pinc, who inspired me to attempt this book – to colleagues and students who read through the book patiently, pen in hand, and many others, alive and dead, who have through the years offered me the pleasure of philosophical conversation and also much food for thought. If I attempted to name some of them, I would certainly forget to name others.

Prague, October 2012

1. Philosophy: between Science, Art and Myth

Art, religion and philosophy differ only in form;
their purpose is the same. (Hegel)

When we are hungry or in dire need of something, we can hardly talk or think about anything else. When we have toothache, when we are scared, or rushing somewhere, conversation stops altogether. But occasionally it might happen that we are in no dire need of anything, and we are in no particular rush to get anywhere, and in those moments philosophy may become possible. Or then again it may not – such free moments can be used in various ways. Often our first thought is to just 'kill time', perhaps by reading a newspaper, solving a crossword, or watching television. And before we know it, it is gone. Why do we seek to 'kill' this free time? For exactly the same reason as we would kill a lion or a snake: we are afraid of it. After all, free time is not as straightforward as we might think. We find ourselves alone with our own company. And this can quickly become intolerable for those of us who do not know how to deal with our own company. We are like a chain-smoker who runs out of cigarettes on Sunday evening when the shops are shut; we feel something akin to withdrawal symptoms. It is a blend of anxiety and boredom. So we bite our nails or drum our fingers on the table. We would dearly love to kill that time – but we don't know how. If only it could be Monday already.

The ancient Greeks had a word to describe this stretch of free time, when we do not have to be anywhere and are lacking nothing – they called it *scholé*. The Romans adopted this word, and everyone else in turn from the Romans, until from *scholé* came our modern word *school*. So *school*, however ironic it may sound, ought to be a place we enjoy going to, where we don't need to hurry, or be afraid of anything, a place where we have the time and leisure to think. But have you ever seen a school that looked like this? I certainly haven't. And yet this is how every school should be. How is this possible? How could it happen that from free time devoted to thinking, from *scholé*, we could end up with *school* – a place where pupils and teachers irritate and bore each other, or worry about exams? If we were to look for a modern equivalent of *scholé* it would be our holidays, the opposite of *school*. How did we reach this state of affairs?

Most likely it has something to do with the fact that there is an art to handling the free moments in one's life. To handle them in such a way that they are not lost to leisure pursuits, while at the same time ensuring that they are not empty, dull or irksome. The people best equipped to manage free time are little children, who are able to take pleasure in the most mundane things: a car passing by, an insect flying through the air, a stone lying on the ground. For the child, each one of these is an event. But over time, as they grow older, children become more used to such things – 'I've seen that, I've done that, it's no big deal'. And we adults provide them with powerful support in this direction: 'Not that car again.', 'OK, so there's a fly buzzing around – so what', 'Stop asking all those silly questions and watch where you're going or you'll fall over!'

And so here we are – 'watch where you're going or you'll fall over.' However strange it might sound, the history of philosophy begins with just such a trivial story, about the Greek philosopher Thales of Miletus. The story tells how he was walking across a courtyard looking so intently at the stars that he tripped over and fell into a well. He had to be rescued by a servant-girl, who mocked him for being so concerned with what was in the sky that he could not see what was at his feet. How Thales answered her, the story does not say. Most likely he was unable to think of a suitable response at that moment and was just glad to be out of the well. But he does not seem to have learned anything from his mishap. After all, if he had abandoned his interest in the stars and the mysteries of the world and simply learned to walk safely across courtyards, it is very unlikely that we would know anything about him today. There have always been plenty of people who know how to walk safely across courtyards.

We will most likely never know what Thales said to the girl. But an answer of sorts is to be found, two hundred years later, with the greatest Greek philosopher, Plato. The answer Plato gives is very surprising and may on the surface appear to be nonsense. He wrote that all philosophy begins in wonder. Now Plato was certainly a great philosopher, but did he not perhaps go a bit overboard here? Surely philosophy is the realm of kindly old eccentrics with long beards who have little interest in (or aptitude for) ordinary, practical things, people who puzzle their heads over questions which nobody else worries about. Is philosophy not something we associate with wisdom, and wise men? And are wise men not men who have seen it all, lived through it all and who can no longer be shocked by anything? And they should be expected to fall over themselves with wonderment and amazement at every little thing, like children? Surely not.

And yet is quite certain that Plato made this statement in all seriousness. Indeed it is possible that he was thinking of Thales' amazement at what was going on over our heads in the sky. Wait, something is going on in the sky? But isn't it just the same thing over and over again, day after day, year after year? Yes it is, and this is precisely what puzzled Thales, and his student Anaximander. From the dawn of time people everywhere have known that the sun comes up in the morning and goes down in the evening, that from sunrise until evening is day and after evening comes night, that evening comes after day and, after night, day again. People have always known that this is simply the way it has always been and always will be and that we have to arrange our affairs accordingly, so we do not end up stranded somewhere in the wilderness when the sun goes down. This is all so simple and natural to us that when we want to say that something is certain we use expressions like 'as sure as night follows day.'

But long ago, even before Anaximander, there were those who realised that there was nothing certain about it whatsoever. And it is those who think that there is any certainty in it who are the foolish ones. Of course, there is a stone lying on the path, it was there yesterday and no doubt it will still be there tomorrow, unless someone picks it up and carries it away. But the sun does not simply lie there like that stone. It is in constant motion, every minute somewhere else. It moves around like an animal, a living thing. It appears somewhere in the east each morning, then climbs higher up in the sky (even higher in the summer) then starts coming down towards the earth again until it finally sets in the evening, disappearing without a trace beyond the horizon. How does it manage to appear again the very next morning – and at the other side of the sky? Where has it been in the meantime? What happened to it? And will the same thing happen again tomorrow? Does it have to happen this way? And what if the sun fails to rise again tomorrow?

If the sun failed to rise again tomorrow, it would be the end of us all. And that is why, thousands of years ago, people started to concern themselves with why it rises. And because the sun's rising was a matter of some importance to them, they also concerned themselves with what needed to be done to ensure it continued to rise. The outcome of their observations and thoughts were the ancient myths. According to the Greek myth the sun is the fire chariot of the god Helios, who travels in it every day across the sky before going down into the sea and the underworld for the evening, where the fiery horses rest before Helios harnesses them to the chariot and rides them out again across the sky. And so that people don't come to take this for granted, the myth also tells of how Helios lent the horses to his son Phaeton. He was not able to control them, however, and the horses took fright, killing the boy. From this time on, Helios knows that he must not lend anyone else his chariot, and so it is certain that he will ride out with them tomorrow, just like yesterday and every day for thousands of years. However, if people were to cause any kind of offence to Helios – who knows what could happen?

Thales' servant most likely heard a story like this in her childhood, and remembered that as long as she behaved respectfully towards Helios, he would come out with his chariot every day, and that there was no need to worry her head about the sun coming up tomorrow. Thales himself probably heard this story as well, but for some reason it struck him as unsatisfactory. Perhaps this was because he had also heard other myths which explained the rising of the sun in some other way. Or perhaps it struck him as peculiar that such an important function should be dependent on one individual – even if he was one of the immortal gods. Does the very regularity of the sun's course through the sky not suggest that something else will be behind it?

We today are unable to read the myth of Helios and Phaeton as anything other than a fairy tale, a more or less entertaining story for children, but one which we would be foolish to take seriously. Like Thales' servant, we do not concern ourselves with whether the sun will rise again tomorrow. And when our own children ask us about it, we will tell them something very different. It will be less entertaining and harder to understand, there will be all sort of difficult concepts and words like 'gravitation', 'momentum' and 'planetary system' involved. We will have to explain to them that it is actually the earth, not the sun, which is moving, although it doesn't seem like that. The servant would laugh heartily at this account, just as we laugh at the story of Phaeton.

But there is a certain difference between the two. These days we have far more knowledge about the stars, the earth and the sun; we have a level of detailed knowledge that would have made Thales' jaw drop. Even those of us who paid no attention to astronomy at school know that there are whole books about it, and that there are people who devote every waking hour to studying, measuring and contemplating the sun. We call these people scientists. And these scientists would perhaps be able to explain to Thales and Anaximander why the sun comes up every day, and even predict to the second when it would occur. They would be able to tell them the life span of our sun, where it gets its energy from, how old it is – a whole host of incredible, and more or less useful, information.

But would they be able to explain all this to people like Thales' servant? Hardly. They would most likely dismiss the scientists outright before they even had a chance to speak. Anything they tried to teach them about the sun would go in one ear and out the other. So a good astronomer, able to give understandable explanations, could have useful conversations with Thales and Anaximander, with Plato and with the youngest children – but they would draw a blank with the people like Thales' servant. Scientists, philosophers and little children – is this not a peculiar group? It might seem so at first sight. But we need only remember Plato's statement about the beginning of philosophy and it all falls into place; these are all people who are capable of experiencing wonder.

There is another, fairly simple, connection between philosophy and science. Just as Thales' interest and uncertainty gave rise to astronomy, much of what we call science has grown out of questions which were originally philosophical in nature. Throughout its whole history philosophy has been a kind of seed-bed of the sciences, a kind of 'Technology Park' dedicated to cultivating the conditions in which science can become possible. In the modern world, science constitutes an entire branch of human activity, employing millions of people. And like any other type of work, it is possible to view it as just work, a way to earn a living. But in our consideration of the dialogue between Thales and the scientist, we of course had in mind a scientist for whom science is something more than just a job. Only such a scientist could understand the questions of a child (or of a philosopher) and answer them in a way that they would be understood. They are able to do this because their science retains inside it something of the philosophy from which it sprang: the ability to understand and the ability to experience wonder.

We have seen that philosophy also developed out of something. The questions that philosophers asked – like, for instance, if and why the sun will come out tomorrow – had previously been answered by myth.

And so as science is the child of philosophy, philosophy is the child of myth. As we know, relations between parents and children are often confrontational; the fifteen-year-old child seeks to break away from his parents, to be different from them, to stand on his own two feet. There are similarities to this in the relationship between myth, philosophy and science. Science, which came last, often seems like it wishes to disown its mother. Her wise old words sound hollow. Just leave behind all this philosophy, it seems to say, and try for once to invent something, measure something, prove something – like us scientists.

And so, by a process of historical justice, philosophy has received the very same treatment it once meted out to myth. This adolescent rebellion against myth is represented by the great flowering of Greek philosophy. The Greek philosophers were merciless in their exposure of the shortcomings of myth. According to them, myth was simply spouting nonsense, and was completely unable to provide reasons for the conclusions it drew. Myth was incapable of distinguishing between the truth and mere fancy. It forced a certain view of the world on people and prevented them from understanding how things actually are. This is what led Heraclitus to the judgement that Homer ought to be expelled and flogged.

And yet, true as all this may be, there is a certain superficiality to it. It hides a far deeper similarity, the fact that there is something very profound that connects myth, philosophy and science: wonder and amazement about the world, about the way things are. This fundamental ability, to see things that the majority of people do not see and to feel wonder in the face of them, is common to all three – myth, philosophy and science – and it is also shared by art. Along with philosophy, art has its wellsprings in myth. Unlike philosophy, however, art has never been ashamed of this origin. But unlike art, philosophy and science have made one significant step forward. After all, it is not enough simply to wonder at the world in which we live; man has also been endowed with the power to think, to contemplate and to evaluate – what we traditionally call reason. Therefore it behoves man to attempt to somehow understand, and communicate, what he has seen. And it is this attempt at understanding and explaining, in a way that others can understand, that separates philosophy and science from art and myth.

And so it is in the space between science, art and myth that philosophy has found its home. There have been entire periods in history where people have got by without philosophy. These were calm times, when nothing much was changing in the world, and people made do with the wisdom that had been passed down from their grandparents. When they could happily walk about their courtyards, devote themselves to running their farms, and the only thing to watch out for was that they didn't go falling into wells. However there have also been other periods in history, when everything seems to be changing, when suddenly children no longer understand their parents and parents no longer understand their children. At such times we have no option but to think, and to find new questions to ask, and new answers to these questions, because the old answers no longer tell us anything. Not that we no longer understand them, but they no longer interest us. Not that we regard the old questions as incorrect, but they are no longer our questions. It was in precisely this kind of period that myth first arose, before giving rise to philosophy and philosophy in turn to science. And it is in precisely this kind of period that we find ourselves today. We do not know where we are meant to be headed. And people who do not know where they belong on this earth are easy prey for demagogues, who will tempt them with all sorts of 'answers' and who can drive them to commit the most awful acts. In the 20th century we saw this over and over again. And it was in part because, in all their rushing around to keep themselves comfortable, people did not find time to think.

And it is for this reason that we need to learn to think, so that we do not fall for false promises in this way again. Now, one can learn to think in two ways. One can learn in the way one learns history; that is, to listen and read about all the interesting things that have happened in the world. Or one can learn in the way one learns to swim or play the piano – that is, by actually doing it. Thinking, by which I mean philosophy, can be done in both ways. One can learn about what the ancient (and not so ancient) philosophers have had to say – that is, learn the history of philosophy. This can be extremely worthwhile and interesting, but it has one shortcoming. The history of philosophy can all too easily become no more than the mindless accumulation of facts – names, dates, mottos and 'famous thoughts'. And in the process the most important thing gets lost – one does not learn to think. It is for that reason that we will attempt the other route here. We will learn to think by thinking about things. We have chosen many important themes that we will learn to ask questions about. All these themes are fairly plain and straightforward, and at first glance may not even appear to be worth talking about. We will aim to prove that this is a mistaken belief. It is in the most ordinary, everyday things that the greatest mysteries are hidden. You would have to be a dull and unobservant person to think that life's mysteries can only be gleaned by exotic travel or the ingestion of certain drugs. If you cannot see secrets and mysteries in the here and now, you will not find them in Tibet either. But if you have learned to see them, then you have learned to think philosophically.

It is the rock-solid belief of all philosophers throughout history that philosophy is the most beautiful thing in the world. But like any meaningful human activity, it cannot be done in a sloppy, cack-handed manner. It demands time, and it demands it all to itself. You cannot philosophise while watching television. You have to dedicate yourself to it. To think philosophically calls for a clear head, concentration, honest endeavour, stamina and curiosity. But, as philosophers will tell you, it has never let anyone down.

Questions:

- Do you know any myths? What are they about? What are they trying to tell us?
- What is the difference between myth and fairy tales?
- How is myth connected to poetry and literature and theatre?
- How did philosophy separate itself from myth and what did it criticise about myth? Was something important lost in this separation?
- How does science differ from philosophy? What questions does it ask? What do these questions deal with? Is there anything these questions ignore?
- Try to compare a philosophical account and a scientific account of the same thing, for example the sun, the earth, or man.

2. How We See and Hear

To comprehend what is, is the task of philosophy.
(Hegel)

We have said that it is possible to philosophise anywhere and about anything. So where do we start? With whatever happens to be in front of us at this moment? We will get to that soon enough, but let us go back one step further – what is it that we have in front of us, and how do we see it? How do we see? Surely that is no kind of question at all. We have two eyes that function like television cameras, giving us a stereoscopic picture of our surroundings. We have ears and we hear sounds, pressure waves in the air. Then we have smell and taste, which in humans do not play as great a role as they do for animals, except when we are eating, and then finally we have touch, with which we experience the surfaces of objects. We have a certain sense of orientation, we know up from down, we have a sense of balance – and that is about it. We have a nervous system which carries information through the body, and finally we have the control centre, the brain, which processes all this information like a computer.

This is roughly what we learned in school and this is how we think of it ourselves – if we bother to think about it at all. For the most part we are too engaged in the business of living to devote much time to such things. But at this moment we are attempting to philosophise – that means that we do have some time. Let us start with the most common and least mysterious of all the senses – sight. We know a great deal about how the eye works and we also know something about how visual information is received, transported to the brain and processed there. We know that for human beings sight is the most important of the senses, the one that receives and processes the most information. It is for this reason that the verb 'to see' has such a wide range of meanings. We can say 'I'd love to see Paris' rather than having to say 'I'd love to travel to Paris'. And if we argue with somebody about something and we turn out to be right we can say 'See? I was right.'

But what is it that we actually see? That is another question. We see what we have in front of us, what we look at. We notice multi-coloured dots as the lens transmits images to the retina. But wait – something is not right here. What the lens transmits to the retina can certainly be described as multi-coloured dots of various shapes, some lighter, some darker. But when we open our eyes we do not see dots, but rather things, objects. Even when we look at an inkblot on paper, we have a tendency to see things in it – one person may see an animal, another may see a car, a third may see a pear, and so on. There are various psychological tests which are based on this. It is only on those rare occasions when we find ourselves looking at something that we know nothing about and which, unlike our inkblot, does not seem to fall naturally into any kind of shape, that we can say that we see nothing but dots or smudges. This may happen if we are looking at an X-ray or a complex electrical schema. In such situations we could just as well say that we see nothing at all. What are all these dots and smudges for? Can we learn anything from them? Are we able to say anything about them? On the other hand an experienced doctor would not see dots but perhaps a spinal fracture. This is not because his eyesight is so much better than ours – he sees the same dots and smudges that we do – but because he has been trained to see fractures in them. Probably in the same way that we learned to see things in our bedroom when we were children.

So from coloured dots on the retina all of a sudden we have objects. We also see them in two-dimensional photographs. Where did they come from? Let us use another example. I walk into the kitchen and I see that the table is set for dinner. On the table are plates and I can see immediately that they are round – even though the retina sees them as elliptical. The table in front of me is a right-angled oblong, even though I see it as a trapezoid. You may well say that this is simply due to the distortion caused by perspective. But if nobody had told me that, I would always have had the impression that I am really *seeing* it as right-angled. I cannot possibly be removing perspective distortion as in projective geometry – anyone who has tried that can tell you how much work is involved. So we are not carrying out any such correction, at least not consciously, but we see the plate as round and a piece of paper as oblong.

You walk into a school classroom and you see tables and chairs. You could easily count how many there are if anyone asked you. Only when you start paying close attention do you notice that you cannot see any of the chairs whole. A part of the backrest sticks out above the table, a part of the leg is visible beneath it. But this would not cause you the slightest difficulty in your task of counting the chairs. It would not even occur to you to count the different parts of the same chair as two separate chairs. You simply know, beyond any doubt, that the armrest and the legs are part of one and the same chair, even though you cannot see the bit in between.

But this simple 'operation', the like of which we carry out a hundred times a day without even needing to think about it, turns out to be anything but simple. This revelation was brought home to us when scientists tried to get a computer to replicate it. You have probably heard of industrial robots. There are also more complex robots, which have within them TV cameras and computers, whose job it is to figure out what is in front of it. Among experts this is known as the 'scene'. And to the great surprise of the scientists, it was discovered that it is extremely difficult for the robot to distinguish the 'scene' from a collection of multi-coloured dots. It turns out that the robot is only able to distinguish a small number of objects, and even then only when they had very simple shapes – cubes, cylinders and pyramids. If there is a larger number of objects in the scene, or if they have more complex shapes, the robot is entirely unable to cope with this task. Even a computer must somehow 'know' in advance what it can expect to see in its environment. The dots on their own are not enough.

For the most part we operate in the environment that we know. Even if we go into a stranger's house or to another town, the things we see strike us as familiar. So the act of 'seeing' is for the most part made out of recognising objects that are already known to us. If we find ourselves face to face with something completely unknown, something we have never seen before, we instinctively try to compare it to something we know. When they first saw a train, Native Americans called it an 'iron horse', and when they first tasted hard drink, they named it 'fire water'. And for the same reason we to this day refer to the dispensers at petrol stations as 'pumps' and we call hand-held computer controllers 'mice'. We do this because 'seeing' consists mostly of recognising objects we know, rather than exploring what is unknown. This is also why we so often overlook and mistake things we know, a failing that makes possible all sorts of illusions, tricks and downright swindles. A fraudster makes a pile of pieces of paper cut to the size of banknotes, at the top and the bottom he places two banknotes of the right size, and then ties it all together with a band, just like bank clerks do. His victim 'sees' a wad of banknotes. On the theatre stage a few props and some painted canvas suffice to make the viewer 'see' a rustic cottage or the tropical rainforest. This may also help to explain why some white people may think that all Africans and Asians look the same (and the other way round, of course) – the white person is unable to distinguish between different faces, and sees only 'an African person' or 'a Chinese person'.

Proof-reading provides us with another good example of how we do not necessarily see what is projected onto the retina. If you do not have any training as a proof-reader, you will often simply fail to see spelling and other typographical mistakes (typos). You will read, 'correctly', what is meant to be there – even if there are letters missing or words are completely misspelt. Clearly this is not being caused by the lens or the retina. If you are unfortunate enough to have impaired vision, you are bound to have difficulty reading – but that will be the case whether the words are spelled correctly or not. The instinctive 'correction' of misspelt words and other typos is further proof of how we often 'see' only what we are meant to see, or indeed what we want to see.

Now to hearing. We have been taught that one hears sounds. Fair enough.

You are sitting at an open window and someone walks past you whistling 'Yellow Submarine'. Let us assume that you are not a musician and know nothing about notes. You would not be able to write the musical notation for 'Yellow Submarine' and you don't know what key it is in. So you are not hearing or recognising individual notes – it is 'Yellow Submarine' that you are hearing. You would recognise it even if it was transposed into a higher or lower key from the original. You would recognise it even if you did not hear it right from the start. However, a song like 'Yellow Submarine' lasts a few minutes and, strictly speaking, it is not possible to 'hear' it all – from moment to moment we can hear only one note or chord. And yet, we do not listen in such a way that we have to remember every note that has gone before. We simply hear and recognise the song as a whole. Let us take another example. Next door a boy is learning to play the piano. He is playing 'Frère Jacques' over and over, and each time he plays the same wrong note in the third bar. When you hear this mistake for the fifth time in a row, you are almost ready to hit the ceiling. Why do we react so strongly? As the boy has never played it properly, how can we know that he is playing a wrong note? And why does it infuriate us so much?

A car is going along the street. It is moving quickly and yet I see it in sharp focus, not blurred as in a photograph. And I see the motionless street, the background in equally sharp focus – not like a photographer who sets up his lens to catch a sharp image of the car against a blurred background. How is it that I see movement, when from second to second the car is always 'somewhere' and film catches it in the same (motionless) way? Only when I look at the film do I see fluent motion – out of motionless pictures.

Our most important senses, sight and hearing, have very different characters. We can point our eyes in more or less any direction and we can even close them. In contrast, our hearing is omnidirectional and never shuts down fully, even during sleep. Our alarm clocks would never manage to wake us up if it did. Sight is the main active sense, whereas hearing is more of a 'defensive' sense. This is why our language gives us, alongside the verb 'to see', a further verb – 'to look at'. We can give 'penetrating stares' and 'glances'. In contrast to this, hearing is associated with paying attention and obedience ('listen to the teacher'). It is interesting to note in this regard that birds of prey have an especially highly developed sense of sight, whereas rodents and the other animals they are likely to prey upon live by their hearing. Sight is what creates our picture of the world around us whereas hearing is the sense of speech and language, of interpersonal communication. The other senses, smell, taste and touch are entirely different again. They are the 'short distance' senses, according to Kant. We cannot give even a rough estimate of the informational content of these senses, as we do not know how to measure it. They do not have anything like the significance of sight and hearing for humans but they give the world the stamp of reality. It is hard to believe in the existence of something that we cannot smell, taste or touch.

There is something eerie about the experience of watching a silent film or the television with the sound turned down – precisely because the people we are watching are 'dumb'. In the same way, there is something odd, even sinister, about hearing noises in the dark – even in the most familiar places. This is because there is no visual accompaniment to the sounds we hear. In normal circumstances, we do not notice sound and image separately – we experience them at the same time. One without the other strikes us as unnatural, sometimes comical and sometimes terrifying. This is why we are so sensitive to any 'disconnect' that occurs between sound and image, for example in a badly dubbed film.

Questions:

- Give some examples of situations where we 'cannot see anything'.
- What do we do in such a situation? How can we orient ourselves in it?
- What changes for us when we learn a new alphabet, like the Cyrillic or Hebrew alphabet? Do we see the same things?
- Notice the difference between live music and recordings and recordings of recordings. Why is it that some sounds bother us when listening to a recording when we would not even notice it in a live performance?
- We often hear people use the word 'unreal' – 'it was unreal', 'an unreal experience', etc. When and why do we say this? Have you ever experienced this for real? How did you deal with it?

3. Perception and Attention

Imagine that you are sitting at home, with a TV wedged amongst the books on the shelves on the wall opposite you. The TV is on but you are reading or doing something else. Suddenly there comes a piercing scream from the TV. You look at the screen and the picture grabs your attention and you start watching. After a while you may lose interest and say to yourself that there is 'nothing on', or you may become engaged in the story. If it is particularly attractive and thrilling, you will soon 'see' only what is happening on the screen – as if you yourself were a part of the action. And only once the detective story is over will you rub your eyes and see the shelves, the books and the TV again. But if you try to recall a scene from the film, it will appear before your eyes without these surroundings – although they surely were registered by your retina at the time.

When concentratedly examining some kind of minute object such as a coin, a postage stamp, an ant or a watch mechanism, we will hold it as close to the eye as possible: the eye has a very wide angle of vision. However our field of vision is still large even at 20 cm: about 60 cm x 30 cm. If I need to focus my attention on an even smaller area, the eye's optics will not help me there, as it does not feature a zoom and it cannot focus at a distance smaller that some 10–15 cm. On such occasions, the 'zoom' of fixed attention kicks in and performs real miracles. If you open, say, a wristwatch, you will see next to nothing at first. After a moment, you will find your bearings and start distinguishing certain shapes. And if you keep up your concentration, you may see minute details of less than a tenth of a millimetre in size. Just the sound of a telephone ringing will be enough to destroy the magic and you will have to start all over again. Although you will likely progress a bit faster the second time round, thanks to the previous experience.

Attention, that is the focusing of your aim at a specific part of your field of vision, probably also somehow governs the focusing of the lens. This is probably based on quite a different principle from the automatic focusing of a photographic camera. The eye does not emit any control beams. Perhaps it works on the basis of trial and error but certainly it happens subconsciously; we simply look here or there and the eye will focus automatically. Only when it cannot do this through loss of flexibility, does one need help in the form of glasses. Glasses do not 'do' anything though, they merely mechanically shorten or lengthen the focal length of the eye's lens.

Even in a noisy environment, we are able to follow what another person is saying, although their voice is many times weaker than the 'background' noise. If such a conversation is recorded, it becomes much more difficult to understand what is being said, while all the distracting noises gain more prominence. This is what makes sound recording such an art. In direct communication we probably employ other senses too. Lip-reading does not only aid the deaf; even a person with unimpaired hearing will understand better when able to watch the speaker's mouth move. We are able to separate a sound which is of interest to us from a concoction of various sounds. It can be one of the people speaking, an instrument in an orchestra, as well as a whistling or rustling noise which will help a mechanic diagnose a fault in an engine. How do we do this?

Perception is not a simple process. Any similarities with visual or sound recording are rather superficial. Our senses are more than just recorders or sensors and we are not recording devices, which would just faithfully record all sound and movement. Even as the act of perception is happening, we are very much able to filter what we will see and hear and what will become of the intrusive background noise. This selection does not in any way resemble the filtering mechanisms used by sound technicians: we do not operate on the basis of the sound's pitch or the direction it is coming from. With a bit of effort, we are able to have a conversation even in a very noisy environment – just as, on other occasions, we can overlook or mishear the most crucial thing. This is why we are so impressed by fictional detectives who excel in noticing that which everybody else has overlooked. A magician can use this to his advantage in his show, making a distracting gesture with his left hand, so that the audience do not notice him pulling a ping-pong ball from inside his sleeve with the right. Our focus, concentration and attention are clearly key here: in other words, that which I do or do not want to hear or see. Philosophers speak of 'intent' – we will return to this term later.

Our remarkable senses and the miracle of focus in particular, must have evolved in an environment quite different to the one we live in now. When we are outside, we tend to look to the distance and follow much larger objects than we do when, say, sitting at home reading. That is why so many city dwellers need glasses. Our gift of attention and focus also developed in an environment much poorer in stimuli. Just a hundred years ago, brightly coloured objects (say flowers, birds or gemstones) were a rarity. Most things were grey, brown or green. In addition, movement in nature tends to be the gentle movement of trees in the wind, of running water and clouds. A bird will fly by overhead or we may catch a glimpse of an animal. Nowadays, our environment hammers us relentlessly with countless stimuli. We have come to take advantage of the gift of perception – often against each other. Brightly coloured spaces, beautiful booming sounds, neon signs, all these draw our attention. It is not just billboards and commercials, but also newspapers and magazines, product packaging, clothing, perfume or makeup, all that can be used to vie for peoples' attention, while dulling the ability to perceive less aggressive impulses. The TV has become the climax of our day, the most effective attention-bait, reducing the viewer to a mere wisp of ever straining perception. Those who have grown fully accustomed to the levels of 'TV attention' can hardly be expected to pay attention to a reality much less bright and colourful, much slower moving and less thrilling. We might well end up like frogs who reportedly do not perceive immobile objects at all. And the providers of bright flickering eye-fodder will be able to manipulate us however they wish.

Questions:

- Pay attention to what you actually hear and see at a given moment.
- What attracts your attention the most?
- What does it mean to overlook something, to not notice it? What does it mean when we did not notice something, when we overlooked it?
- How can you tell if somebody's attention has been attracted by something?
- Describe how you navigate your way around a supermarket, in a bookshop, when leafing through a magazine?
- How does advertising hook us in?
- What will you do to attract somebody's attention?

4. Things, Words and Names

The man gave names to all livestock and to the birds
of the heavens and to every beast of the field. (Bible)

We have established that we see and perceive 'things' – we see a table, we see the sun in the sky, we hear the sound of an ambulance. Where do these 'things' come from? A TV camera does not recognise them, and robots find it extremely difficult. People, on the other hand, cannot help but see just that – things. Even if we cannot remember what a thing is called, we see 'this thing here' and we can point at it. If we look at a microphotograph, an X-ray or an abstract painting, we are, in a way, seeing 'nothing'. If we were to remember what we have seen or to describe it to someone else, we would first have to name the confusion of lines and colours for ourselves, dissect it into segments which would remind us of something, thus turning them into 'things'. It was in this way that constellations of stars were named many years ago and it still is how every child interprets the shapes that clouds make in the sky, stains on the ceiling or cracks in the plaster on the wall. Just think of how Europe used to be depicted in old maps, as a queen with Spain for a head, Italy her right hand – and Czechs to this day proudly declare themselves to be 'in the heart of Europe'.

In a familiar environment on the other hand, things simply 'jump out' from their surroundings: there is the table, the chair, the potted plant, the rug. Each of these things however contains parts which form the whole: a table has legs, a top and (sometimes) a drawer. Why do we see a table as a thing, and not each individual leg? This may be because all these parts are joined together – you can only move it from place to place as a whole. Also we can clearly identify the function of a table, why we need it and what for. Now a carpenter who makes tables most likely thinks of a table leg or a drawer as 'things'.

This is the environment to which we have been accustomed since childhood and where we have learned to understand the world – in other words, our home, where we view the arrangements as beautifully uncomplicated and straightforward. If someone asked me to describe what our kitchen looks like, I would immediately say there is a table, a cooker, a sink, a shelving unit, a fridge, three chairs, and a bench. Things which you can move, separate from their surroundings, regard individually. I might add the window, the light, the door, although these cannot be moved so easily. The list of things would definitely not be infinite or particularly 'subjective'. You could find a list like that on the wall of a hotel room; factories will have an inventory number for each 'thing' and the accounting department will have a copy of their list.

And what about the rest? The walls and the ceiling, are they 'things' too? Perhaps. And what if a young child notices a scratched surface on the cooker or a bit of fluff on the rug (something a grown-up will not notice)? What is that? 'Well – how can I explain it to you – it's ... nothing.' This answer is not as silly as it might seem at first glance. A scratch is really not a thing. And a bit of fluff? Is that a thing? It does not serve any purpose and it should not be on the rug in the first place. Just as when we are asked what's in the paper today, or what we did at work or school, we tend to reply 'nothing' – by which we actually mean 'nothing special', nothing worth mentioning, easy to label and describe. After all, the Greek *logos* mean word, as well as sense and reason. Even the word 'thing' does not simply mean that which you can grasp with your hands, but more importantly the thing which is of interest to us, the thing we focus on, the thing that is being talked about.

So there are a certain number of 'things' in the kitchen. That does not mean the place looks like some sort of warehouse. These things contain other things – there are hobs on the cooker, it has an integrated oven (which I cannot pick up and hold on its own), the table has a drawer with cutlery in it. Also, these things are arranged in a certain way, you can relate them to one another; they all occupy their designated space. The crockery shelf is over the sink, the unit containing bags of flour and sugar is above the fridge. Everything has its place and everybody understands what it means to 'tidy up'. And amongst all this, 'we', that is I, my wife and children, navigate our way around. We all have our favourite, or at least habitual, spots and if we need something, we know where to reach for it. 'Our kitchen' – that is not just a pile of things (what a mathematician might call a 'set') but also the sum of what they contain, the way they are arranged, the relations and spaces between them. The place where pots and cutlery go, the place where you do the dishes, Dad's favourite seat, the corner where the dog usually sleeps. Young children are very sensitive about maintaining this usual order of things and, likewise, elderly people dislike changes to it.

The environment in which we spent our childhood is where we first learned about things: what a table is, a chair, a grater, a tea towel. And incidentally, the table we sat at while learning all this, 'our table', will for many of us remain the very embodiment of a table, somehow more table-like than any other. As time went by, other 'things' started to emerge, some of them not as precisely separated from one another, ones which are less clearly outlined, impossible to pick up or move from place to place: the steps and the street, the tree, the garden and the wood, a cloud in the sky, a puddle and the pavement. And then there are 'things' which really need to be in inverted commas, for they are actually not things at all: wind and rain, heat and cold, morning and night, joy and anger. But by that time we already knew that to be able to talk about something, it has to have name – and so they, too, were named.

We learned quite early on that there is a similar table at Granny's house, that there are tables all over the place and that all of them really are tables. Suddenly, the word does not denote just one particular thing but a number of others and maybe all of them together, too. That is what we grown-ups then call a concept. A concept will mean more or less the same to all of us and in all situations: the word 'table' denotes a table not just when there is one right in front of us but equally when there are none and I ask somebody to 'bring over a table'. And geographers refer to a raised plateau as 'tableland'

When we were discussing how we see, we simply said that we see things. That is true, but only partly and in the most straightforward cases at that. We usually see things in a context, which will mostly be that of their function, what makes them useful to us. Otherwise we might not even notice them. So a chair is not just defined by a description of what it looks like but by the fact that we can sit on it. I will most likely notice it when I am looking for a place to sit down. But the very same chair can serve other purposes, too. We may have ridden it like a horse when we were children. If there is no table, I can put my plate on a chair. It can be used as a prop for exercising, or as a useful weapon in a pub brawl. A number of similar examples can be found. When I go into a cake shop, I do not see carbohydrates, I see cakes and pastries. I have come not to examine them but to satisfy my craving for something sweet. If

I overindulge however, I will lose my interest in them and I may even find the thought of them off-putting for a while.

A cake can change its meaning in other ways, too. If it gets dropped on the floor, it will suddenly become a mess, a piece of rubbish that some people might not want to touch. A scientist would have us know that it is still the same substance, just somewhat splattered, but it has acquired a new context and thus a new meaning. It is because young children chiefly perceive meanings that they can play with anything. A cardboard box can become a house, a bed, or a car – whatever it needs to be. A beautiful electric toy car, on the other hand, is far less universal and therefore also less usable. It could at a push become a table or a boat but it would serve that purpose a lot better if we first broke the wheels off.

It is an important fact that things can acquire different meanings and that it is meanings rather than things as such that we usually work with. This allows us to understand children's games as well as the poetic and symbolic use of things, theatre and religious symbolism – wherever everyday things can be used to mean something unusual, acquiring a different meaning. Culture and civilisation, however, also surround us with objects which only acquire their meaning through convention. If a policeman asks 'did you not notice anything?' to a driver who has just driven through a red light, he is not enquiring about the clouds, the trees or a good-looking woman walking past, he is referring to the cheerfully-coloured lights which tend to be found at traffic junctions. For they are not there for the amusement of passers-by, rather they carry a conventional meaning, such as 'stop'. And a flashing amber light on the left bumper is not a form of greeting to fellow drivers (although Prague tram drivers have come to use it as such), it is an expression of the driver's intention to turn left at the nearest available opportunity.

That we come to see the world largely through meanings can sometimes complicate matters. The very same thing can have different meanings to different people and we can only get the verification of the meaning from the person in question. Who knows if a matchbox is just a matchbox at a given moment, or whether it is a boat or a car. And even if you ask the child who is playing with it, you might not get a definitive answer. For children (and adults too) savour the chance to switch between multiple meanings. This forms the basis of many a joke. A lunatic is walking a toothbrush (whom he calls Rover) on a leash, calling on him to hurry up. A warden trained in psychology tries to start a conversation, asking how the dog is doing. Remaining aloof, the lunatic denies any knowledge of Rover – why, anybody can see this is just a toothbrush. Once the warden is out of earshot, the lunatic remarks over his shoulder: 'We fooled him today Rover!'

Such games with meanings and ambiguity are all very well but they are a hindrance when it comes to efficiently conveying precise information which has a particular purpose. That is why science, unlike everyday life, tries to find ways to 'tame' the meanings of words and introduce unambiguous terminology, independent of context and games we might play with them. If you think back to Rover, this might not seem so difficult; just strip the thing of its meanings and regard it as it is. But what is a toothbrush devoid of its purpose, i.e., to brush one's teeth? How would a native of the Brazilian rainforest see it? Or closer to home, look at almost everything growing in your vegetable garden – kale, cabbage, cauliflower, kohlrabi and goodness knows what else – from the botanical point of view, all of these are just cultivars of the same 'thing' the plant *Brassica oleracea* L., i. e., the wild cabbage. Try suggesting this to a greengrocer or a cook. On the other hand, all the plants which a gardener might dismiss with the word 'weed' will be scrupulously classified into dozens of species, genera and families by a botanist. Which one of them is right and what is the 'thing as such'?

We probably have to concede that both are different meanings of the same thing. Scientific taxonomy operates according to its own rules, which are independent of everyday contexts and sometimes (as we have just seen) in direct contrast to it. As science lavishes great and unfailing attention on the meanings of the terms it uses, their culinary or gardening usage may be rendered somewhat limited, but these meanings and terms are unambiguous (all good botanists will use the same term when shown a particular plant) as well as precise (said botanists will take good care to distinguish it from all the other manners of weeds). Older sciences, such as botany, which as a starting point based their observations on everyday experience, used already existing words, attributing to them a greater precision. This approach can however lead to a rift between the language of science and that of everyday use. Experience of such confusions has led science to rely on unusual or foreign words (borrowed from Greek or simply made up in physics, Latin words in botany and zoology), which prevents the possibility of such misunderstandings.

Using precise, unambiguous terms is a simple and effective way to navigate through a given field with the same ease as in our own kitchen, where most of us first came across the idea in the first place. The Czech writer Richard Weiner likens them to pins, as they help to hold things in their place. That is why each and every field of science must first of all make an inventory of its area, to demarcate its scope and introduce terms for everything within that scope. This is why you can easily distinguish an expert from a layperson. If you open the bonnet of a car, most of us might point to 'that round black thing down there', a mechanic will drily utter the magical word 'distributor'. A layman needs to have 'the thing' in front of him in order to point at it, whereas an expert will be able to correctly identify it in any circumstance. If you have never had to contend with an area where such a body of vocabulary is not yet available you will find it hard to appreciate just how helpful it is to have.

The effort of science to make terms exact and unambiguous makes them different in nature to the names and vocabulary of everyday life. First of all, the possibility of interchanging them should never arise. Areas such as law, government and administration have similar goals. In a nutshell, in ordinary discourse our chief aim is to know what we want to express and to successfully convey this to someone else. If my wife asks me to fetch a chair and I can only see a stool, I can assume what I am supposed to do or I can ask. It is not a problem that she was not 'unambiguous' about it. Science (like courts or administrative bodies) cannot and does not afford any such assumptions; their statements should be formulated clearly so they can be understood by everybody. This drives the effort to coin and define terms so that all ambiguity is eliminated. All relevant things can either be precisely listed or pointed out, or a precise definition can be created which will divide the whole world into two parts: chairs and non-chairs. A scientific term actually strongly resembles the intuitive concept of a mathematical set. While an ordinary word will emphasise the typical characteristics of a given object (a dog has four legs and barks; it is irrelevant that some dogs do not bark at all), a scientific or administrative term must state conditions and limitations. We can sometimes distinguish between the 'content' and 'scope' of a certain term. The scope tends to be the harder one to demarcate and it is rarely clear. An exception can be found in legal and administrative terminologies which factor it in: 'persons born between 1951–1962', 'permanent residents of Essex', or 'a company with 15–25 employees'.

There is a lot to be said for scientific terminology: it is succinct, exact and precise. Being more or less clearly defined saves a lot of talking and writing and the terms may be universally conveyed and explained – possibly because they do not draw on our subjective experiences. Let us use an example from botany again, a science which is not particularly abstract. In a botanical guide, a tree that we are able to recognise will be classified among vascular, spermatophytic, magnoliophyta, dicotyledonous plants and it might be described as follows: 'Small leaved lime (*Tilia cordata*) is a hardy, deciduous tree, the leaves are alternately arranged, stalked, rounded to triangular-ovate, 3–8 cm long and broad, mostly hairless except for small tufts of brown hair on the leaf vein axils. The small yellow-green hermaphrodite flowers are produced in clusters of three to sixteen in early summer with a leafy subtending bract.' This is certainly a thorough description. If you are confronted with a tree and you are not sure if it is a lime tree, this description will, supposing you know some basic botanical terms, help you identify it.

But if you had no idea what a lime tree was, this description would probably not be of much use to you. How would you even arrive at it? And why should you be interested at all, unless you are just about to sit a botany exam? Most of us know what a lime tree looks like but we have come to know it in a different way. Such as when walking through a park, we saw a beautiful and majestic tree. The sun was shining and the tree was in bloom. It gave off a beautiful smell and when we came a bit closer, we could hear the buzzing of swarms of bees attracted by the smell. And that was how we first learned what a lime tree was. Later, we got to see it in various guises, in the autumn, in winter, so now we can recognise it even when it has no leaves, from a distance, just by the shape of its crown and branches, its bark and roots. Then, if we are unsure or confuse two different trees, botanical descriptions can be very helpful. But not before then.

If you take a child to a river and show him a family of ducks, he will immediately grasp the concept and start asking relevant questions. Who is the mummy duck and daddy duck, where do they live, what do they eat and when do they go to bed? If you ask the child where the duck's bill is, he will without a moment's hesitation point at his own nose (and the majority of grown-ups would do the same). Where are the wings? He will flap his arms. This is precisely in accordance with evolutionary biology. The child has taken to the ducks and feels involved with them, because he has rightly guessed that there is a connection – and he focuses his questions in that direction. This is how people usually learn about new things – by comparing them to things they already know. A child will usually use his own self as a point of comparison. Science does not favour this particular method of exploration. It is referred to as anthropomorphism. As long as people were convinced there was no link between humans and animals, such objections were perhaps justified. Nowadays, however, we take it as a given that humans are a part of nature and that they share a great number of things with animals. And if that is so, why would it be wrong to learn about animals through what we have in common?

Questions:

- Think about all that we refer to as a 'thing'. Is there a common feature?
- We said that things sometimes 'jump out' from the surroundings. Could it sometimes be a problem? Why do soldiers wear camouflage?
- Have you ever had to give a name to something you were not familiar with?
- How did our ancestors deal with such situations? Can you find examples which would demonstrate this?
- In what circumstances could you say that a word is a "thing"?
- What is the difference between sign-things, such as traffic lights, and "ordinary" things in your kitchen?
- Explain some scientific terms and demonstrate how they could have been based on everyday experience (e.g., 'chord' in geometry, 'crane' in machinery, legal 'person', 'branch' of a graph).
- What is the difference between a definition of a term and its meaning in everyday language? Would you be able to give a definition of a table?
- Why would we sometimes talk about the "objective" meaning of a word?

5. Language and Thought

The boundaries of my language are the boundaries of my world. (Wittgenstein)

Things and meanings are rarely discussed outside philosophy, but we all learned about language as schoolchildren. We therefore have some theoretical notion of it, which we will now look at. First and foremost, we have learned to equate language with communication, the conveying of thoughts. That seems fair enough, albeit somewhat incomplete and one-sided. If I ask you the way or damn you to hell, I am not exactly conveying a thought. Secondly, we have made a connection between language and a set of grammatical rules, which will immediately spring to mind. But when we were first learning to speak, we did not learn any rules. These came later, once we were at school. When we speak, we should no doubt do so in a correct way; this however does not mean that we are able to construct our utterances based on these rules. Finally, many people's ideas about language are these days steeped in computing metaphors, such as programming 'languages', 'information', 'encoding', etc. So, in order to get closer to language, we must adopt a different approach.

Having just reached the summit of a high mountain, one will stand there 'wordlessly', as the Romantic poets would say. A strong experience or emotion, whether it be horrifying or beautiful, an idea, a thought, a discovery, all this is 'wordless' to begin with. Only once we have recovered from the initial impulse and we start thinking things over, will words come to the fore. For such an impression or idea is at first like a flash of lightning. It's all too much and all jumbled before our eyes, 'in the original', as Edmund Husserl calls it. And to digest it somehow, one must then attempt to unscramble the jumble piece by piece. But you cannot do this with an impression, or idea, you can only achieve it with the help of words and terms, Weiner's 'pins'.

We have said that an experience, just like a thought or an idea, contains everything at once. It is comprised of numerous things and ingredients, references to other things and connections to this and that. To think it all over and digest it then means taking these ingredients one by one, starting from one end (or beginning), independently of each other, yet keeping them connected, so that finally the whole fabric gets processed and strung together like beads. For only then can we start talking about this thing, let alone writing about it. And that is no mean feat. It is like journeying through a landscape place by place, without missing a spot while never passing through the same spot twice. I am sure you have all witnessed somebody having just experienced some strong emotion and as yet unable to relate this experience in an intelligible manner. They will mangle their words, gabble and get all muddled up, while nobody is quite able to follow what they are trying to say. Only when they have calmed down are they able to distinguish the more important facts from the less important ones, compose themselves, and relate their experience to someone else, for they themselves are just beginning to comprehend it.

Thinking does not start with us coming up with something and then needing words and terms to communicate it to others. It is not like encoding and dispatching a message. Thinking requires speech well before we start speaking and communicating. We need it to be able to 'articulate' the thing, to break it down and arrange it in some sort of sequence – what is the most important part, what comes first, what later. And only once a thought has been processed in this way does it deserve to be called a thought, for a great many brilliant ideas burst like a bubble during this first processing, they turn out to be no good, a mistake, or pure rubbish.

The journey which leads from an experience or an idea to a fully-fledged thought is long and requires a lot of hard work. This is equally so for a poet, a musician, a technician, or a philosopher. And only once this journey is at an end and the work is done, will it become clear whether it has been worth the bother. For an idea which we fail to articulate properly, may not have been worth much, but it is certainly of not much use to us. Einstein once said that a scientist's work consists of 10% talent and ideas, and of 90% effort and hard work. Thus every sort of creative work requires a certain mastery of appropriate language necessary for carrying out the aforementioned 90%. For a musician, this will be the language of musical sounds, the language of symbols for a mathematician, but for a philosopher – and for a poet alike – it is always the everyday, the natural language of words that we speak.

The language we speak has certain given and fixed rules. Not just spelling, but other, much more fundamental rules too. We speak in sentences and these consist of words. Each word has its role within the sentence and we cannot combine them just any old way. 'The dog is running' is a sentence, while 'The dog the cat' is not. We recognise various parts of speech – 'dog' and 'cat' are nouns, 'to run' or 'to be running' are verbs. For a sentence to be complete, it has to contain a verb (predicate) and a noun (subject). If necessary, these two parts can be expanded by the addition of other words, such as other nouns in the role of the object or complement, adjectives in the capacity of attributes, the nouns can be further replaced by pronouns. At the same time, the language has ingenious ways of flouting its own rules. Think of the idiom 'the more the merrier'. It has no subject, verb or object, but it makes sense and can be easily understood. Is it also a correct sentence? According to which rules?

We only become fully aware of a set of linguistic rules when we try to learn a foreign language. In our own language, our mother tongue, we only learned them incidentally, while learning to speak. This is because these rules do not just govern our language, they also govern our thinking. At the beginning, we talked about how we perceive 'things'. Some of them are solid objects, such as a chair or a spoon, others are not. But they all behave in the same way from the linguistic point of view – they are described with nouns. We have already said that we would not be able to talk about anything without such words. Thus even our very perception of the world, from the moment we open our eyes, is bound up in language and its rules. Even if we are not talking about what we see, the world around us still opens up to us through the use of words and names. The connection between language and thinking and even intelligence is best illustrated by the (perhaps paradoxical) fact that hearing impairments have a far more acute impact than blindness on a child's mental development. Although sight is our major source of information, speech is the basis of our thinking and the development of speech normally evolves from our ability to hear and form sounds. Children with impaired hearing find it much harder to learn a replacement sign language which enables them to develop normal thought-formation. Until sign language was developed, such children remained disabled not only by the fact that it was more difficult for them to communicate; it was actually more difficult for them to form thoughts.

People who have had dealings with computers sometimes succumb to the naive illusion that language is a purely neutral instrument, allowing us to simply express or 'encode' whatever comes into our minds. But in fact our language does, ever so inconspicuously and subtly and in so many ways, guide us and make us talk in a certain specific way. Each language has its phonetic system, an 'alphabet' of sounds, which are allowed to be used, while others do not belong to it. You can observe the way in which young children, who experiment with all sorts of sounds until they learn to speak, gradually mastering the relevant phonetic system and eliminating the other sounds from their usage.

Then there is vocabulary, a set of words each person has at their disposal in a given language, with each individual's vocabulary varying in size and scope. Our personal vocabulary, or idiolect, which we substantially enlarge through reading and study, also significantly influences our thinking – if we lack a word to label or evoke something, unless we have it right in front of us, it might as well not exist as far as we are concerned. Even less conspicuous – and all the more effective – are the rules which govern the way in which words string themselves into sentences, permissible combinations of words, parts of speech, phrases etc. However, these are not rules devised consciously by an individual or a group of individuals, these rules have been created anonymously, over a long period of time, like tracks for our thinking processes to move along. Thus they contain traces of the ways our fathers and forefathers thought, and these still lead us on, while some of us expand, enrich and reshape them, be they poets or philosophers. Let us look at several examples of what language structures tell us about the characteristics and possibilities of the process of thinking, and also about its past.

Language makes us express what we see in a certain way. If I see a crow flying past, I have to divide this monolithic experience into 'a crow', that is, a noun, the act of 'flying', perhaps the crow being black, etc. It is useful to recognise that we never see a crow 'as such' but rather always in the context of some action, adorned with some properties, and it is language which forces us to dissect the originally monolithic experience in this way. Language has succeeded in this so perfectly that we cannot even think of doing it otherwise. Not only language, but also our thinking creates forms of X is doing Y, Z is W etc.

Some of the properties which we associate with nouns are such as can be expressed directly by the noun itself. Or rather the properties of the thing are denoted by the given noun. Some languages make the distinction between animate and inanimate objects directly in the forms of these nouns. That is perhaps easy enough to understand. The grammatical gender of nouns, on the other hand, is a real conundrum. Unlike modern English, many other languages distinguish masculine and feminine (and possibly also neuter) noun gender forms (such as *der, die, das* in German or *le, la* in French). This distinction seems to point back at where our language originated – and where it originates for every new person: that is, the experience of home and family. That is where the categories of 'man', 'woman', and 'child' make sense. As soon as we leave the haven of the family though, the division becomes more problematic – still understandable when applied to animals, an expert will be able to apply it to plants, but beyond that, it is a sheer mystery.

While many languages distinguish genders as a matter of fact, the way in which various languages have dealt with the issue differs. It is quite natural for a native speaker to know if a noun is 'masculine', 'feminine', or 'neuter', and he or she is not likely to make a mistake in that respect. But the same area is a veritable minefield when we are speaking in a foreign language. Who can possibly remember that the word for 'sun', a neuter noun in Czech, is feminine in German, and masculine in French? It was the structuralist ethnographers who partly uncovered this mystery when they described the strange 'logic' of thinking in primitive peoples. They explained that the world of primitive peoples is inevitably divided into opposing groups of things, animals, plants, etc, where fairly intricate rules apply as to what belongs where, what can be combined with what, and what is mutually exclusive. What we should take from this is that grammatical gender is a vestige of pre-rational thinking, a trace of the way our ancient ancestors dissected the world – and that this original trace still bears a lot of influence on the way we think and speak today.

But the things that surround us do not just lie around. Some move and change shape, others are moved by us, made into something else, picked up and used. After all, when we were talking about names, we said that we refer to as 'things' above all those objects which are of some use to us, or to which we have an important relationship. This basic relationship is expressed by another word class – the verb. In everyday speech, the verb is probably the most essential part of a sentence, as we can see in sentences, where the subject is only formally present as 'it' – 'It's raining', or when grammar does without one altogether – 'Go!'

Notice what features or traits of action, changes and activities were considered of such importance that they have been incorporated directly into the properties of verbs. Let us start with the most basic category, the person. The name 'person' is perhaps not quite accurate, as language does not distinguish if it is Tom, Dick or Harry doing something, but it does make a distinction between me, you, or him. Is there really so much of a difference? Judging by the language of science or that of administration, which use the third person almost exclusively, it might appear that it actually does not matter very much. But language is prepared for all eventualities. In the most basic language situation, dialogue, person is used to denote three fundamental roles: that who is speaking (I), that who I am speaking to (you), and that who I am talking about (he, she, it). After all, a mere change of person can result in a huge difference in the content and meaning of an utterance.

Let us consider a simple example – 'He is a thief' is a sentence we can hear ten times a day and not pay much attention to. Whether it be truth or slander, it does not take much courage to utter (as 'he' is most likely to be absent) and the utterance itself will probably not change anything about the situation. The person in question will not give up their thieving ways. Change the sentence to the 2nd person, however, and immediately you have a sentence which most of us would not dare to utter for fear of being too frank or too rude, for now you have to take into account a possible reaction, even retribution. And to say 'I am a thief' in earnest, indicative mode, well, most of us have probably never said it or heard it said, unusual as it would be. And if somebody did say it, they were most likely a saint or a neurotic individual, who has just reached some sort of breaking point in their life by uttering those words.

So, grammatical person captures the basic speech situation when the speaker is talking to someone about someone or something. It is there because these three roles are neither the same, nor equal, on the contrary, they express the fundamental differences between these roles. It is an interesting fact that in English, the only person retaining a distinctive form is the 3rd person singular, as if the language wanted to stress that it is the most different one. Similarly, we could demonstrate the difference between 'I' and 'we' in a situation involving some sort of problem, responsibility, or pledge – 'We guarantee..., we shall not allow...., we shall ensure...' – politicians say these things every day. 'We', of course, why not? But 'I'? Why just me?

An important category which no Indo-European language can do without is tense. The German name for 'verb' is *das Zeitwort*, 'time-word'. Tense expresses the relationship between the time of the action described and the time of utterance. Some tense systems also incorporate a tense expressing a relationship between two actions or differentiate between a complete or incomplete action. Based on language observations, tense too, is a fundamental category of our thinking. If in doubt, just consider the differences between 'I had', 'I have', and ' I will have', where the first and the last sentences also imply, paradoxically, 'I do not have'. Unlike the category of person, where there is a clear-cut division, different tenses may overlap, but they will not bleed into each other; they each express something slightly different. For example the use of future tense can imply a degree of uncertainty: 'From here to the city centre? That will take a good half-hour.'

Each grammatical category bears testimony to a great feat of abstract thinking, which puts aside what is different in order to stress what is shared. For example, language has taken notice of certain symmetry of actions – a horse is pulling a cart, a cart is being pulled by a horse. This is expressed by the active or passive voice of the verb. We can also observe, in various languages, how the tendency towards regularity gradually takes over, with only the most common (and therefore most likely the oldest) verbs maintaining their cumbersome irregularity, sometimes even to the extent of different forms having different roots ('to be', 'I am', 'I was'). And one of the utmost achievements of language abstraction is surely negation. This apparently simple operation, which is so universal, actually happens exclusively within the sphere of thinking and it contains many hidden hurdles. For now, let us consider that a negative sentence (e.g., 'It isn't raining') does not have 'an original' to follow, but rather evokes a perceived occurrence or state which is absent at the given moment.

In philosophy, the direct connection between language structures and rules of thinking was discovered by Aristotle. A considerable part of his system of thought can be best understood if we equate his terms with linguistic ones – for example, the Aristotelian *substance* bears many similarities to the noun, *accident* to attributive adjectives, and so on. From this discovery springs logic, one of the first sciences to be separated from philosophy (thanks largely to Aristotle), to develop independently, paving their way with results, statements and answers which they gained from their starting point, that is philosophy. And it was this aspect of Aristotle's teaching that the Viennese neopositivists took as their own starting point in the early 20th century, as well as the philosophy of language, which is now the most widespread philosophical school in the Anglo-Saxon world.

Questions:

- Look at a picture of a landscape and try to describe what you see in it. What did you start with and why? What did you need in order to do it?
- How does our knowledge help when processing an idea or an experience? Is there a difference between a layman and an expert?
- Why does language distinguish between things (i.e., nouns), actions (i.e., verbs), characteristics (adjectives) etc.? What experience is this differentiation based on?
- In English, the word 'man' means both a male human being and mankind as a whole. This is not the case in German or in Slavic languages. Could this peculiarity somehow be connected to the feminist movement originating in England?
- What does grammatical person express? What about singular and plural?

6. Man in the World

The waking have one common world, but the sleeping turn
aside each into a world of his own. (Heraclitus)

When I wake up and open my eyes in the morning, all around me I can see familiar objects: the furniture, plants, windows, books. This is my world. The world I can find my way in, where I know what is what, where not much is likely to surprise me for I feel 'at home' here. Very young children know no other world and very old people find it reassuring. If for some reason I have to stay overnight at a hotel or in someone else's house, it takes me a while to realise where I am. But it is also the world. I get dressed, go out into the streets, to school, to work. From time to time I go visiting people or take a trip to another town, or go on a holiday to the seaside. All this, too, becomes my world, it piles onto and merges with it, and my world becomes wider and more complex. I have learned at school that the world reaches further still, to places where I have never been, beyond the sea, to the tropics, to the Polar regions. I know that all of this is a part of our planet, the Earth, which we live on. When I look up at the sky at night, I can see the Moon and the stars, the universe which I shall never visit but still, it is a part of the world.

The world in the philosophical sense is with us from morning till night, from childhood to adulthood, it is a counterpart of our waking consciousness – we can never get rid of it, unless we fall asleep, faint or drink ourselves senseless, thus ridding ourselves temporarily of our consciousness. Everything we come across, everything we need or take an interest in, everything we try to avoid, it is all included in the world. We have already mentioned how things and meanings 'jump out' when we focus on them. But they could not even be things if they lacked this ever-present background, the floor and the ground which they stand on, the space and light which enable us to see, hear and feel them. The Czech philosopher Jan Patočka observed the connection between the Czech words *svět* (world) and *světlo* (light). Think of a rabbit frozen in the headlights of an approaching car, unable to make the jump into the dark to save itself. Even for the rabbit, the world only exists where there is light. The Greeks called the world *cosmos*, which also means beauty, a pleasing arrangement, order. The Latin *mundus* also means 'clean', and the German word *Welt* is connected with the English *wealth*. Well, is that not a nice bit of philosophy in a nutshell?

The world is not just a random jumble of things; it is organised and there are rules. These apply not only to our home, the garden, or the park, but, say, to a dump site in equal measure. The necessary and inevitable centre of my world is I myself. That cannot be avoided and it is not necessarily a sign of egocentrism, although it may easily lead us to it. The 'I' does not exist in the world floating freely, like some sort of spectre, but always within a body, always here at this very spot. That is always my vantage point and it is always my view. We should take this into account and be aware that other people view things from other standpoints, and therefore perhaps differently, and there is nothing we can do to change that. 'I' means always 'I – here', or as we shall see later, 'I – here – now'.

There is always an up and a down, which I am always aware of and reminded of by the Earth's gravity – should I just for a moment not be sure, in an avalanche maybe, I could just drop something and watch which way it falls. The distinction between the up and down is very important to humans, who take an enormous pride in their upright gait and who have, unlike their four-legged relatives, always endeavoured to be remote from the ground. We use words such as high and low, up and down in countless metaphors, where they do not refer to plain spatial orientation. Think of base motives, aiming high, low life etc. 'Down' means to sink low, going downhill, from bad to worse, possibly into or even under the ground, 'up' stands for a higher position, more power, closer to the sun and sky.

My body is shaped in response to the world in a way characteristic of humans. Let us make a few comparisons with animals. We have already mentioned the upright gait. While it renders us less nimble than a mountain goat or a dog, it enables us to see far and wide and it has freed our hands for other uses. Unlike animals, whose eyes are usually positioned to look to the sides, our eyes look forward. Thus we do not see to the sides or behind us, but our spatial vision is superior. Instead of a snout or a trunk, a beak or a proboscis, we have been equipped with a rather inconspicuous mouth, hardly best designed for picking up food with; we have to use our hands or even cutlery. However, we manage to process everything that we cannot put straight into our mouth; we can break it up, chop it, or even boil and bake it. Our eyes look forward and humans are probably the only creatures who can see what they are eating. Have you ever observed a blackbird struggling, not being able to see where it is pecking at? We humans have our hands in this space in front of us. That gives us a unique skill to pick things up, pass them on, look at them closely. Thanks to hand – eye coordination a small area has been created where we can best focus our attention and exercise our abilities, whether it be a work-desk for an adult or a sandpit for a child. No animal can match us in this respect.

Like most animals, our bodies, too, are oriented forward. That is the direction in which we most often move, look, throw, and also think. The word 'forward', too, carries a strong potential for metaphor. We use the phrase 'a step forward' to describe progress. Since we move forward, we also visualise our life in this way. The past is 'behind us' and that which still awaits, what we anticipate, desire or dread, is somewhere 'ahead of us'.

Thus what we call 'space' spreads in front of us, from the nearest, which we can reach out into, to the furthest away, as far as the eye can see to the horizon. And then further still, too far for us to see. It has its up and down, closer and further, right and left, which, through abstraction and ingenious simplification employed by the great philosophers Euclid, Descartes and Newton, came to be described as 'three-dimensional space'. It was Descartes who observed that each possible direction can be described as a combination of three basic directions – if we are walking up a hill, the direction is partly up and partly forward. This 'space' is then so simplified that it is possible to express it mathematically and to carry out numerical operations within it. This geometrical space will then become common, not connected with the orientation of our own body any more. For we are usually not alone in the world and space. There are other people, whom we encounter, co-operate with or fight against. As the famous quotation from Heraclitus puts it, 'all the waking have one world in common'. How does this come about, since each and every one of us has our own world with ourselves as its natural centre?

We do not enter the world alone and into solitude, we enter amongst other people and through their endeavour. Our parents awaited our arrival and then spent years looking after us. Besides, man is a creature which has adapted to life in a group in order to survive. Therefore, communication with others is of utmost importance to us. But if I want communication to be successful, I have to bridge the gap between my world and that of the other person's. For if we are facing each other, my 'right' is their 'left', what is closer for me can be further for them. Only if we are stood side by side do our 'worlds' roughly correspond. The general urge to communicate experience and knowledge has compelled us to develop the capacity for abstraction, so characteristic of humans. But what do we actually abstract from? First and foremost from ourselves, our point of view, the orientation of our body, our person. From the way we see our world to the way it is. Fortunately, the ground for abstraction is prepared by the way we perceive things.

We have already spoken about how, if we pay close attention, we realise that we see the world and the things in it in perspective. The task 'draw the inside of this room' will be interpreted by the realist painter and by most adults alike – to create on paper something that would resemble a photograph, that is to employ perspective, with objects appearing smaller the further they are, parallel lines converging and angles variously distorted. A small child, however, or a medieval painter, would approach such a task quite differently. They would want to draw the thing 'as it is'. The largest object will be not that which is the closest but that which is the most important. A house may be drawn with all four walls in view, for even though I cannot see them all at once, I do know they are there. A plate will be round, of course, as I know it to be round. The fact that one thing blocks another from view will present certain difficulties, resulting in an effort to arrange them so that, if possible, all are visible. Notice that in such a picture it is impossible to say where the artist's viewpoint is – he or she simply draws things, not his or her view of them.

That is certainly a surprising discovery. For it would seem easiest to draw 'what I see'. But that is precisely the question: 'What exactly do I see?' Or rather, what experience or memory will I have left of what I have seen? To draw the room as it looks from my perspective is not easy and requires some practice. Few of us could tackle the task with confidence. That is why children draw things as they are (like the medieval painters). Their aim is not to portray the world, the space as it is projected onto the retina, but rather individual things, the way they belong together and the way we remember them.

The modern adult still has the same problem but would probably opt for a different approach, perhaps some sort of abstraction: a ground plan or a bird's eye view. Not that it is something he will have seen, as it would require the ability to look from above through the ceiling, but it is also an attempt to capture the situation 'as it is'. There will be the table and the chairs, the windows and the door, everything in its correct place and size ratio. Also, such a diagram will be the same for everybody. A perspective view is always different from each spot and so each of us sees the same room differently. But a bird's-eye view is the same for everyone and if I make a mistake in it, anybody can correct it. It is as if the 'one world' of Heraclitus was not created retrospectively, when I need to interact with somebody. It is as if our very experience and perception worked towards making the world we see and live in possible to be shared with others. This ability to depersonalise our experience also forms the basis of the 'objective view' of science.

The surrounding world accompanies us all our waking life. We cannot rid ourselves of it. After all, our physical being is firmly anchored in it and as we go through life, we continue to discover it further and become intertwined in it. The body is extended into hairstyle, clothing, jewellery and accessories, furniture and our abode. As we get older, we become attached to countless objects; they 'grow on us' you might say, and likewise, these objects get attached to us. Our world is with us at all times then. But our relationship towards it may be different every time. The most frequent is, as Martin Heidegger puts it, the relationship of procuration. When we wake up in the morning, we stumble into our slippers and go to the bathroom to wash ourselves. We reach for the toothbrush or the shaver, we grab a towel, put the kettle on. The 'world' in this case consists of the bedroom, bathroom and kitchen, it houses the objects which we need and which fulfil a certain function. Apart from that, they do not interest us greatly. Many people might not be able to say what their slippers look like. They will only notice them properly when they become worn out and no longer serve their purpose. The toothbrush is of interest only when it is not to be found in its allocated place. Then we might start wondering what it actually looked like.

Where we busy ourselves with procuring the most, in our home or workplace, we create around us a characteristic arrangement of things which we use. The bathroom, kitchen, workshop or the office desk all bear the clear mark of their 'master'. Each household bears the clear imprint of its inhabitants, who create it in their own image. An engraver I worked with in a goldsmith's workshop was well-known for the amazing orderliness of his workbench – the chisels were arranged in a perfect semi-circle within easy reach, and each of them always in the same spot. Out of mischief, we sometimes tried to spoil this perfect order. Each time, he would grumble but instead of tidying up, he just set about his work. At first he would have to look for his tools, but within half an hour, they were all back in their place. Order is not external (on the desk), rather it resides in our head and it is from there that it goes out into the world (or onto our desk).

The interesting and intimate connection between a person and their closest surroundings is accentuated if we enter the house of somebody who has just passed away. Everything is just as it was, only the very person who created and maintained it and who was the reason for it all being there, is no longer there. The difference between the 'living' world of an actual person and a lifeless assortment of objects, which are to be found in various open-air museums, where they pretend to be a 'typical agricultural homestead', in imposing displays in chateaux and palaces, or in memorials to the famous – a sensitive person can immediately sense that nobody has ever really lived in these surroundings.

There is another kind of relating to the world, which characterises a scientist researching something. Unlike the intimate closeness typical for the homely world of procuring, a scientist has to keep a detached attitude towards his or her subject. He rarely observes the object of his research in its natural environment – the need to repeat experiments and observations causes the requirement of a simplified, artificial environment, with the exclusion of external influences. Live objects are frequently killed and preserved to that purpose. A botanist prefers to work with dried plants and an entomologist with prepared beetles. Detachment aside, another attitude typical of a scientist is their desire for a clear overview – a scientist comparing various specimens, preferably pinned up in one box in an orderly manner.

We could find a host of more or less different attitudes towards the world. Let us consider the noncommittal attitude of a tourist looking around a place knowing they are never going to live there. The 'attitude' of a person lying on a beach, not wishing for anything, not needing anything, just having a good time. The attitude of a child, who, while having various sorrows and anxieties, does not really know what worry is. Or the attitude of a landlord who experiences physical suffering at the sight of his lodgers demolishing his 'world'.

Here is another interesting thing – language makes a distinction between 'to be' and 'to have' in man's attitude towards the world. Gabriel Marcel noted this difference and Erich Fromm wrote an acclaimed book about it. The difference is certainly there. For example, I am Czech, I am a mechanic, I am a keen philatelist. But I have a car, I have a holiday home. Surprisingly perhaps, I have two eyes, I have hair, I have a body – it would appear then that I 'am' something separate from all that. Both verbs are used to express the past 'I have been'. French and German actually use both 'be' and 'have', 'to be' for verbs expressing movement, 'to have' for everything else. As if movement was the most intrinsic form of 'being'.

Our brief look at the position of man in the world shows that there is no clear-cut boundary defining the 'I' – it is positioned somewhere in the middle, it 'has' its body and its worries first of all, then its clothing, followed by the place to live and the rest. Man is thus firmly planted into the world, taking root in it and extending it further. That is why the right to ownership – as an extension of our own being – counts among the basic human rights. There are people for whom a particular material loss can be more acutely painful than the loss of a limb. While there is not a clear boundary, there are undoubtedly certain differences. Differences between what is our 'own', such as a leg, the bed, a pipe, that which we constantly need and what we live in, our house or pots and pans, and that which we have 'in store', in the cellar or at our weekend house, and finally that which we have remotely so to speak, what we may not even know about and what interests us merely in relation to its extent or value, possessions, riches in the narrow sense of the word. There are differences in how we treat what we have and what role it plays in our lives. Possessions can certainly make our life more comfortable, but on the other hand, they require us to take care of them. Thus on the one hand, things become ours, on the other hand, we equally become 'theirs'. In the end, it is a matter of how well we are able to withstand the natural tendency regarding things and possessions, that is for the roles to be reversed and for us to become enslaved – or possessed – by what we own.

Questions:

- Describe the way in which our bodies are set within the world and our orientation towards it.
- How would you explain that while each of us has their own world, we are able to meet in a shared one?
- Think about the difference between 'to be' and 'to have'. Can man be without having anything? What is the danger of great wealth?
- Explain the relation between the world and things, which we have earlier described as 'jumping out' from it.

- Would you be able to describe the world in a dream? How is it different from the waking world?
- A sofa belongs in a sitting room, while it would look ridiculous in a meadow. How can this be utilised, e.g., in art?
- Can we sometimes encounter a thing without the world? Consider drawings in an encyclopaedia.

7. Holiday and Everyday, Myth and Logos

Life without festivity is a long road without an inn.
(Democritus)

The nice thing about travelling by train is that you can look out of the window and observe things that have little relation to you. You do not have to drive as the train takes care of that, and so your only concern is that you do not miss your stop. For those of us who do not need to take the train every day it can be like a holiday. When we get off the train, we will once again enter the workaday world, with our head full of worries and concerns. We do not merely go around observing the world, however; we must first of all try to find a way to survive in it. But man is a thinking creature and so more complicated questions may interest him. Before he starts on something, he will try to figure out the best way of doing it, and, once he has done it, he will ask himself whether he was right to do it in that way. And even if everything is perfectly taken care of and we have managed to obtain everything that we need, sooner or later the question is bound to arise: what about *me*? How are things in that department? Am I merely a machine built for work? And is the world merely a source of food?

Strictly speaking, we do not concern ourselves with survival every hour of the day, but during daytime, when the sun is out. Then night comes, and we go to sleep and forget about it all until the morning. People have also arranged longer time scales into a similar pattern. A long time ago they learned to divide their time into the working week, in which they concern themselves with earning a living, and holidays and festivals, during which everything is entirely different. Whatever they have earned in their work time, they can spend during their holidays. The time in which we must concentrate on work alternates with time which we have to ourselves – time in which we can do the things we enjoy, when we have time for other people, for playing and for other impractical things, when we can celebrate and enjoy ourselves, tell and listen to stories, reminisce or even think. Only in our free time can we lift our heads from our work and our day-to-day worries and notice those things that we have not had the time to notice – things that are of no immediate concern to us.

Only in our free time, the time we have to ourselves, can we look around us and notice that we exist in this world. Such banality! And yet the world is more than just the things we have around us, things that serve some kind of purpose; there are also clouds, the sky, the sun, light, the stars and the universe. Those who look well may notice how it all fits together and forms a whole – a grand, somewhat frightening and mysterious whole, from which we have our own existence and upon which we depend. There have always been people who have been drawn to this and have tried to somehow express it, whether it be in the form of music and dance, poetry or storytelling. This kind of sacred storytelling, which aims to present and grasp the mystery of this world and life in it, the origins of things and relationships between them, the relationship of man to the world, his fate, and many other fundamental things, is what we call myth. Myths originally belonged to religious ceremonies and celebrations, and only later did they become separate enough from them that they could be freely recited, and later written down – becoming in the process accessible to everyone at any time. Myth is not an explanation in today's meaning of the word (Greek *mythos* means speech, a tale), nor is it a description. It is an attempt to understand and express the mystery of the world and man's place in it through the use of something transparent and familiar, of human language.* We have already mentioned the myth of Phaeton and the golden sun-chariot. To a modern person these myths seem at first sight naively anthropomorphic; they see in everything the existence of familiar beings who live, act, love and hate like we do. But ancient man had no other way of expressing things. The abstract terms used by science and philosophy today arrived much later – partly on the back of myth. Myth presents the universe and the natural world as something close and familiar to man. It does not break down nature into its constituent parts, but shows it as a human (or rather superhuman) story.

---

* 'Myths tell us what we already know. That is their way of reproducing the unfamiliar in the well known. They reproduce solidarity, not information.' (Niklas Luhmann)

In its use of language to depict nature and bring it closer to us, myth is in fact a testimony to the way in which man separates himself from nature, and has begun to observe it from a certain distance. The art of telling such stories itself involves a striking degree of abstraction. But myth is more than simple abstraction, description or art. It is, first and foremost, an attempt to glimpse the depths of the world, its foundations and the divine forces that shape it. It is through the actions of the gods that the world is brought into being, out of the primaeval darkness; and it is the actions of the gods that maintain order in it. And it is the task of all those who depend upon the maintenance of this order to support the good gods, to help them fend off the wicked gods, to ensure that this primary divine act, the creation of the world, is maintained. This is why ancient man was compelled to repeat this act regularly in a symbolic manner. In many ancient tribes there appear myths about evil gods who want to swallow up the moon. And in the critical moments of the new moon, when it has almost entirely disappeared from the sky, the tribespeople chase away the evil gods by shouting and screaming, in order that the moon may be saved (or rather renewed).

So myth is something more than mere storytelling – it demonstrates a particular understanding of the world and our place in it, an understanding which has certain characteristic features. Firstly, it is intuitive and sees things as wholes; it does not analyse or compare, but sees things largely on the basis of closeness and familiarity. Secondly, it is symbolic. It does not communicate its meaning through conceptual language but through images, archetypal situations and characters. It has, from our viewpoint, a dreamlike quality – you will find no rational principles like identity, cause and effect or the excluded middle at work in myth. Thirdly, myth says what it says and permits of no questions, let alone doubts or criticism. It offers, on the other hand, a feeling of security and safety. Fourthly, it is an extremely powerful and effective art form, having matured over thousands of years of telling and retelling, making it close to what Carl Gustav Jung would later refer to as archetypes. And it is precisely this that makes myth so convincing. Fifth, myth is collective. It cannot be the property of any one individual; it brings together the entire tribe without exception. It takes just one member of the tribe to refute myth to endanger its entire validity. Finally, myth teaches the individual that his fundamental responsibility is to ensure the continuation of the original *status quo*, the golden age that pertained at the start of things, and which remains forever the model of correct behaviour. Our everyday world changes, of course, and we ourselves change and grow old, but it is for precisely this reason that we need to constantly renew the original state. The emphasis placed on the idea of this golden age belonging somewhere in the past means that myth supports the granting of authority to our elders (who are closer than us to the golden age), or to those of noble birth who know the long list of their forebears and are thereby also connected to the golden age.

New-year rituals are a typical example of mythical treatment of the renewal of the world. In every ancient society there is a certain order; there are certain rules and authorities. However, like all the things of this Earth, they too become blemished, they weaken and decay (like nature itself). And as nature renews itself with the coming of spring, so too must the society, the tribe, the world, renew itself. And to this effect, in the days before the festival of renewal – namely, the New Year – the blemished and decaying order is overturned and abolished. The young instruct the old, women rule over men, and all that is normally forbidden is permitted. Nobody works during the day and nobody sleeps during the night. The meagre remains of those ceremonies that have survived to this day, such as Lent, Carnival and New Year's Eve, give us no clue to the seriousness of what was at stake when our ancestors performed them. The future of the entire tribe depended upon their perfectly accurate and successful performance. The more perfectly the old order can be abolished and cleared away, the greater the chance that it can be renewed in its original, flawless state. It is perhaps only in the mythical idea of revolution, that sweeps away all before it, that there is maintained something of the seriousness of these renewal rituals. But revolutions, of course, cannot be regularly repeated without ceasing to be revolutions.

Mankind was sustained for thousands of years by this mythical understanding of the world, so perhaps it is no surprise that certain traces of it, such as customs and superstitions, remain in our modern society (especially those surrounding the new year, Easter, weddings and funerals) and in the human subconscious they continue to appear in the form of symbols and archetypes. Few may know it, but the ordinary round tarts that you see in the windows of Czech bakeries symbolise the spring sun, as does the planting of eggs in the ground, while the smashing of plates at weddings is a throwback to the noise with which our ancestors sought to ward off evil spirits.

As human life has changed, especially with the growth of cities and mass migration, myth has lost a great deal of its persuasive hold on us. Despite the attempts of rulers and tyrants to prop it up with violence, we have reached a stage where myth has ceased to carry weight and has become no more than a peculiar kind of superstition. This change was largely brought about by a new understanding of the world, one based on observation, critical debate and the methodical application of reason. Now, reason also has its categorical certainties. If I am here, I cannot also be somewhere else; if something is a stone, it cannot suddenly then become a princess; if something is a wolf, it cannot also be a prince; a stone cannot start moving all by itself, and so on.

The Greek word *logos* means 'word', but it also means 'sense', 'reason'; later on it also came to mean 'measure', 'number' and even 'account'. It is as if the whole history of human knowledge has been compressed into a single word. This new way of understanding the world also has its characteristic features. Firstly, it is based on verbal expression, the verbal description of reality. But as we have seen, the mere exercise of verbal description divides reality into separate parts, with the result that the whole becomes lost to view. Secondly, verbal description allows for discussion, questioning and criticism. Verbal claims invite questioning. Thirdly, once we start operating in descriptive language, we are also operating in the sphere of reason; language is the means through which the rules of reason are asserted. Whatever is not accessible to reason is to be treated with suspicion. Fourthly, reason makes no appeal to collective authority, but rather to our own ability to think, so it is up to each individual to convince himself of the certainties of reason. The individual can, and must, reach these certainties freely. And finally, learning, observation and contemplation are all directed to what is here and now, not to the distant past. The goal of learning is of course to guide human behaviour, to find the right road into the future, or even to predict it. For nobody knows the road to the future and it cannot be imitated, as the ancient archetypes were imitated. It must be found over and over again. It must be created and examined through rational thought. It is for this reason that the leading role in society is no longer with the elderly and noble, but has been taken over by creative, inventive, enterprising and educated people.

The whole of classical philosophy, particularly the dialogues of Plato, bear witness to this transformation. The modern reader may find it hard to appreciate, having grown up in this way of thinking, that it was just coming into full fruition in Plato's time. And it is very interesting to observe how Plato himself struggles with it and in some books (especially in *Timaeus* or the *Laws*) seems unable to decide. But the status of myth as a source of certainties and social cohesion was gone forever. The conditions in which it had developed no longer applied, man had begun to see his place in the world in a new light and all efforts to maintain the validity of myth, through force, authority and the poetic arts, had failed. Man was alone in the world, with only his reason and his word. And he was no longer bound to others through blood or tribal unity but, again, purely through word and reason – *logos*.

Some features of the mythic understanding of the world lived on however, and not only among small children. Art, both visual and verbal, continues to be characterised by the holistic vision, symbolism and use of archetypal images and characters that constituted myth. The experience of viewing or reading is more about seeing things from the artist's viewpoint rather than learning anything. The reader of Shakespeare and Dostoyevsky enters the world of myth, albeit on his own (it is only in the theatre that a kind of community of myth can exist, and even then only exceptionally) and it does not occur to him that these stories should be regarded as a model of correct behaviour or a source of existential certainties. The figures of Falstaff, Shylock or Prince Myshkin may however come to his mind as an embodiment of certain outlooks on life.

The sense that something has been lost with the collapse of myth has reached not only the arts but also philosophy and science. Conceptual, discursive thought, aiming at control and criticism, misses the whole and the sense of what it is investigating. For this reason philosophy in the 20ᵗʰ century became closely bound up with poetry, literature and art. Heidegger dedicated himself in later years to the interpretation of poetry, Sartre was a literary man as well as a philosopher and Paul Ricoeur studied storytelling *per se* – story and narrative. In science, major breakthroughs were made by Sigmund Freud, who was the first to recognise the scientific value of dream symbols, albeit as symptoms of illness, and Carl Gustav Jung, who brought about their complete rehabilitation. And the utterances of theoretical physicists and cosmologists have a similarly 'mythic', dreamlike quality, as these scientists are unable to communicate their ideas in descriptive language. This is largely because current notions of microphysical reality are not governed by the laws of common sense: electrons do not look much like us and can only be said to be here now with a degree of probability, and their location is not determined until the moment when we attempt to locate it.

This is very different to the attempts to renew myth as a source of collective existential certainties, which absolves man of the responsibility to think for himself. Such attempts occur frequently throughout history. We have already seen it in Plato and even Christianity, which did much to cause the collapse of myth, did not escape it. And the further from myth our understanding of the world has taken us, the more violent and monstrous these attempts have become. In the 20th century these attempts met with the greatest success in the 'myths' of totalitarian regimes, in Alfred Rosenberg's 'Myth of the 20th century' and in the mythical strand of communism. Precisely because myth *per se* is no longer convincing, it becomes in these caricatures a means of suppressing thought and argument. These false myths are no more than ideological manipulation, a means of forcibly rounding people up into a herd. And the 'certainty' that they offer is in fact entirely cynical – it is merely the brutal strength of the dictator, who crushes all dissent. When the dictator falls, on the other hand, the whole myth bursts like a bubble, leaving behind nothing but a pile of ruins. These horrific experiences are a dire warning to us not to abandon our critical faculties. Reason, argument and criticism, as tools of discovery, may seem difficult and laborious (and even reason can be mythologised), but without them we become easy prey to the most evil forces.

Questions:

- What do you understand by myth? Give an example of a mythic story.
- Would you be able to invent a myth? What would your partner or your friends say to it?
- What must society be like, in order to depend on myths?
- When and why did myth collapse? What was it replaced with?
- Jean-Francois Lyotard spoke of 'metanarrative'; does this have any relation to myth?
- Can we return to myth? Why would we?
- Is science-fiction myth? Or Tolkien? Or Harry Potter? How do they differ from each other?
- Why are contemporary attempts at creating artistic myths so popular? What is that we seek in them?

8. You and I

Whenever I am thinking, it is always me that is thinking – even if I am not fully conscious of it. Descartes based all his philosophical certainty upon this. This on its own does not make us egocentric or selfish. My thoughts necessarily come from me (who else could do my thinking for me?) and they return, in a roundabout way, to me. This is in fact why we refer to it as 'reflection'. But now it is time for us to focus our attention on the fact that we are not alone in this world. From the viewpoint of our own personal development it is the case that others – for example our parents – were here before us. We could not have survived without them, we know what we know from them, and we wouldn't have even been here if it wasn't for them. Small children are entirely taken up with themselves. It is one of the first tasks of parents – and later, teachers – to take children out of this state, and to give them the opportunity to learn and take an interest in the world outside. In short, to help them create and discover their world – to be in the world. We have mentioned this before, when we spoke of knowledge.

In a certain sense, others appeared in our lives even before we did. It is only by a roundabout route, through what we hear from our parents that a child learns to identify itself as 'Margaret', and even later that it learns to call itself 'I'. This is not simply a matter of language or words, because this 'I' does not come ready-made into the world. It exists in the child only as a potential, which needs to be encouraged and cultivated. Some mentally ill people never manage this task. Even mentally healthy individuals never fully achieve it.

With our scientific education we would like to be able to say what this 'I' really is. But for all our countless use of the word in everyday life, we are unable to find any simple answer to this question.* We could say

---

* 'That which I cannot rid myself of – that is I.' (Emmanuel Lévinas)

that 'I' is not a thing that we can point our finger at; although we often accompany the word 'I' by pointing towards our chest, we can hardly say that it resides there. 'I' is always 'here', never 'there' and always 'now'. To put it more precisely, our conscious 'I' defines where is 'here' and what is 'now'.

When we encounter difficulties defining an object, it helps to contrast it with its opposite, or counterpart. So what is the counterpart of 'I'? Surely such a counterpart must exist or else we would not need to talk about 'I'. We use it whenever we need to distinguish ourselves from the person we are speaking to ('you') or the object of our conversation ('these', 'those'). So 'I' always appears in relation to something, as one of the poles of the relationship. And as there is a countless number of such relationships, and 'I' is the intersection common to them all, it becomes something more definite and stable for us. It is through this process that what we call a 'person' develops. As we have seen, even grammar refers to 'I' as the 'first person'.

However, 'I' is only the first person from the perspective of the adult or the adolescent. We have seen how this role was first taken by the mother, the one who first spoke to us and who became our first 'you'. Most philosophers, especially in the modern era, have taken their adult perspective as their starting point and therefore it has perhaps seemed to them that the fundamental, defining counterpart is the thing they are investigating and talking about – 'it', 'that', 'these', or even 'the world'. Philosophical speech – and, to a far greater extent, scientific speech – is aimed, it would seem, at anybody and at nobody in particular. This is what gives it its characteristic feature of being (at best) *about* something but not *to* anybody. It therefore mostly takes the form of the third person, with just the rarest intrusion of 'I'. The second person is almost never used.

In our everyday lives, in literature and poetry and in religious life, the exact opposite is the case. Here, speech revolves entirely around 'I' and 'you'. We may be speaking *about* something, but we are always speaking *to* somebody. When we encounter somebody speaking to nobody or just to themselves, our first judgment is that there is something wrong with them. In our discussion of language, we saw the difference between the second and third person. Now we shall develop this further, and find out the reasons for the difference.

It is always 'I' who speaks and acts, but also who observes and listens. The difference is in the character of the counterpart to whom I relate in the given activity. It is highly likely from a developmental viewpoint (but also from an objective viewpoint) that we should start with the counterpart we are speaking to – 'you'. 'You' is always a living person. When a child addresses a doll, and a grown man addresses a dog, as 'you', they always imagine that they are talking to a living person. There is only ever one of them, they have their own name and I know that they see me the same way I see them. The symmetry of this 'I' – 'you' relationship is expressed by looking into the other's eyes, something which many people have great difficulty with. The common perception that inability to maintain eye contact is a sign of guilt or suspicious intent may not be valid, but it creates difficulties which almost everyone can feel. The Czech writer Jan Neruda once wrote that 'in two is born seriousness'. When the tension becomes too much we seek to draw attention elsewhere or simply laugh it off, make fun of it. On the other hand, a steady fixed stare into someone's eyes can sometimes have a hint of aggression in it, something that animals also feel.

In the 'I' – 'you' relationship there are always two concrete people, each alone, and so there develops a certain responsibility for what we say or do – we cannot blame anyone else. In my encounters with 'you', it is not only 'I' who does the talking – I must also listen. And I am constantly distracted from my own thoughts, and forced to think of things that have never occurred to me, or which I would prefer to avoid, by the retorts and rejoinders offered by 'you'. This is why such dialogue is so valuable – and often so unpleasant. This symmetrical 'I' – 'you' relationship holds up a mirror to us all: 'I' see 'you' but also think about how 'you' see 'me'. This picture matters to me and so I attempt to somehow influence it. I anticipate 'your' feelings and attempt to reckon with them. Not in a calculating manner – that is what con-men do – but in an entirely natural way. I observe that 'you' are doing the same thing, and so in this way we reveal ourselves to each other, and come to know ourselves more deeply. It is in front of 'you' that I would, for example, be ashamed if I had failed to deliver on a commitment I had made. It is 'you' that I confide in because there is nobody else around; and I trust that 'you' will say nothing to anyone else.

We have so far been describing the 'I' – 'you' relationship as symmetrical, as Martin Buber described it. But it is often a great deal more complicated than that; and some philosophers are convinced that this more complicated relationship is the rule rather than the exception. According to Emmanuel Lévinas 'the other' stands always 'above me', as my mother and father once did. In any case the 'I' – 'you' relationship is always various and secret, it may possess an unexpected depth and it plays a large role in all philosophical attempts to establish and justify codes of ethics. The scriptural 'do to others as you would have them do to you' is based on this, as is morality in general – no matter how much Kant may have tried to avoid it.* According to Lévinas, peace is the 'ability and willingness to debate' and justice consists of approaching others face to face, and not sideways or from the back.

The relationship towards a counterpart with whom I am not speaking, the 'I' – 'it' relationship, is, while also capable of complexity, much simpler. All the thinking, speaking and acting come from the 'I' – the 'it' by definition does not speak and 'he' may not even be here. There is nothing for him to hear and he cannot reply. I speak of him, not to him. This relationship, which of course may have any number of variants, is the basis of the modern concept of the thinking, discovering, active 'subject' (me) as opposed to the passive, discovered 'object' – 'it'. This relationship obscures the difference between person and object. 'He' and 'they' also exist somewhere 'there', I can see them and they can see me, but I speak about them as if they were objects. We say that such talk is 'objectivising' them – like the plantation owner selecting strong and healthy slaves at the slave market. This is why we regard it as unfair play when we hear bad things being said about people in their absence and we object: 'Why are you telling me that? Tell him!'

I can address an individual or a small group of people as 'you'. But when there start to be too many people in the group, I can no longer identify each member and hear what they each want to say. At this point I must learn to see 'them' as I would a herd of cattle, and behave towards them accordingly. The first in history to encounter this problem were military leaders and rulers. But the number of cases where we have to deal with people in this collective, objectivising manner has been multiplying ever since. Not only generals and politicians, but also businesspeople, company directors, statisticians, journalists, scientists and even school teachers have to deal with masses of people – 'a contingent of 600 men,' '37.2% of the population,' 127,000 OAPs,' 'the pupils of class 4b'. These are groups without a face, who do not speak and who have no names. We will return to the problems generated by this in our discussions of government and power.

In our modern mass society we cannot completely avoid this, but we should always keep in mind that it is in some respects a makeshift

---

*   Kant wanted us to be governed, not by 'you', but by that which is universal and common to everyone: 'Act only according to that maxim whereby you can, at the same time, will that it should become a universal law.'

measure; furthermore it is imperfect, undignified and dangerous. The concentration camps of the last century implemented perfectly thought-out systems of depriving people of words, then names, faces, individuality and dignity; then, when they were no more than numbered 'häftlings' or 'zeks', they were murdered in cold blood and even used as raw material. Such things are always possible in mass societies, and people who become used to manipulating nameless masses naturally lose their human inhibitions.

For entirely different reasons, this 'collective' relationship has also established itself in science. According to Aristotle, science 'cannot be about individual things'. The demand for objectivity in science is legitimate and even a doctor examining a relative must often forget that this is a person close to him. For the time being it is simply 'a patient' or 'an inflamed gallbladder'. However, the influence of the scientific view of reality, human and non-human (there is no difference for science between the two) has recently begun to spread into areas beyond science – phrases such as 'scientific management' have entered our language. This of course also increases the danger of the objectivising view of man and especially the 'objective' treatment of people. It is one of philosophy's most urgent tasks in the present day to warn us of these dangers and help us to face them. Who else will do it?

Questions:

- How can you explain that 'I' is not an object?
- Explain the difference between the 'I' – 'you' relationship and the 'I' – 'it' relationship.
- What does your name mean to you? What do others use it for?
- Why do we give names to our pets and to things that we are fond of?
- Why were concentration camp inmates given numbers?

9. Action and Freedom

If somebody insults me, I will most likely return the insult; I will say something even more hurtful to him, preferably in an even harsher voice. I will not have helped either him or myself in so doing, but I will have vented my anger: I will have reacted. In much the same way as oxygen reacts with hydrogene or a car reacts to its driver stepping on the accelerator – these things simply 'do' what they must, and they do it instantaneously. This immediate, instantaneous reaction to various stimuli – to prey, to food, to a mate, to danger – is typical of animals. But man has other possibilities open to him. He may pretend not to have heard and ask 'sorry, what was that?' He may crush his opponent with a glance then turn away. He may snarl through gritted teeth, 'just you wait!' He may whistle quietly, or he may simply sink into thought and do nothing at all. In each case, he makes use of his human advantages – the ability to think and to weigh up options – in many cases successfully. Every good poker player knows that the secret to his success is never to react and to leave his opponents wondering what he has planned for them. Even if he has nothing at all planned for them, his silence can give them plenty to worry about.

The main characteristic of authentic human action is that it is more than merely a reaction to stimuli. Such action is the result of man being able to maintain a certain distance from such stimuli. First of all, he evaluates the situation, then considers a number of options before settling on one. He is acting with deliberation and judgment. This certain knowledge, that I can act in more than one way, either now or later, alone or together with another person, that I can act according to my own judgment, that the stimulus need not determine how I choose to act (or not act) – this is the basis of what we call freedom. For centuries, philosophers have debated whether this freedom is genuine –

that man really is not determined by circumstances – or whether it is simply a fantasy. Today we tend to be of the opinion that this question is unanswerable (how should we decide?) and that the wisest course is to learn from our own experience, which teaches us that we can think and make decisions.

We have seen that action is more than just reaction. What makes it more than just reaction is that it follows a goal – a goal that is mine, not one that is forced upon me by my surroundings. This ability to find, evaluate and consistently follow a goal, especially one that is remote, is also a distinguishing feature of man and human action. It is something so markedly different from mere reaction to stimuli that man has always considered himself alone in the possession of such a faculty, and has always tried to find something in nature that at least comes close to it. Whenever he has found such a characteristic – spiders' webs, beaver dams or beehives – he has always paid it close attention. Spiders, beavers and bees are not reacting to anything when they build their structures; on the contrary they are preparing for something, something which will not happen until later on. The spider, for example, spins its webs at a time moment when there are no flies anywhere in sight – but when they do arrive, the spider is superbly prepared for them. As opposed to reaction, which is an answer to something which is happening or has just happened, true action is a preparation for something which only comes later, or a path to a desired goal. To put it in more philosophical terms, reaction is a response to a cause, whereas action always leads to some kind of goal. Even if the action was brought about by some stimulus, it has extended beyond that stimulus and cannot be entirely explained by it.

Such action, which is not provoked or brought about by any obvious stimulus, has evidently been thought out in advance by the person who carries it out. And it is for this reason that we can consider it to be free, which also means that its originator carries full responsibility for it. Young children are aware of this, and when they are caught doing something bad they always try to blame it on someone else ('he started it!'). They do this because they know that those who initiate an action, whether good or bad, take the greater responsibility for it. Similar arguments are also conducted by nation states or other groups in conflicts, because those who started the conflict deserve to be punished. Other people may argue about who was the first to think of a certain idea, who was its originator or inventor. For this reason it is important to bear in mind that simple reaction to stimulus is not the norm for human beings and even those who did not 'start it' can have great influence over the course of a conflict or argument. Even if they do no more than simply return insults, blows or kicks, they are still acting and therefore also carry their share of responsibility.

My freedom, which I perceive as being something internal, is for the most part pleasant and valuable to me, and it confers upon me certain considerable advantages, such as making my intentions towards potential opponents unknown to them until the very last minute. For this same reason the freedom of others can be an unpleasant thing for me, even a threat. This is why people, especially those in the ruling classes, have since time immemorial sought to extend their own freedom and limit the freedom of others. What can be more flattering to a man than the power to quash another's freedom? And is there something that can be done to limit this natural inclination, to avoid it leading to catastrophe? Or is freedom necessarily a source of chaos in society, of conflicts of all against all, where the winners are always the most brutish and least self-restrained? And are those who identify freedom with anarchy, and wish to deny it to us, right to think so?

As we have just seen, freedom is most of all limited within itself; the only action that can be called free is that which is carried out with a sense of distance and a cool head. That is why we tell ourselves to 'count to ten' when we feel angry. A man who is merely reacting does what first occurs to him, and he may give vent to his anger, but he is not free; he is doing what he must. That freedom mostly means the overcoming of the 'passions' is the main theme of late Greek philosophy, later to be adopted by Christianity. So freedom is closely connected with judgment and reason, and education, in the ancient conception, was education towards freedom, mainly as self-control.

Further, action is free only when it is accompanied by the responsibility of the person who is acting. A vandal who spray-paints a wall and then runs away is not acting like a free person – whether he is fifteen or fifty. So freedom is bound up with some person, some 'I', who remembers his actions and who attributes to himself even the more remote consequences of his actions. This connection is naturally far less pleasant, especially at times when it is invoked by someone else. This responsibility towards consequences is in fact the main reason why people are often fearful of their freedom and why they sometimes willingly forego it.

Ordinary civic relations between people are only possible to the extent that we all regard each other as free and act accordingly. When a man makes a promise, signs a contract or a bill of exchange, purchases goods and deposits money in a bank, we naturally assume that he is free, in the sense that it really is he himself who is doing these things. And we do not, as a rule, probe too far into whether he is capable of doing such things. In the criminal justice system, however, modern ideas of justice require that no such assumption can be made about criminals. The extent of a criminal's 'objective' responsibility and sanity is examined by psychologists, who occasionally find that the defendant cannot take responsibility for his actions. This may be due to insufficient intellectual ability, or it may be because at the time the crime was committed he was 'not himself', therefore not a free person. This 'double standard' most likely has its roots in the modern belief that people are fundamentally good and if they commit a crime the likelihood is that they were not in full control of their faculties.

The area where human freedom causes the greatest difficulty is science. This is not because scientists are a group of obscurantists who would wish to deprive us of our freedom – quite the opposite. It is simply that freedom, by definition, refers to action that cannot be fully explained by causes, action that is unpredictable and unrepeatable. The consequence of this is that it makes no sense to examine scientifically action which we regard as free. Sciences which cannot operate without the assumption of freedom – for example, history – must solve this problem in another way, whereas medicine and psychology have a tendency to simply ignore freedom altogether and to regard human action simply as *behaviour*– a response to stimuli. As long as everyone involved in such research understands that this is a methodological simplification, there can be no objection to it. But when a school of thought (for example behaviourism) believes that man as a whole can be understood in this way, the result is a series of absurd misunderstandings and ludicrous paradoxes. If all human action could be reduced to a series of responses to stimuli, and if it could be understood purely on grounds of cause and effect, this would undermine all opinions, including behaviourism, and all those who broadcast them. Their speech would be no more than a response to a stimulus, mere 'phonation', and could impart nothing of any use to us. Imagine an impassioned speaker, using the most rhetorical language to convince listeners that the word *freedom* has no meaning – one can only laugh.

The classic question of whether man is or is not free, which has occupied so many great philosophers and theologians from the Middle Ages, can now be seen as a question of perspective. So a mathematician has no problem understanding that he himself is free, while his linear functions are not. The physicist and the chemist need not ascribe 'freedom' to the subject of their investigations, whereas this approach would cause some difficulty to a biologist, anthropologist or doctor. And at the other end of the spectrum, it is impossible for a historian or political scientist to work without assuming the freedom of others. However, even the most conscientious historians must resort to using methods that regard their human 'subjects' as determined. I mean primarily statistical methods. For instance, it has been demonstrated in opinion polls that large numbers of 'free' people, taken as an aggregate, behave in ways that are predictable, and therefore by definition not quite 'free'. Similarly, it can be demonstrated that many of the great historical movements were influenced by preceding social crises, economic decline, or rapid growth or decline of population. However, we must bear in mind here that 'influenced by' and 'caused by' are not the same thing.

The rise of depth psychology in the 20th century was an even greater challenge to our notions of the free 'I'. The founder of depth psychology, Sigmund Freud, was able not only to understand, but also to cure, a great many psychic ailments on the basis of his interpretation. He was also able to offer a convincing explanation of many minor acts ('Freudian slips') to which we do not normally attribute any significance – slips of the tongue, for example. According to Freud, psychiatric illnesses and slips of the tongue are expressions of the unconscious mind, the place where, under societal pressure, we repress undesirable thoughts and wishes – especially sexual thoughts and wishes. And so the core of the human personality is not the conscious, mature 'I', but rather the unconscious and suppressed 'id' and the suppressing 'superego', which corresponds to our conscious ideas of how we ought to be. The unconscious comes to the fore in dreams and whenever the control of the conscious mind is weakened. If the unconscious is too heavily suppressed, this manifests itself in psychiatric disorder. And so Freud's work was, in its own way, an updating of the Stoics' philosophy of overcoming the passions, although he solved the problem in the opposite way – difficulties are overcome by accepting and becoming aware of our suppressed longings. The philosophical consequence of Freud's work is that the traditional notion of the free and responsible 'I', who is in control of his actions, is also probably a methodological simplification, and not the full reality.

Freud's pupil Carl Gustav Jung came from a wider experience than that of a psychologist treating the Viennese middle classes. The phenomenon of the unconscious, which he significantly expanded, was not for him merely a dumping-ground for undesirable thoughts, but also the source of ideas and creativity. Jung discovered a significant layer of the unconscious mind, the contents of which are not specific to each individual but rather to people from the same culture or community – the *collective unconscious*. This layer is closely bound up with man's religious and cultural expression. This seems to render unsustainable the traditional concept of European individualism and the sovereignty of the individual, who stands alone and needs nobody else. After all, people have always lived in groups and communities, not only those of the family but of the wider culture, nation and so on. People think through language and their actions are carried out in an environment which they did not create themselves. Even art and culture are not merely the work of outstanding individuals; on the contrary, these individuals grew out of the surrounding shared culture of their communities.

Questions:

- What is the difference between reaction, behaviour and action?
- Explain the difference between cause and purpose.
- What is characteristic of human action?
- What do you think of the opinion that freedom is impossible because no-one can just do what they want all the time?
- Does the phrase 'absolute freedom' have any meaning?
- Why can freedom never mean the same as licence or arbitrary behaviour?
- Why are people afraid of freedom? Why do they give it up?
- Find some examples of situations where we want to rid ourselves of freedom. How do we do it?
- Why did the unconscious start to make its presence felt so much in Freud's time and among the urban middle classes?

10. Play

The phenomenon of play, so diverse and so ubiquitous, bears witness to how man has envisaged his life and his humanity throughout the ages. Moralists have always warned against it and condemned it as a waste of time; but curiously enough, the common people have paid no heed, and adults and children alike have indulged in play with passion and abandon. Even the worst dictators have not dared to take this entertainment away; on the contrary, they have realised that apart from bread, it is the one thing necessary to keep the people docile. While it does seem difficult at a glance to find what links such activities, from children's games, to theatre, playing a musical instrument, sport, card games, and even gambling, there must be a link, for the language has good reasons for combining them in the same word. So let us put the question another way – what is the opposite of play? What is not play?

'This isn't a game, this is a matter of life and death.' Yes, there is something at stake in life, sometimes even life itself. Do we mean to say by this, though, that play is not serious, that it is something to be done casually? Hardly. Only a person who has never played anything could think so. A player who does not approach a game with all seriousness and commitment will only spoil it for others; a game played too casually is no game at all. There is a difference though. An actor who dies on stage can do so over and over again. The loser of a chess game will not become a captive of the winner, like an unsuccessful general, they will merely swap colours and start another game.

Play is not 'life' and life is most likely not play, as the Romantics sometimes claim, but there is a definite connection. Theatre plays evolved from the religious mystery plays, which sought to show us the deepest secrets of life and the world. Perhaps play is fundamentally something that acts out real life, which presents a sort of artificial model of life and the world. Even playing music creates something of its own 'world' which the musicians and listeners alike enter for a while, in order to free themselves from the everyday world 'out there'. This is even more the case with theatre or sport. It is play, in relation to life, which strives to differentiate itself from life, not the other way round. That is why people often dress up in costumes to play, and often play in separate places designed purely for that activity and no other. In this, the world of play resembles that of religion.

Every game is strictly limited, in both space and time, usually in advance. The clearly defined space and time are set apart from the rest of the world – by a white line, or a curtain, a whistle or a bell. While many of parallels can be drawn between the 'world' of play and of real life, there are no direct links. A sales person can play a queen, a president can play a brewery worker.* But when they have finished acting, they will go back to being what they were before. Actors in Ancient Greece wore masks on their faces so that nobody could confuse them with real-life people. It was the advent of television, offering as it does a close-up of the actors' faces, which destroyed this important distance, so a TV actor remains 'the doctor' or 'the executive' from a TV series, even if we meet them in the street. If you beat your boss at tennis or chess, it does not mean that you will be able to order him about tomorrow. Even the result remains in the realm of play and does not transfer into the outside world. That is why gambling is in fact a misunderstanding of the concept of play. Playing something professionally is a different matter; there, playing becomes a show in which the spectators' participation is mediated, and they then have to give vent to their fighting spirit somewhere on the streets or on a train.

Play is then set apart from the rest of the world while holding up a mirror to it. Why is that? What do we see in that mirror? Even that which makes play different form 'life' clearly shows how we regard life, what we consider important and what we would like to change. The spatial and temporal separation of play stresses that everything will be different here – do not confuse play and life. There is no transition between the two and the obligations and duties we have in the world of play do not apply outside it (and vice versa). Our positions and privileges are not transferable between the two worlds. They do not have anything in common. Those of play mean nothing in 'life' and the 'real' ones mean nothing in a game. This means that you must not be afraid

* As Václav Havel did in his autobiographical play *Audience*.

to be free while at play. What you may do within a game, provided it is according to its rules, will have no bearing on your life. Win or lose, it will have no permanent consequences.

Every type of game accentuates some aspect of life and provides the participants, and perhaps the spectators, with an opportunity to exercise these without worrying about the consequences, and in appropriately idealised conditions. Let us look at an example which everybody is familiar with – competitive games such as football, tennis, or chess. All of them simulate conflict or battle in its simplest form, one on one, the red team against the blue team. The advantage of play in this case is very obvious, as few people leave a real battlefield in one piece. Of course the players of such games must put their body and soul into the fight, from the first whistle to the last, but when it is over, it is as if nothing has happened. That is why 'fighting' games can afford the luxury of rules. For in a real battle, the participants would probably wish for rules too, but who would stick to them, really, whether winning or losing? Life is not at stake in a game, and that is why there can be rules and moreover an impartial referee who would make sure they are upheld and whose decisions would be final.

The presence of rules and referees sets play markedly apart from real life. Our options are more limited, and therefore easier to survey. In chess, for example, the number of possible moves is finite (albeit huge). A superficial observer might think that such limitations would impair creativity, but in fact the opposite is true. Nothing spurs human creativity like good and firm restrictions. This is why, for example, experiments with larger chessboards have never been successful. In music, this restricting function is fulfilled by the tonal system and the choice of instruments, and here, too, atonal music did not usher in a new era, rather a loss of clarity. The presence of a referee and rules stresses further the uncompromising desire for justice or fairness, yet another contrast to real life. For justice is possible within the simplified conditions stipulated by the rules of a game, and it is interesting to note just how important this is for play.

It is worth noting how various games understand justice differently. In a tennis match, the player who has lost a game, loses all the points won in that game and whether the player lost the game closely, or to love, this will not in any way be reflected in the result of the match. The same also goes for winning a set and the match. Such a concept of 'fairness' would surely be unacceptable to any rationalist, as it is blatantly unfair – a player who actually lost more points than his opponent can win the match. But this system has the virtue of maintaining suspense. In each and every game, everything is at stake. It is also very realistic and teaches the players something which is nearly enough a rule in real life. And it also bears a resemblance to the concept of 'fairness' inherent in the British 'first-past-the-post' voting system – which is perhaps no coincidence.

In every game, one of the players starts and the other responds. This regular turn-taking is most clearly seen in chess or bridge, but it is there in tennis and other games too. By incorporating it, play employs a typical aspect of human behaviour, something we might call 'demarcated freedom'. In tennis, the player serving has the freedom to choose how to hit the ball, and the receiving player has somehow to deal with this shot, which he himself did not choose. Provided he can get to the ball, he then has a certain amount of choice – where to place the ball, how much spin to put on it, and so on. Similarly in chess, white has the choice of the opening move; but every other move is influenced by what black chooses to do in response to this opening. Both players have their general plans and strategies, and these confront each other constantly on the chess board, where one player's plan presents an obstacle for the other to overcome, and vice versa. So each player views the game as a continual alternation of moments of decision (within the given limits, and always restricted by the opponent's actions) and moments of response to the opponent's plan, as it gradually takes shape on the board.

In chess, it is only white's first move which is entirely 'free'; all the following moves are partly necessitated by the opponent's previous moves. Having the first move therefore confers a certain advantage, obvious for example in tennis, for the player who serves, and the rules applying to the serve have to be markedly restrictive. The taking of turns on serve further dissipates this advantage, as does rotating the serve, as in volleyball. We have already discussed the confrontation of freedoms, about one person's desire to assert his or her freedom against the freedom of others, and to 'trump' theirs if necessary. It is this aspect of conflict and warfare that competitive games reflect – and their enduring popularity demonstrates their success in so doing. Using the benign circumstances of play as such (in a just environment and without lasting consequences), people can repeatedly experience and practise one of the fundamental features of their life, namely the confrontation of freedoms, the collision of which causes mutual limitation. This is often more important than winning or losing. If we want to 'have a good game', we will choose an opponent at a similar level of ability, not a beginner or an inept player that we can easily beat.

If we want to win, we have to possess some skill, for sure, but we also have to have some luck – the crucially important ingredient so emphasised in gambling, where the opponent might be the fate, embodied by a slot machine. In collective sports like football people learn to collaborate, to pass the ball and to participate in common strategies. Finally, in play, one gets used not only to be glorious in victory, but also dignified in defeat. It is not by accident that games became a part of education, at schools and universities. Wherever this happened, playing games cultivated the public life and opened the road to the rule of law. According to Plato, a well-designed game is of paramount importance for the legislator.

Questions:

- What do children's games and playing a sport have in common? In what they differ?
- What features of play can you identify in a theatre performance, a violinist's performance, or card playing?
- What does play tell us about the nature of human freedom? What is the role of rules and judges there?
- Where else have people managed to introduce rules, a referee?
- Why is it that we do not view rule in a game as restrictive? What do they have to be like in order to promote and not restrict the freedom of a game?
- Name different examples of 'justice' as expressed in the rules of games.

11. Language as Play

At school, or when we are reading, we mostly encounter language in its written (that is, permanent) form, which is however also more impersonal and less 'live'. We have mentioned that language has its formal, syntactical aspect and its semantic aspect, the creation of meaning. We encounter both when learning a foreign language, acquiring a 'language competence'. However, the most fundamental language situation is the spoken language: speech, dialogue, Chomsky's 'performance'. And there, the third aspect of language comes in – how and why we utilise language, the discipline known as pragmatics. Grammar, phonetics, and vocabulary, all these are just a set of rules and options which allow us to think, speak, write, and understand. As any other 'option' though, language only really 'exists' when it is used, when it has some speakers.

In this, language bears a remarkable resemblance to play; that too is a set of options and rules which the players themselves usually did not invent, but which they accept, and with which they start their own individual and unique games, within the framework provided by these rules. Similarly to the way players enter a game, people engaging in a conversation enter the world of speech rules and start a sort of game, whose participants take turns to make their respective 'moves', that is, utterances. There are countless possible kinds of language game available to us, from the quite 'playful' to the competitive and confrontational, to the frighteningly serious and tragic. For language play is usually not separated from the rest of life and it cannot be said that its results have no permanent bearing on it; quite the opposite is true.

Language play is usually not played for its own sake. It is always within a context and its participants have their interests and aims in sight. After all, language is hardly a mere conveyor of information, as it might seem to be when we read textbooks. Most often, people just chat, simply because they are together – at home, on a bus, at the office. It is language which creates and maintains human society. If we are 'not speaking' to someone, it can be very serious indeed, a (so far) non-violent declaration of war. Then we have the language of narrative, from fairy-tales to drama and fiction, which transports us to another world, a world constructed by language play. A quite different kind of language is spoken in the office, in court, at school, in shops, in church, or between lovers. That is why language has such rich diversity of vocabulary at its disposal, to suffice for all the speaking, talking, speech-making, chatting, nattering and blethering, gossiping and slandering, ratting and whistle-blowing, for incantation and bewitching, for talking back, haggling and for reaching agreement. You can talk down to people, speak up or misspeak. Also you can call something off, call somebody up or call on them instead. So our ancestors, while not knowing much about grammar, or semantics, nevertheless understood pragmatics quite comprehensively.

We have also mentioned that language distinguishes three 'persons', the first, second, and third. Linguists refer to an *addresser* (speaker, 'I'), who directs his utterance at an *addressee* '(you'), talking about the *referens*, the subject in the broadest meaning. Utterances, too, can be of different types. The most common one is denotative, which corresponds to the indicative mode in grammar: 'the window is open.' In such an utterance, the addresser imparts the information to the addressee, who previously did not know it. The emphasis here is on the subject, the *referent*, and the question of veracity arises – is it really true? For the same construction could be used to express the truth or a mistake, just as a lie or deception; they all *denote* something. It is then left to the addressee to process it somehow, to either accept the utterance or reject it, to ask something or just snigger, simply to respond within the framework of the given rules, thus himself becoming the addresser. Denotative utterances are characteristic of 'factual' speech, they tend to be long and frequently occur in books, lectures, and other monologues where the addressee is restricted to the role of listener. We might then ask who actually is the addressee, and how much the addresser knows about them. That is what Nietzsche had in mind when he described *Thus Spoke Zarathustra* as 'a book for everybody and nobody'. In a televised dialogue, the participants may speak directly to each other, but the real addressees sit at home in front of their TV sets, a fact which any canny politician will be well aware of.

The opposite situation in relation to the referent is supposed by the utterance: 'is the window open?' At least at a first sight, on the basic level, the addresser seeks to learn something. But not always, we can use the same form to pose a rhetorical question, or an ironic one, or the addresser may not really be concerned about the window being open or not but might instead be trying to find out something else – whether the addressee can speak English for example. Such confusion of the referent is in fact quite common, particularly in questions. The Czech philosopher and scientist Emanuel Rádl frequently said that the answer to the question 'what is it like outside?' could easily be 'put a coat on'. When we ask 'can you tell me what time the next train leaves?' we do not really expect the answer 'yes, I can.' On the other hand, the utterance 'can you open the window?' is not properly a question but nearly the same as 'open the window!' – a prescriptive utterance. In a prescriptive utterance, the addresser acts as a person with some degree of authority, ordering, requesting, or asking, he simply wants something done (or not done), the addressee being in a position to bring it about. The addresser may be in a superior position to the addressee, like a boss or a commanding officer, or he can be addressing him like a beggar with a plea, he can twist and modify this relationship in order to achieve his goal, for that is the point here. Contrastingly, truth, mistakes, and lies make little sense in these circumstances. True questions as well as prescriptions tend to be succinct, grammatically in the second person and most often to be found in a conversation.

There is a further specific type of utterance, namely those which are not about something, but bring something about by the mere act of utterance: 'Can I go out?' 'You can.' The addressee of such a performative utterance is clearly some sort of authorised person, while the addresser can remain quite vague: 'I declare this exhibition open'. And so the king of a certain small planet tells Exupéry's *Little Prince* how the sun always sets on his command, he just has to be careful to utter the command at the right time. There is another kind of performative utterance worth noting, and that is promise. A promise is characteristically always in the future tense and it creates an obligation for the addresser. It may not be as frequent, but it has always been considered so important, that it is in many languages expressed by the phrase 'to give one's word'. Curious, is it not?

But let us return to conversation, which is the fundamental form of language play. Unlike lectures and other monologues, which, as Franz Rosenzweig put it, reduce most participants to a mere pair of ears, conversation has a much richer fabric and contains a strong element of the unexpected. We can reasonably expect a person who is about to give a lecture, or write something, to be able to say what topic it is going to be on. With a conversation, we can never tell beforehand what it is going to be about. Therein lies the excitement – and likewise the risk and danger – of conversation. It is not as if those who embark on a conversation have no idea what they want to talk about, but a conversation depends on each and every participant, and never solely on a single one of them. None of them can completely prepare all their arguments and points beforehand, none know where the conversation might take them to.

For a conversation to become established, the participants' role is really to provide ideas and topics, and once the conversation is going, it flows by itself and leads from one plot to another, based on its own internal logic, based on its underlying theme. And if the participants really give in to it, it will lead them somewhere where none of them would get on their own, so much so that a good conversation may leave you unable to clearly remember who exactly said something, but you will know that it has been said. That is precisely what Plato meant in the famous passage from his seventh letter, about the spark which jumps across two pieces of wood rubbed together. That is precisely what we rely on when we want to have a talk about something, and that is what T. G. Masaryk meant when he said that 'democracy is a discussion' – for it to happen, all participants must have roughly the same understanding of it – something of a rarity in politics.

As a conversation is purely in the present moment, a true temporal action in which nothing can be skipped or speeded up, everything must happen at its natural pace and in its natural order – therefore, it can also not be infinite. While the dialogue was the basic means for philosophy, there was no room for lengthy tomes and philosophers had to make do with the format of Platonic dialogues. A monologue, a lecture, and a treaty are created in advance, whether in writing or not, but they are all ready and thought through; and the lecturer then only feigns to be speaking to his audience. A recording would do just as good a job. This is why it can be such an ordeal to follow lectures.

What conversation could and should be, can be best seen when something goes awry. This is most often the case in stage-managed dialogues, such as can be seen often on TV, where the participants feign to be addressing each other, while in fact they are not interested in each other at all as their real target is the viewers and voters in front of the TV set. Interrupting another speaker is a typical sign of a fake dialogue. It proves that those doing the interrupting care little about what the other person is saying, and are not interested in it. As a result, they cannot really learn anything and they render the dialogue useless – not only for the person that they have interrupted, but also for themselves.

Dialogue is a truly democratic, even egalitarian institution. That is why it does not fare well if it has an audience. The presence of any kind of authority (real or imagined) is also detrimental, either because it asserts itself too much or because it causes the others to cower. A dialogue may be heated, but it must never be personal; it remains a dialogue only when it is something that is shared, never as a verbal shooting match or mudslinging in front of others. Just like some people are said to have no sense of fair play, others have the reputation that 'there's no talking to them', you cannot lead a dialogue with them. For dialogue is really a speech game, a non-zero-sum game, which can yield more than the sum of what its participants put into it, provided they themselves will allow it to happen.

Questions:

- Why do we say that speech is originally a dialogue?
- Try to formulate rules of a dialogue as a speech game. What would merit a yellow or a red card?
- Name different types of speech games and utterances. Explain the differences.
- Consider the temporal structure of a promise at the moment it is created and when it is supposed to be fulfilled.
- Why is it said that democracy is a dialogue? What are its strengths and weaknesses?
- How can a dialogue become more than what its participants put into it? Have you ever experienced it?

12. Time

'If no one asks me, I know what it is. If I wish to explain it to him, who asks, I do not know,' the great Christian philosopher St. Augustine said of time. Fifteen centuries on, his words are still as valid as when he wrote them. Time is something so self-evident and trivial that our inability to say exactly what it is can be infuriating. We have mentioned the expression of time in grammatical tenses, the radio announces the 'exact time', sprinters can achieve their personal best time, some of us feel they have 'all the time in the world' to do something. Grown-ups usually 'don't have time', older people like to reminisce about 'old times'; we may hear that perhaps this is not 'the right time' for something. What does it all mean? Does it all mean the same? Hardly. And do all these expressions even have anything in common?

There was a fictional radio station which featured in many Russian jokes, called Radio Yerevan. The time announcement would come on like this: 'It is exactly ten o'clock, beep-beep-beep. I repeat, it is exactly ten o'clock...' Why is that funny? Because time passes all the time, the exact time is always 'now' and it cannot be repeated. The exact time is simply a piece of data, a number, which was once calculated in relation to the Sun – and that is why we still count in years, months, days, and hours, although they are nowadays measured by a precise electronic clock, with the numerals showing on a display. This image can be traced back to Aristotle, who said that time is some measured motion in relation to what precedes and what follows. By 'motion', he meant the movement of the Sun, the perpetual alternation of day and night, but it would be a valid description even if we imagine it as the movement of a pendulum, or any other steady movement which repeats itself and is, therefore, possible to count. This is in fact just what an electronic clock does.

So we know that time gets measured. But what is time? Is it just this measuring, which says what time it is 'now'? And when is 'now', anyway? We can only experience our own 'now'. Science does not consider it either, for the 'now' is probably 'my now', of which I know it will never return. A person steeped in science might imagine 'now' as sort of point moving along the time line, always exactly where I am, where you are, where everybody is. After all the whole world is there, because the past is always 'to the left' of this point, that which is gone, while 'to the right', there is what is to come, the future. But the past is gone and the future has not yet arrived, it is only the present that exists.

So what is present? You are reading a book right now. You are reading word after word, as they appear on the lines; you put them together into sentences, trying to understand what they mean. When I am reading, speaking or listening, I am always doing so 'now'. When I am listening to a word and a sentence, I would in a 'point of time', a moment without dimensions, hear only just a sound, a tone, perhaps only a mere oscillation. It takes a certain time to utter a sentence, word by word, sound by sound; it is not possible to say it all at once. But at the same time, I do hear the sentence 'now', without feeling I need to search my memory for the previous sound or word. This is even more notable in a melody, as once described by St. Augustine and analyzed by Edmund Husserl. Imagine you hear somebody whistle a tune. You immediately recognise it as, say, Yellow Submarine. You will recognise it even if you cannot read music or tell a G from a C sharp. That person is whistling it 'now', and it is how I hear it, as if all of it in the present moment.

We should say 'the present' then, rather than 'now', and that is certainly not a point on a time line, as imagined by physics, rather something which possesses a certain depth and breadth, a certain duration. The extent of the duration depends on what it is we are doing. After all, the word 'present', from the Latin *prae-sum*, I am in front of, denotes what we are confronted with, engaged in, what we are focusing on at a given moment. We have discussed how focusing our attention can select the subject of our interest within the field of vision. Also, the way in which we perceive the present moment is crucial. A person waiting for a train, and with no work to do, will find the time dragging on, and the span of his present very short, there being nothing to join it together. On the other hand, if I am watching a gripping detective story on TV, it is all 'in front of me', as if present, and I am 'with it' from the very start. When the film is over, I rub my eyes and wonder at how late it has become: 'how the time flies!' So for a viewer fully engaged by the plot of such a story, the present can easily span over a couple of hours. The same goes for a concert-goer, a chess player or a lecturer – their present must comprise the whole of what they are doing or taking part in, otherwise it would make no sense. As people have ascertained over the centuries that a normal human being is able to pay attention for about an hour, or two at a push, it has been established that a school lesson, a film, a concert, a mass, or a football match should not last longer than that, otherwise the participants might start nodding off.

And so the present, which we constantly live in, is a fairly complicated structure. On the one hand, we keep hold of what has already passed; on the other, we anticipate that which is coming. We have a certain idea about it, which is usually fulfilled in everyday life. Things run along as expected, to the extent that it is almost boring. That is why we will gladly watch a western, where it will not be so. The hero is sitting at a bar, enjoying his drink, when suddenly – BANG! Something surprising happens. If we were not anticipating what happens next, there would be no scope for surprise. Somebody is learning to play the piano next door and always makes a mistake in the third bar. Why is it so unbearable? Because we know what 'should' be there, and it goes wrong.

This curious conjunction of what has passed and what is anticipated (Husserl calls it 'retention' and 'protention') in the unity of the present, is the core of the phenomenon of time. Only once a film has finished does it truly become 'the past' for me, a closed lapse of time, a former present. It is now a coherent story, which I will remember and will be able to relate to others. Similarly to the way the past and the future conjoin in the present, individual time units conjoin into larger ones – school lessons form the school day, days grow into seasons and years, years create the whole of our life experience. On closer inspection, this ability to retain as present that which has passed enables us to 'count' movements. Aristotle says that there has to be something beside the counted movements, and that is the soul which retains them. That is how we are able to – up to a certain limit – carry out mental counting of movements, e.g., steps or heartbeats, as long as we still view them as present, while to count days and weeks, we would have to make marks on a tree trunk, after the fashion of Robinson Crusoe.

We have touched upon an important distinction here – retention is something other than memory or recollection. I cannot very well say of the past section of a present action, that I 'remember' it; I remember things which have passed for good. The current act, crime story, drama or game is before me, for I am keeping my focus on it right now. I can only speak of memory when I have to recall each individual moment, once my attention has been diverted from the subject. And if I want to go back to it, I have to jog my memory: 'how did it go?' or 'where did we leave off the last time?'

A memory will show that what we remember is not a linear recording of events, an unbroken trace of the time passed. The 'boring phases' of our life will be projected quite sketchily, or not at all, while dramatic and interesting moments, especially those from our childhood, can be recalled with astonishing detail. It is extremely difficult, nigh impossible, to reconstruct our own life as it really happened. For our memory is neither continuous, nor dated, as a historian might put it. I might recall a distant event and see it vividly before my eyes, but my memory may give me no clues as to when it actually happened. I have to ponder whether it was before I was married, or how old my children were at the time, and so on – like looking at an old photograph with no date on it. Likewise, the order of events, unless they bear some direct connection, may be lost or confused in our memory.

As we have just seen, the phenomenon of time is created by retention of what has passed and anticipation of the future.[*] But that which has been has quite a different meaning for us than that which will be. Past experience may have equipped us for this moment, has formed us in a certain way, but it is itself over and gone. We do not have much knowledge of the future on the other hand, of that which is to come and what is ahead of us. We project our ideas, worries, and hopes into it. It is of importance to us to gauge correctly, to be prepared for it, when it arrives as the present. But it is not a pre-recorded film, on show just for each of us individually – although some philosophers did imagine it in this way. The future only happens when it becomes the present, and it is up to us what we make of it.

The way in which the future becomes the present has been described by Heidegger as an alternation and collision of two different elements. There are, first of all, our plans and ideas, our activities, which we project into the future, that which we wish to happen. At the same time, however, we keep coming up against things we have not chosen for ourselves, various restrictions, hurdles, but also unexpected opportunities. Sometimes we may feel as if we have been thrown into a world which nobody consulted us about (Heidegger's 'thrown-ness'), but which we nevertheless have to accept for what it is. And only in this collision and mingling of our

---

[*]   'Time is the life of the soul in movement'. (Plotinus)

projections and our 'being thrown', our activity and passive acceptance of given circumstances, can something real happen and the imagined future become the real present, whether we like it or not. We could illustrate these two important elements with any number of examples, but let us return to the subject we were discussing a while ago: play. When we wanted to describe the peculiar nature of human behaviour as revealed by play, we used the phrase 'demarcated freedom'. Now we can be a bit more specific. In chess or tennis, the players experience alternation and collision of their projections – such as the serve, strategy, goal – and their 'thrown-ness', their being 'thrown' into a situation which is not shaped according to their wishes, but which are formed by the opponent, by their returns and counter-moves. At the same time, we are creating the situation of being thrown for the opponent. The principle of turn-taking, which differentiates such games from reality, allows us to glimpse, in a simplified form, something which is inherent in the human situation under any circumstances. Only it is not always so readily visible.

Let us now return to the temporal nature of our existence. We have noted that moments of full attention and focus on the present alternate with moments of 'emptiness', when we are just looking around waiting for the next thing to happen, and also moments when we take a step back and regard ourselves more distantly, which enables us to see further. And so our projections can be cast at closer or further horizons and aims; and we can try to gauge what possibilities the future itself will bring us when we reach a certain horizon. When the lecture is over, I'll go for a bite to eat, I am planning to go to a concert tomorrow, next week I should go to see my aunt, I would like to finish writing a book by next year. In ten years' time... will I still be alive? Maybe, but in fifty years' time definitely not. We may not know when, but we do know for certain that we are going to die. Whatever notions we have of death, we are aware that it means the end of our projections, our human possibilities. Although we speak little of this certainty, and we do not think about it too often either, we are constantly aware of it. That is why it can sometimes happen that we 'have no time'. And it is also another feature which sets us apart from animals.

Awareness of the finite nature of our life lends a characteristic form to our time and temporality. A picture or a shape must be finite and limited, in order for us to perceive it as a shape, that is, to see it in its entirety at one glance, while only a line or an ever-repeating pattern can be infinite. Similarly, it is the finite nature of life which allows us to attempt to form it into some sort of overall shape; the very fact actually spurs us on and obliges us to try. If life is finite, we should treat it as such, try to shape it as a whole, one form, or to be more precise, as it is a temporal form, keep it as one story. We have already touched on the paradoxical fact that restrictions actually significantly stimulate human creativity. Now we shall have a closer look at a particular manifestation of this fact.

If life is to be perceived as a whole, it should be in one way or another always present. To put it simply, a person should always be able to own up to their past, and always act in such a way so as not to be ashamed of it in future, so that each action strings on to one storyline. Naturally, that does not mean that life should from start to finish trot along a straight line, a story does not do that either, there is complication, there is drama. Some elements, however, must hold the story together. One of them is giving one's word. A person who keeps his promises, actually acknowledges the validity of something which has already passed. But he has given his word and it belongs in the story of his life, therefore it is still valid. Every one of us is sure to have events in our life which we would much rather not have in it. But they did happen, and what is more, it was us who did them. If we want our life to be a story, we have to acknowledge them and bear any possible consequences.

You may have noticed that our explanation of time keeps straying into explanations of behaviour, life, human existence. That is not by accident. According to Heidegger, it is not accurate to say that we live 'in time,' rather, our life is time. Does this seem strange to you? A number of quite ordinary things appear to prove him right. A person who says they do not 'have time' for one thing or another, is not saying that they do not know the time or have lost the sense of time, rather that they cannot find a free slot in their life (in their diary, so to speak) to do it. It is to say that the person cannot or is not willing to devote such and such portion of their life to the matter in question. This is also the thinking underlying the modern idea of punishing criminals by 'taking away their freedom' for a certain period of time. In the old days, crime used to be punished by death, or perhaps the chopping off of the offender's hand. Over time, Europeans began to view the practice of removing people's body parts as barbaric, and introduced the notion of confiscating part of a person's life instead. When we speak of imprisonment as taking away somebody's freedom, it really means taking away a piece of their life. The American saying 'time is money' is not suggesting that a clock will shed coins. It suggests that we can – and do – turn our time, part of our life, into money. We sell a considerable portion of our lives to our employers, doing things we would not do otherwise, in order to be able to spend the rest of the time doing what we really want to do, such as playing games, where time is not money.

We have said that 'now' is always 'my now', my present time. But it is in the present time that we meet the world and other people in it; it is not possible otherwise. The present is the time of meeting, when our respective 'nows' intersect and where we can act together. To do so we need a sort of synchronisation: the sound of the starter's gun or a shout of 'ready-steady-GO!' will cause the athletes in a race to start running. This sound is an event, a shared marker in the area of our individual 'presents', which makes a shared activity and synchronisation possible (e.g., 'heave-ho!'). A watch fulfils a similar purpose, enabling us to agree to meet at the school exactly when the big hand is pointing up and the small hand is at the number which resembles a snowman, at eight o'clock, to put it plainly. With the help of a clock and a calendar, we are able to synchronise even outside the present. The history of this shared (Heidegger calls it 'public') time shows its connection to shared activity. Until not that long ago, the sun was that clock hand, the event determining the shared time, and its culmination, the noon. It happens at a different time at each meridian, with the difference of about four minutes per degree of longitude, which is about 75 kilometres in the Central European latitudes. It was the expansion of fast travel, rail travel in this case, which necessitated the introduction of time zones, so now time is not governed by the sun, but is the same in each zone, with a whole hour difference from zone to zone, which is less confusing.

Time is not only shared in the present. We have already spoken about giving one's word. By doing so, we create a sort of time community with the person we have given our word to: 'I'll see you at nine at the bus stop.' Thus, originally for practical reasons, a shared worldwide method of counting time was created, which became known as GMT. It is no longer governed by the sun, as the movement of the sun is not regular enough, but it has, for the same practical reasons, upheld the traditional way of counting days and hours, and strives to make the differences from the time as shown by the sun almost invisible to us. So while noon on the clock comes a few minutes before or after the sun peaks in the sky, it ensures that it is not dark at noon and that the sun does not rise at midnight. It is not an easy task and something similar has already happened with the counting of years when the Julian calendar had to be reformed as it had become a shocking two weeks removed from solar time.

It seems however that we can experience shared time at a much more profound and basic level, when we share the experience of rhythm. Human time is constantly accompanied by the 'chanting' of the rhythms of our bodies – the heartbeat, the rhythm of our breath, our walking. This is what musical time is based on: the Italian word *tempo* means time, the neutral *allegro moderato* is close to the rhythm of the heart and the somewhat slower *andante* means literally walking. Musical rhythm synchronises us almost involuntarily. Just try marching or even walking down the street when there is a marching band playing; it is almost impossible *not* to walk in time to the music. Singing together, chanting slogans, or merely uttering noises such as 'heave-ho!' – all of this creates a special kind of unwitting *togetherness*, much stronger than many bonds which we are aware of. That is why rhythmic sounds and songs have always accompanied hard labour, and why they are an indispensable technique in military psychology, they always feature in rallies, demonstrations, and revolutions, and generally rank among the stock of weaponry used in the manipulation of the masses. It is thanks to rhythm that when dancing, people are together in a different way than when they are talking, and they can indeed feel as if they have shed their loneliness, perhaps even their ego.

Questions:

- Consider in which circumstances we use the word *time* and words and phrases derived from it (*on time, timely, untimely, good time, three times*)
- Note how 'large' our present can be in different circumstances.
- Describe temporal synchronisation between people, for example when a sprint race is started.
- What effect might the concept that the future is (or is not) 'pre-programmed' have on our freedom?
- What is memory good for, and awareness of events passed? What is experience?
- How does time awareness of a young child differ from that of a grown-up person or an elderly person?
- What do rhythms do to us? Is there a way we can influence it?
- Notice how bodily rhythms connect us with nature and other human beings.

13. Science and Knowledge

'Do you think so?' – 'I don't think so, I know so.' To know something, unlike to suppose, believe, or think it, means not only to be firmly convinced of something, but moreover to have the certainty that we are able to support this opinion, to prove it, show the reasoning behind it and convince others of its veracity. What I know is not only my certainty, but is supported by indisputable reasoning, proof, experience. A person can lead their life by merely repeating what they have been told, and many people do just that. If it turns out not to be true, well, it is just what I have heard. But to know something requires some courage. The courage to independently observe, analyse, think. The courage to rely not only on what I know from others, but what I know myself.

How have I learned what I know? Leaving aside what we have learned from others (e.g., that the Earth is round), we learn from experience. I can put my hand out of the window and find out if it is raining or not. I can look in my wallet and see if there is any money in it or not. The experience in such cases is the experience of the senses. Senses can, however, deceive us too – in blistering heat, a tarmac road can appear wet. A sensible person will pause for thought – how could it get wet, in such heat? On closer inspection, it turns out to be dry. The diffraction of light causes the hot tarmac surface to 'reflect' like a wet surface. An occurrence which I have seen may have various causes, and my first inference was wrong because I had uncritically selected the most common one. The mistake, then, is not due to my eyesight, but rather due to the wrong judgement I have made based on incomplete sensory experience. We are not so much deceived by our senses, as by our judgement. As we already know, however, we do not separate the two in our everyday life; we do not see the bending of light rays, from which we would later infer the road being wet, we see a 'wet road'.

How can we uncover such mistakes? We need, first of all, the experience of such things happening – 'all that glitters is not gold'. In other words, we need to be critical. Secondly, we have to be able to combine our experiences – a wet road while the sun is beating down? There is something not right about that! As soon as a suspicion arises, or if it is a matter of importance, we will endeavour to prove or refute the original impression by gaining further experience of it – such as having a closer look, looking from a different angle, feeling the surface of the road. Our judgement will become more certain the greater variety of experience will support it. And should we feel that our own experience is insufficient, we will go and seek advice from someone else.

The first immediate impression does not require any particular conscious activity on my side – I just look and see. That is why some people consider it to be the most reliable: 'I've seen it with my own eyes!' Our sensory perception is however programmed for the most common situations, when it must function quickly and reliably. That is why it 'takes shortcuts' and also often sees things which are not really there, such as a wet road. If I want to safeguard myself from such rash judgements, I must employ my rational faculties as well. Then I can no longer rely just on what I have 'seen', but I must in some way articulate the content of my sensory experience, as we have already discussed when we were talking about terms. Only then can the experience, as expressed in words, be compared to and confronted with other experiences, or the experiences of others for that matter. To formulate an experience is, as we know, not an easy task. So a person grappling with some unusual experience may often mutter under their breath the summary of where they got so far: 'I'll be... The money was right here. Or hang on, was it in the other room?' Pretending that we are consulting the matter with someone else helps us proceed step by step and not be fooled by some rash judgement again.

The form of play which best demonstrates and illustrates this approach is the crime story. It juxtaposes 'facts' discovered at the scene of the crime, the experiences of the detective, the police, and the witnesses. What ensues is usually that both the police and guiltless witnesses are misguided by ambiguous facts, which the culprit arranged so as to lead them astray and throw them off the right track. This is because they allow themselves to be contented with first impressions, with what Plato would call 'a mere opinion', thus arriving at a dead end – why, at the time of the murder, there was nobody in the banker's mansion. It is left to the critically thinking, cunning and crafty detective to realise that in the eyes of the upper crust witnesses, there really was 'nobody' else, not one of them, that is to say, but what about the gardener? Bingo! A reader of crime fiction is, however, very particular that it should only be for the culprit and the police to play this game, not for the author to play it with his readership. If the author does withhold what the detective has uncovered, we will quickly put the book down on the grounds that it is badly written and makes no sense.

Detective thrillers describe difficult situations where everyday life comes up short, where it cannot cope, and where the help of critical reason, in the shape the great expert Sherlock Holmes, must be sought. Magnates and noblemen beseech this shabby-looking intellectual as their only hope. As such a clear demonstration of the usefulness (necessity, even) of critical intellect, in undeniably grave matters, it is dream material for many an intellectual who may otherwise feel undervalued and frustrated in real life. This also explains the undying popularity of the genre.

So far, we have been talking about situations where experience is obtained through the senses. As that is most often the case in everyday life, some philosophers believe that the senses are our only source of knowledge. There are cases, however, when we learn something without the involvement of the senses. These are fairly rare, but very interesting nevertheless, and therefore a point of interest for philosophers throughout the ages. A classic example is the answer to the question 'how many diagonals are there in a pentagon?' A person who does not know the answer by heart only needs to think for a moment to come up with the correct answer. If they are smart enough and able to generalise, they can put together the formula which enabled them to find the answer, and which is valid for all polygons. If they do not possess a strong imagination, they can help themselves by drawing a diagram. Note that even now, no sensory experience is involved; the picture is merely there to aid the thinking process.

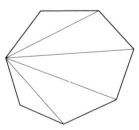

Fig. 1. Diagonals in a heptagon

How do we go about such deliberation? There is an equal number of diagonals starting from each apex, thus their number will correlate to the number of vertexes. They will lead to all vertexes, with the exception of the adjoining ones and the starting one. The number of diagonals then equals the number of vertexes minus three. (Note that this only applies to shapes where none of the vertexes are inverted so as to be in the way of some diagonals. This means the polygon has to be convex, with all the vertex angles smaller than 180 degrees.) Each diagonal connects two vertexes and would therefore feature twice in the total number. The result, which will in any case be an even number, then has to be divided by two. In mathematical terms, the resulting formula will look like this: $N \times (N-3) / 2$. The thought process which we have just recapitulated is the answer to our question, actually a general answer to a whole category of questions, and more besides that. As it is based on indisputable facts and general rules, it is at the same time a proof. Anyone who knows a little bit about geometry, who knows what a polygon, a vertex and a diagonal are, must acknowledge its correctness.

This way of knowing, which is traditionally called 'rational' (Leibniz distinguishes between the 'truth of reason' and the 'truth of fact'), is interesting in that it is something that we have in fact always possessed (*a priori* knowledge, as Immanuel Kant calls it), we just have not been aware of it, or rather, it refers to knowledge which can be gained without further external experience. Indeed, Descartes talks of 'innate ideas'. A sceptic might counter that everything which our thought process has led to is already included in the definition of a polygon and a diagonal. But that is precisely the point. If something is included in or implied by something else, somebody has to be able to explicate it – to unravel it, we might say. Most human activities involve such unravelling, whether it be taking fish from water, starch from grain, or chemicals from coal. That is not to say that such activity may not be creative, even just to find out what can be unravelled from where can be an exceptional feat. Let alone to discover how to go about it. Socrates, the father of western philosophy, actually saw his activity as helping his fellow citizens bring to light ideas which they carry within themselves, and he likened his role to that of a midwife.

The appeal of rational thought lies above all in that is in its own way general and certain. It does not rely on any changeable sensory findings, which can moreover merge in various ways; from a sensory experience we must, as we have seen, pick out individual objects through recognising them. Rational thought, on the other hand, does not involve any unchecked judgements, which are the most common root of mistakes of 'mere opinion'. Each step is critically regarded, and it is carried out in unambiguous terms, and it can be checked by others, too. It uses terminology which is thoroughly clear and which, once understood, provides all the necessary knowledge. Unlike a piece of rock or a dog, which can always surprise me in some way, a triangle hides no secrets. I know 'everything' there is to know about it, immediately, all at once. As it is so simple, I can hardly forget it either. Therein, however, also lies the strongest limitation of rational knowledge – it can only be applied to logical, mathematical, or geometrical objects, that is to say objects which are ideal or rational. The discovery of rational knowledge, its generality and reliability, is the starting point for science, too.

The aim of science, as established by Greek philosophers and classical scientists, was to gain true and certain knowledge and understanding of the world. Such knowledge is only possible where the objects themselves are precisely defined, unchangeable and eternal – in an ideal domain, such as geometry. The Pythagorean conviction, that the very foundations of the world are determined by numerical laws, was probably grounded in the discovery of the numerical principles governing the tones created on the string of a musical instrument. A string shortened by a half sounds an octave higher; a three-fifth length gives a sound a fifth higher, and so on. The whole scale can be formulated in fractions with very small denominators. The Pythagoreans suggested that, similarly to the arrangement of the tones of a scale on a string, the planets are arranged so that their motion creates the 'music of the spheres'. Further remarkable discoveries in geometry followed, such as the discovery of five regular polyhedrons, which would, two thousand years later, serve the young Johannes Kepler as the model for the arrangement of the planetary system.

If we speak about the Greek roots of science, we do not mean to say that there was no such thing before the Greeks. The Middle-Eastern cultures, especially the Babylonians and Egyptians, had already cultivated astronomy and geometry with astonishing results. However, their approach always led to a specific method of solving the given problem. Thus the Egyptians knew that if they measured out three sections on a string, in the ratio of 3:4:5, and formed a triangle out of them, it would be a rectangular one. But it was only the Greeks who understood that this is not an isolated coincidence but rather a general principle, as formulated in Pythagoras' theorem. So it was in Greece that science was born as a system of exact knowledge, with Euclid even attempting to ground it in several basic and indisputable postulates, or axioms.

The beauty of the axiomatic system rests in the ability to further deduce more complex postulates from basic axioms, which in themselves are no longer so obvious. We can see this in two simple examples, which also demonstrate the way in which the Ancient Greeks envisaged the construction of proof as a sequence of steps which cannot be disputed, as they are plainly visible to the eye. Refer to figure 2 for the geometrical proof of Thales' theorem, which we are all familiar with from high school. It states that if A, B, and C are points on a circle, with the line AC being the diameter of the circle, then the angle ABC is a right angle. In other words, the points A, B, and C form a right angled triangle. This is no trivial claim; it is not immediately obvious why it should be so. But we only need to look at the diagram and it becomes quite clear – the aforementioned triangle is in fact one half of a quadrangle, whose diagonals are of equal length (they are diameters of the circle) and they intersect in the middle, with the resulting triangle being inevitably a right angled one. If your geometry textbook only showed the upper half of the diagram, this connection was not obvious and you just had to trust the teacher that they are telling you the truth about Thales' theorem.

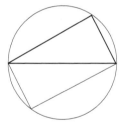

Fig. 2 Thales' theorem

Pythagoras' theorem presents a slightly harder nut to crack – in any right triangle, the area of the square whose side is the hypotenuse (the side opposite the right angle) is equal to the sum of the areas of the squares whose sides are the two legs (the two sides which meet at the right angle). We have the triangle with the sides a, b, and c (drawn in bold). Both squares in figure 3 have the sides of the length equal to $a+b$. The one on the left shows the squares with the legs of the triangle (sides a and b), whose areas thus being a squared and b squared respectively. The rest of the big square is filled with four triangles identical to ABC, just as it is the case with the square on the right, where these four triangles surround the square over the hypotenuse (c^2). It then follows that $a^2 + b^2 = c^2$. You can even try this with paper and scissors. If you were never shown this proof at school, then only now do you really know that Pythagoras' theorem is valid. You know it because you have seen it with your own eyes. Nevertheless, it is likely that none of us could have come up with this elegant proof independently.

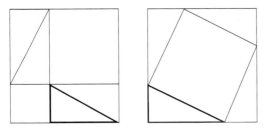

Fig. 3 Pythagoras' theorem: $(a+b)^2 = a^2+b^2+2ab = c^2+2ab$

Aristotle significantly extended the concept of science, applying it to any area of experience, as long as it is possible to categorise systematically. Thus logic was founded as the science of language rules and argumentation, physics as the science of nature, and psychology, zoology, politics, rhetoric, poetics, and ethics. He too regarded science as a systematic exploration of reality, whose aim is true and certain understanding and knowledge. Instead of working on the basis of fundamental axioms, which understandably were not available, Aristotle satisfied himself with the knowledge that the observed realities are universally true and that anyone can verify them. He organised his subjects according to a principle which never varies: we can describe each subject by finding the nearest hypernymous (superordinate) term in which it is included, together with subjects similar to it, then formulating the specific features which distinguish it from all the others in that category. Thus man is an animal (generic term) with the ability to speak (specific feature). Aristotle's concept of science still forms the foundation of linguistics, natural sciences and the study of human society. In scientific terms, all bacteria, plants, and animals still receive two names, a species name and a family name; such as *Taraxacum officinale*, dandelion.

Pythagoras' and Plato's idea of a single hidden rational foundation of the world and Aristotle's idea of order as a systematic organisation of our experiences forms the two classical roots of science. The modern age has modified them in an interesting fashion, and added to them. Modern science still sees the very basis of the world mathematically, although it no longer means only 'beautiful' relationships between small whole numbers and regular geometrical objects, but rather the relationship of quantities, which are entirely variable. Where the numerical and geometrical basis of reality is not immediately obvious (such as, say, in crystals), we must establish it by weighing and measuring, just as a market-stall vendor would. After all, it was from merchants that science borrowed the new and vastly more practical way of numerical transcription in the decimal system, using Arabic numbers. It is of no concern that the measuring does not yield convenient round numbers, their relationship remains the same and owing to the decimal system, we can easily operate with them. The particular numerical value is after all secondary, a fact which is stressed by the use of variables – it is the correspondence and ratio what really matters, whatever numbers we choose to substitute. The mathematical foundation of the world should thus not be quantified by numbers and fractions, rather by functions; that is, the correspondence between variables. So when Descartes joined function with geometry, the road ahead was clear.

As the modern age only busies itself with the 'scientific', that is to say reliably measurable, part of our experience, the mere observation of nature, as Aristotle envisaged it, loses its meaning and is duly replaced by experimentation. Unlike pure observation, an experiment does not focus on everything which we can observe; it seeks numerical answers *to the questions posed*. If possible, then, modern science prefers an artificially controlled experiment to direct observation. Consider a sheet of paper, falling to the ground at a speed slower than that of a stone. But Galileo stipulated that objects should fall to the ground at the same speed, regardless of their weight. The difference in speed is caused by air friction, a force which we are not concerned with at the moment. Properly, a free fall experiment should be carried out in a vacuum, where such 'side effects' would not confuse us. It also goes to show how science gets into conflict with everyday experience – was Galileo right, or should we just believe our own eyes? There, the Greek tradition, as well as Scholasticism, was helpful, as it was very sceptical towards immediate impressions and sought truth as usually contrasting with what seems to be the case at first glance. A similar, but even graver, conflict arose from the question of the Sun's movement. People always saw it rise and set above the steadfast Earth, until a certain Copernicus started to affirm that it is just the opposite. But there, too, the Galilean science emerged victorious, while at the same time further eroding trust in everyday experience. It achieved its victory by being able to predict what is going to happen, e.g., an eclipse – an ability bordering on the superhuman. Francis Bacon was the first to note that the scope of science offers man a hitherto unheard of power over nature. And that seems to be its main goal in modern times.[*]

The success of this modern-day mathematisation of science lies very much in that once it is possible to mathematise the relationships between objects, it is possible to explore them further, to the extent of being able to predict their behaviour and characteristics, and to do so in a mathematical way. If we are able to calculate and quantify the load-carrying capacity of a girder, we can tell in advance whether a bridge will fall down or not, without actually having to build it and then relying on our sensory experience to find out. Moreover, we are able to carry out the same calculation for any given bridge. And so the problem of taming nature is a problem of mathematisation. Scientific fields which were not able to mathematise and had to make do with the Aristotelian organisation of facts, such as botany, have been sidelined. Those sciences which were able to mathematise inevitably sought to widen their scope. Up until Renaissance times, science distinguished between measurable quantities (e.g., length) and immeasurable qualities (e.g., colour). Modern science managed to quantify many qualities, first weight, then temperature and tone frequency, and it was Newton who boldly suggested that colour too may be something like a tone frequency. It turned out he was right.

With the discovery of statistics came another great breakthrough in the programme of mathematisation. Even the behaviour of subjects, which superficially does not show any signs of regularity, can be subsequently mathematised, provided we gather enough data. This can be the movement of molecules in a gas, hereditary traits in plants, or the behaviour of shoppers in a shopping centre. As early as the 19th century, the mathematisation of almost all reality was achieved, at least as a mass phenomenon. All it takes is to formulate a hypothesis, state what is dependent on what, then collect data and find out to what extent (what percentage and relevance) the hypothesis holds. This represents a significant advance in our understanding of what science is; Galileo and Newton had perceived the laws of nature as a precise project, on the basis of which God Himself created nature. He who has understood the

---

[*] „The true aim of the science is to enrich mankind with new forces and inventions." (Francis Bacon)

laws of nature comes to view it through God's eyes, and therefore with a perfection which cannot be surpassed. That is the Platonic heritage of modern-day science. The law of statistics assumes much less; it only states the degree of co-dependency between two measurable quantities and that is it. This law applies within the given scope, and it can be used to make more or less accurate predictions; but as to the nature of what it describes, it remains silent. Even what is a cause and what is an effect has to be added later, through a hypothesis, or measuring with a control group.*

The mathematisation of science forms the basis of technology – industrial, social, financial – thus influencing our everyday life. Within science itself, new, truly philosophical, ideas have been formed. At the beginning of the 19th century, Hegel created a grand concept of the world as evolving in time. Up until that point, science had, in accordance with its Ancient Greek heritage, took note only of principles which were unchangeable and perpetual; any change was seen as a film of dirt obscuring the true, eternal being. Hegel's original idea, which proposed the evolution of Spirit, was soon abandoned and it was change which became the focal point of a number of scientific fields. Not any change, however, but change which is perpetual, irreversible, which leads on to something. It is not that which is constant and never-changing which is substantial and of interest to us, but rather that which evolves. This idea, which was previously contained in historical studies, then quickly spread into linguistic disciplines, geology, and the study of animate nature. Darwin would make it the key to the understanding of species and Comte would use it as the foundation of his vision of social development. Without most of the participants noticing it very much, our view of the world has undergone substantial changes in the last two hundred years, largely under the influence of this concept of evolution. You will even find businesses stressing their developmental trends and tendencies over their current standing and results. Percentages of growth or decrease are more important than the absolute figures.

The twentieth century ushered in the idea of structure and information *per se*. It was partly a reaction to the preceding Historicism, the interest in evolvement and change in time. Structuralism, on the other hand, focuses on principles and regularities which are not of temporal nature; rather, they are 'structural'. All around us, especially

---

* The effectiveness of a medicine is established by comparing the development of an illness in the group which received the medicine with a control group who did not receive it.

in living organisms, in human societies and culture, there are noticeable similarities and structures, which manifest themselves in a similar way. Language, mathematics, or the structural rules of native tribal societies all show similarities. A living organism is neither a mechanical machine, as Descartes believed, nor a system of chemicals and energy; life is above all an organisation of molecules, cells and organs governed by the exchange of information. Nothing is unchangeable or constant; there is, however the ability to regulate and balance out the fluctuations which occur. A warm-blooded creature does not need to maintain its constant bodily temperature by protecting itself from external changes of temperature, as it is able to 'monitor' these changes and actively compensates for them. That is called feedback and it is not a chemical or energy link. It is an information link, albeit one carried out by means of chemicals or electricity.

The concept of information has changed the world in our lifetime. It was not there eighty years ago. It, too, is mathematised and still closely connected to mathematics, but it is a different kind of mathematics. It is not concerned with measuring quantities; it deals with formulating the regularity of structures. In place of differential equations, algebra comes to the fore, as well as informational statistics. A good example is provided by the Markov chains – in each language, it is possible to determine the average word length or the probability of a given speech sound being followed by another. If we let a computer generate a random sequence of letters with the same statistical properties, the resulting text will not make sense, but it will, at a casual glance, strongly resemble writing in German or English. Information and the processing of it nowadays dominates not only administration and all levels of government, it also sustains a vast industry, as well as providing the foundations of molecular biology and genetics. Moreover, the concepts of structure and information have helped bring about interdisciplinary scientific projects and endeavours, often motivated by environmental concerns, perceiving nature, and the Earth, as a whole, something which frequently slips off the radar of the specialised disciplines.

The aim of this ridiculously short summary of the ideological history of science is merely to demonstrate that 'science' today is anything but monolithic, that there is a constant flow of new ideas and concepts, which retroactively affect even everyday existence. In this way, science constantly touches on and grapples with philosophy, which should not only act as a nutrient medium for science, and provide new ideas, but which should also monitor the direction which science is taking. For all their natural tensions and misunderstandings, the two disciplines belong together. Not only through philosophers offering criticism of how blind or fragmented science is, nor just on the strength of the frequent excursions into the realm of philosophy so beloved of many scientists. They should recognise their shared responsibility for the future of our world. To reach interesting and useful results, science has to simplify. It has to neglect various aspects of reality, as they are not measurable, not useful for its purposes, not general and necessary enough. But it is perhaps one of the tasks of philosophy to remind us that these models are methodological simplifications, not reality as a whole.

The astonishing success of European science owes much to Descartes' discovery that no reality need be examined as a whole. We can pick out the tiniest section or feature of it, and provided that we stick to an exact method, our results will be valid, and applicable. The individual findings and discoveries may be stacked up, and one person's research may provide a springboard for another's, while an ever-growing body of reliable and exact findings is created. Naturally, through the division of reality into particular items, aspects, and principles, a certain loss is sustained – as if we were carrying out a post mortem. An exact method must simplify and disregard that which cannot be ascertained. That is why the scientific picture of reality is the more satisfying the simpler the object of its examination. The most serious consequence of the scientific method is, however, the strict separation of the scientist from his subject, the separation of the scientific result from its practical usage. A physicist describes the properties of matter, he proves that it can be split – and the technicians will build a bomb or a power station. It follows from the definition of their task that it is of no concern to them, whether it is right or wrong. That is up to others to decide.

And yet the scientist is a human being too, and once he leaves his laboratory, he re-enters our shared world, where the question of right and wrong must be constantly posed and responsibility must be assumed for the answer we have given. The core of the problem lies in the tendency of modern organisation to compartmentalise, thus separating activity from responsibility. The scientist researches the splitting of the atom, the technician builds the equipment, the politician makes the decision whether to use the bomb or not. The guard in a concentration camp complies with orders, while his commander has actually not killed anyone in person. Where does the responsibility lie? Millions killed and no murderer to be seen. The same goes for less drastic examples – think of the automobile, one of the most successful technical inventions, which is each year responsible for tens of thousands of deaths and has the lion's share of responsibility for our cities not being fit for living in. Is this good or not? And above all, whose problem is it anyway? Who should be racking their brains over it? Who makes the decisions and who bears the responsibility? Is it possible to attribute it to anyone?

Questions:

- We know many scientific disciplines; what do they have in common and how do they differ from one another? Could they be arranged in some order?
- Is mathematics a science? A natural science? What is specific about it?
- What is the difference between conventional and alternative medicines? Can they reach some understanding?
- It is essential for science to know that there are boundaries to its remit. How is this reflected in science, in the thought processes of a scientist, in his life?
- Can science pass a value judgement? Why so, or why not? Based on what reasons?
- Can a scientist withhold judgement? Does his particular field make a difference to this?

14. Truth

In our discussion of science it was impossible for us to avoid the concept of truth – and in fact we should have spoken about it in connection with language. Like science, speech itself only makes sense when something is – or is not – true. This is so obvious that, for the most part, we don't even pay it any notice. 'It is true that grass is green' means exactly the same as 'grass is green'. Even a liar expects to be believed, or else there would be no point in lying. But as for truth itself – what is it? This has been a classic philosophical problem throughout the ages. At first glance it all appears so straightforward; truthful speech is speech which corresponds to how things are – to reality. A sentence or utterance is true when it says what is the case. So the sentence 'it is raining' is true only when it really is raining. Other sentences, such as 'one and one is two', are true always. This is the basis of the oldest and most widely accepted definition of truth – correspondence, the agreement of intellect and reality, as Thomas Aquinas says.

This definition reflects the remarkable fact that real knowledge is governed, not by its own interests, but by the reality being learned about, the thing which we dedicate ourselves to. And so truth is that which separates genuine, unbiased and unselfish knowledge of a subject in itself, for what it is, from the casual violence with which man habitually treats the things surrounding him. Real knowledge attempts to penetrate the secrets of its object, but always tries to leave it as is. Only then can we really come to know something that we didn't before and be saved from our misunderstanding. This conception of truth and truthfulness as the truth of knowledge is the basis of the ethos of science: the emphasis on impartiality, the strictness of the scientist (or investigator, or judge) regarding his own biases, the attempt to gain knowledge in such a way that anyone could repeat the same steps and find out for themselves.

The difficulty arises when we speak of things which do not exist. That a round square is impossible is certainly true, but where is the 'reality' with which such a sentence should correspond? And what do we even mean by 'correspondence'? 'This is a one-pound coin' may be a true sentence, but Kant noticed that it does not actually resemble a one-pound coin in any way – the latter is a round, metallic object, with which something can be bought. But I cannot buy anything with a sentence – so where is the correspondence? And in any case, where everything is clear we will most likey not speak of truth at all. We only become aware of it when we do not know, when we experience doubt – in short, only when we start looking for it. If somebody tells me 'it's raining,' I can stick my hand out of the window and find out for myself. But what about the sentence 'it's going to rain'? This sentence tells me something which may have great interest for me – but this is precisely because I cannot verify it.

If I am uncertain about something, I can ask others: 'is this mushroom edible?' If I receive confirmation from them, we can act accordingly. Another theory of truth has its basis in this. If we have difficulty establishing a correspondence between judgement and reality, we can establish this correspondence between two judgements – two sentences. Truth would therefore mean agreement, consensus between people. From this comes the consensual theory of truth. This theory will not take us very far, however; if our mushroom turns out to be a toadstool, the fact that we all agreed it was edible will not prevent us from becoming poisoned. It is also well known that nothing arouses greater anger than the truth. If my wife tells me that I have behaved like a hooligan she may well be right, but we are unlikely to reach agreement.

The difficulty with truth may well be in the fact that we use the same word – *truth* – to describe various different relationships. Let us begin with the most certain of these relationships, such as mathematical or logical truths. These are true everywhere and at all times, they are true for everybody and can usually be proven. Where there exists a whole system of such sentences – for example in mathematics – truth becomes any utterance that is not in conflict with the others within the system and which cannot be refuted. This is known as the coherence theory of truth: truth as a property of internally consistent systems. The world we live in, however, is most certainly not a system of internally consistent utterances, so this theory can only be used for axiomatic systems. But it is precisely because these assertions are derived from basic utterances and axioms, and because they are always with us and always at our disposal, we feel that there is nothing dramatic about them; they rarely excite us.

That two and two are four is certainly true but it will hardly win you the Nobel Prize. To the extent that we utter such truths at all, we do so in a wry, indifferent manner, and our interlocutors will most likely ask themselves why we are bothering them with it. Two times three is six – so what? Is that truth?

Then there are the interesting bits of truth that we can read in various magazines, when we have nothing else to do with our time. They make for good reading but have no great significance in our lives. We could do just as well without them. Then we have the important, weighty truths on which a great deal depends – like with our mushroom. Here we must do something in order to find out what the truth is. Some pragmatists insist that truth is what has been *proven*, what has been seen to work. But in the case of our toadstool that kind of truth does not help us as it only becomes apparent *post mortem*. There are also some truths which may only apply at some times and in some situations, but which can utterly transform our lives. And finally, there are those truths on which all depends: truths for which people have given their lives. They may not have proved by so doing that the truth was on their side, but they have shown how important the truth was to them. To take an example – we may no longer value Giordano Bruno's scientific theories, but we continue to admire his courage.

This is why people who like to play at being philosophers often say things like 'everyone has their own truth'. Indeed this stance has become fashionable. But no philosopher can ever allow himself to say this; he would have to stop speaking at once. Every sentence, or rather, every denotative utterance and every question, is made with the presupposition of truth – a truth that is not mine alone. The idea that everyone has their own truth was referred to by Plato as a 'mere opinion' and those who have not learned to distinguish this from truth has not begun to learn philosophy. Platonic dialogues always begin with such an opinion or conviction, but the truth is only revealed when the person in question begins to doubt his opinion under the pressure of questioning and argument – when he or she realises that they were not right after all. The phrase 'I am right' says very little about truth, whereas when somebody says 'you were right' something fundamental to do with the truth has occurred.

Truth, at least truth of the interesting and non-banal variety, apparently occurs somewhere, it shows itself in language. But where does it come from? The Czech word *pravda* (truth) is connected with the verb *pravit*, which means to make a judicial utterance. The German words

Wahrheit (truth) and *wahr* (real, genuine) stem from the old Germanic word *waer*, which originally meant something to be relied on, a contract or a promise. Along with the Latin *verus* (genuine, real) it has the same Indo-European root as the old Slavonic word *viera*, and the modern Czech word *víra* (belief). This word meant something which we believe and which we can rely upon.

This is an interesting trail. Let us now try to turn it around: what can we *not* rely upon, what is the opposite of truth? Is it an error? That two plus two make seven is certainly not true, but for the most part it is not really a lie either; it is a mistake, an untruth, a nonsense – depending on the situation. In school it is a mistake, in science it is an untruth and we could only regard it as a 'lie' when we overhear a waiter saying it while counting up our bill. If we catch him at it, he will most likely apologise and say he got mixed up – in short, he will try to explain it away as a mistake. But there remains the unpleasant feeling that someone has tried to cheat us, that we have been lied to (albeit unsuccessfully). If an actor says 'I am the prince of Denmark' he is certainly not lying, even if he cannot speak a word of Danish and has never been to Denmark. When children find a piece of pyrite in a stream, they may think that they have struck gold. They are of course wrong but they are not doing the same thing as the fraudster who sells 'guaranteed' real gold rings at the side of the road. That truth is not just a neutral correspondence which we merely state, that it is something on which a great deal depends and which (depending on the circumstances) may have a greater or lesser value, is shown by the fact that the truth 'holds good'.

Let us return now to the reliability of truth. At first glance, it might seem that what is reliable is that which is always and everywhere the same, that which never changes. In this sense the truths of mathematics and science are reliable – they must by definition remain valid in all circumstances. Is it like this with truth in general? We have already seen that sentences like 'it is raining' are sometimes true and sometimes not. By Sunday night everybody knows which numbers came up in the lottery. If only there was a way of knowing it a couple of days earlier! According to the logical positivists, this was exactly the same truth as it is now on Monday. But back then it was worth millions to somebody, whereas now it is worth nothing to anybody. But there are more serious and dramatic cases than this. That the Titanic sank in 1912 may excite some people even today. But what would such an utterance have done to people a week before the ship left port? It could have saved hundreds of lives; it could have bankrupted the company who owned the ship;

and it could have led the person who uttered it into an insane asylum – especially if the person knew just how much was at stake and if he or she uttered the sentence with enough urgency. The declarative sentence that Adolf Hitler is a villain is certainly true. But was it always so? A hundred years ago it made no sense. Only in the 1930s did there emerge a few wise individuals who noticed it. Those who flocked to Hitler violently disagreed with it and those few brave souls in Germany who insisted upon it paid for it with their lives. Then the war came, and when it was over suddenly it was clear to everyone. To say that Hitler was a villain no longer cost anybody anything – indeed it could prove helpful as a career move. But for the truth of the sentence it was already somewhat late: the war lost, the Jews exterminated, Germany destroyed. None of it needed to happen, if only more Germans had realised in time the truth that some of them had glimpsed. Only later did it become clear that this truth was not only reliable, but it could have saved millions of human lives: such was its value. But only then. Not later.*

In the Bible, truth is spoken of in this sense. A prophet, as long as he lives, is an extremely unpopular person who tells everyone very unpleasant things. He even says them to kings, so it is little wonder that few prophets live to enjoy a peaceful old age. The Ancient Jews, however, maintained a collective memory and when they faced a catastrophe, they would remember the unpleasant man: 'he was right all along!' Such people, upon whom others should have relied but who they (to their own cost) ignored, became known as prophets. Prophets were people who offered rare and unpleasant truth – and in time. In the gospels Jesus says 'the truth will set you free'. This is something that cannot be said for those unchanging, always true utterances such as two and two is four.

It seems to be the case that if we want to 'use' a genuinely valuable truth, we must do so in time. We must grasp it before it becomes clear to everyone, before it becomes visible to the naked eye. In short, we must gamble upon it at the right moment – in the knowledge that we may be mistaken. This is the approach of inventors and great scientists, who do not know yet for certain, but who have a hunch that they have hit upon something. It is the approach of the great politician who guesses what dangers lie ahead and begins to prepare for them. Those who simply wait until they know everything to a certainty will in the end be left with nothing but what we call 'bitter truth': that which is left after everything

---

* 'God, return truth to the world! That will be more than peace treaties, it will be more valuable than any alliance. To rid the world of lies is worth more than disarmament.' (Karel Čapek 1938)

else is frittered away, as the Czech writer Ludvík Vaculík once wrote. Perhaps Masaryk had the same thought when he had the slogan 'truth will prevail' on the presidential flag – which itself is a quote from one of the Hebrew books which did not make it into the Bible. This is no statement of correspondence, but rather an expression of the conviction that when a person glimpses the truth, he or she should follow it. The truth will win in the end. Truth which has prevailed, i.e., which has been proved and has become established, still remains the truth, but of a different kind, as there is no longer anything to be gambled over; everyone knows it. If it continues to be trotted out for a long period of time, however, it becomes merely trite and tiresome 'wisdom', to be greeted with sneering derision. This is perhaps why many people prefer not to speak at all of the most serious things, or only in quiet among close friends or loved ones. Not because they care nothing for them, but on the contrary because they have such respect for them.

Truth is then not only an attribute of a truthful utterance, something that can be expressed with ones and zeroes in a logical formulation. Rather it is the very possibility of distinguishing that some things are valid and some are not; the hope and belief that 'the truth will out', that it will eventually come out, disputes will be settled and uncertainties will dissolve away in its light. For the most part, this possibility is not in our hands – otherwise there would be no need to talk of truth at all – and yet we reckon with it every time we say anything. It is never 'our truth' but rather something we seek and something we expect. This is what Feurbach had in mind when he said 'I do not have the truth, the truth has me'. But if truth were something that we merely waited on, it would come to us only in the unfortunate likeness of something we have already missed.

Questions:

- Consider when the different demarcations of truth are most useful and when they are inconvenient.
- Why do we say that 'two and two is four' is a true sentence?
- Why can we say that a novel or a picture is 'truthful'? What do we mean by that?
- What does the 'requirement of truthfulness' mean for a doctor who has just discovered that his patient has an incurable disease? Or for the captain of the Titanic, who has just learned that the ship is sinking?

- Confrontational, unpleasant truths can be dangerous for a society. How to deal with this? Can we afford to ignore or suppress them?
- What does the sentence 'I am right' (in Czech and German 'I have the truth') tell us? When does it make sense? Why do some philosophers say on the contrary 'the truth has me'?
- Can truth win? Can truth prevail? What then happens to it?

15. Scale and Ratio

When Descartes speaks of corporeal objects, he says they are 'extended things', *res extensae* in Latin. In other words, any material object can be characterised by a certain expanse, and hence also by size. In mathematics and geometry, the prevailing opinion is that size is not of much importance – a triangle can be enlarged or reduced without any of its properties being affected. Is that really true, though? Let us consider any given triangle and imagine reducing it a hundred thousand times. Would it still be a triangle? In what sense? From the geometrical viewpoint, if we were only concerned with ideal shapes, it certainly would. But as a thing, as an 'extended thing', a triangle thus reduced in size would not be at all visible, as it would have lost all expanse. Or let us take the letter W, with which this paragraph begins. If we were to enlarge it a million times, it would measure about three kilometres in height and nobody would recognise it as a letter any more, unless they were observing it from a satellite. Is it then still meaningful to call it a letter?

A similar situation arises when we do not increase or reduce the size of things themselves, but the way we see them; by using a magnifying glass, a microscope or a telescope. This enables us to see something which would not be visible to the naked eye, but we will at the same time lose what we did see before. Looking at a finger through a strong magnifying glass, we will be able to see the fine ridges which are used to identify criminals, but we will not see the finger as such. A telescope may show us wondrous spiral nebulae, but we will not be able to see a stellar constellation or the Milky Way. Each and every time, a considerable increase or decrease of scale ushers us into a different world. When we were children, all of us probably imagined what it would be like to be the size of a bug, or quite the opposite, to stride over whole mountains like a giant. Many children's stories, like Tom Thumb or Jack and the Beanstalk, are in fact thought experiments about scale.

Fairy tale imagination overlooks one important aspect however. With each increase of size, all three-dimensional volume increases to the power of three, while two-dimensional areas, such as cross sections etc., only increase to the power of two. Hence the weight of the human body enlarged lineally five times would increase one hundred and twenty-five times (five cubed), while the cross section area of the bones, which determines the strength of the skeleton, would only increase twenty-five times (five squared). Each real-life object, whether natural or man-made, must be 'constructed' according to a certain scale and cannot be significantly enlarged or decreased with impunity. The dimensions of living organisms are strictly limited by the properties of the materials and construction elements which nature has at its disposal. They are limited at the bottom end of the scale, too, for a cell, the building block of all living organisms, cannot be smaller than the dimensions of protein molecules allow it to be, which is counted in microns (micrometres). A plant can grow up to two metres, and then it has to start producing cellulose, wood fibre, to reach the size of a fifty-metre tree. The chitinous construction of an insect's body does not afford enough space for a brain, and so the insect must make do with a nerve ganglion. There are also likely to be some sort of 'strength limits' restricting the structure of atoms. Elements with an atomic number higher than 90 are no longer stable and fall apart spontaneously.

Different 'scales' in the natural world then appear to have corresponding types of constructions, various types of binding and forces. Classical physics, nevertheless, supposed the basic principles, which underlie it and which govern all rational thinking, to be universally valid. It was not until the 20th century that this stipulation was definitively disproved. We cannot say of an electron that it is 'here', and not 'there', or that its speed is such and such. The image of a particle as a sort of microscopic body or a ball is probably a very rough approximation. A photon can manifest itself as a particle or as a wave, depending on how we examine it. The statistical behaviour of particles often leads to seemingly irrational results; however, these can be not only reliably proven, but also practically utilised (e.g., quantum tunnelling). There is then nothing for it but to reconcile ourselves to the notion that what is considered obvious and certain within the limits of everyday human experience, may in other scales apply differently or not at all. Hence scale is not just a 'subjective' result of our anthropocentric way of thinking; it can cause a qualitative difference too.

It is worth noting that we do not perceive the intensity of light or sound in a linear way but rather in a logarithmic fashion – if we want to replicate the impression created by doubling the volume of sound, we will have to turn up the volume by four times, then by eight etc. Correspondingly, the decibel scales, which are also arranged logarithmically (a difference of 10dB equals a double output). Thus our eyesight and hearing can span a vast scope of intensity (roughly 1:1000 in sound), something even modern humans need in their life. It remains to be seen what impact the current overabundance of decibel and lux units will have on the sensory faculties of our descendants.

We can count how many eggs there are in a basket – there are three, or four, but not anything in between. Meat, milk, or cloth has to be measured, that is compared against a conventionally agreed measure or unit. The result can be anything: 'slightly over two pounds, is that alright?' Units were originally derived from various body parts (an inch, an ell, a foot), later by local convention (for example the iron 'elbow' rods on the wall of Prague's New Town Hall). It seemed unacceptable to the Enlightenment rationalists that scientific measurements should have such an unscientific origin, so they decided to redress the situation. Thus the metre was created as one ten thousandth of a half meridian (from the Equator to the Pole). They however overlooked the fact that we are able to (and need to) measure many things with a much higher degree of precision than we are able to measure Mother Earth, which makes the result of their efforts just another linear measuring unit. It may be made of invar and stored in a cellar, but it is just as conventional as the fathom or the inch. Nowadays it is defined by a quite unrounded ratio to the wavelength equal to the frequency of a Caesium atom, a thoroughly technical improvement. Moreover, it has the advantage of being describable in the same way as a unit of time, as that is no longer governed by the Sun, but by the Caesium atom.

Measuring, too, is comparing, setting a ratio, albeit against something conventional, which does not have a meaning of its own. A philosopher or a mathematician, looking for a numerical order of the world, could never be fully satisfied with it. Even the oldest ones we are aware of, the Pythagoreans, endeavoured to find neat, preferably nicely rounded, ratios between natural phenomena. We have already mentioned their most outstanding achievement, the discovery of the musical scales on a string. All other areas presented more difficulty. They did however manage to establish the ratio of the orbit times of the Moon and the Sun as 19:235. That does not look particularly pretty and besides, it is only approximate. They faced their biggest disappointments in geometry though. It proved impossible to calculate even such a simple thing as the ratio between the radius and circumference of a circle. And the last straw came with the failure to quantify the ratio of the length of a diagonal and the side of a square, which actually led to the conclusion that it is not possible to calculate. At that point, the Pythagorean programme of mathematisation of the world collapsed.

The need to *mathematise*, that is, to uncover exact principles which we did not think up ourselves and which we can rely on, was nevertheless stronger. The next attempt, carried out by Plato, was not based on numbers but on geometrical shapes and constructions. It is a shame that the diagonal is not commensurable with the side of the square, but never mind, their ratio is still obvious to the eye. It seems that Plato came up with a number of similar ingenious constructions, which bypass the irrationality issue, and attempted to mathematise the world by employing symmetrical polygons and polyhedrons. While he did not get very far, Euclid embraced his ideas, although he took them in a slightly different direction, and even Kepler was convinced at first, that symmetrical polyhedrons were the way forward. However, the difference between the merchant and the scientist was no longer so unsurpassable in early modern times, and a merchant's manners came to the fore: 'it's slightly over, is that alright?' The difference between the number of eggs in the basket and any ratio or measuring is naturally obvious. But a merchant's ratio can be accurate with arbitrarily high degree of precision. The 'unlimited' degree of accuracy is key here. Just define what 'accurate' is and we will build the scales and weights, and we will be able to measure to that specification. Thus we all know that the ratio between the circumference and diameter of a circle is the number *pi*, approximately 3.14. The more diligent pupils among you may remember it as 3.1416, or even 3.141592. But if that were not precise enough, just look it up and there you will find as many decimal places as you could possibly wish for. Who cares that it is not the exact number, even with a thousand decimal places? So what? That is what the modern operative definition of exactness is based on – an error smaller that an *a priori* given number. Accurate measurement is a measurement with a known uncertainty or error.

However, those ratios which are difficult to quantify are just as important. Thus artists still utilise the 'golden section' rule, that is the division of a line into two parts so that the ratio of the shorter part to the longer part is the same as that of the longer part to the whole length of the given line, that is to say at the ratio of √2, roughly 3:5 or 0.618, as it has been shown to have a particularly harmonious and well-balanced effect. Aesthetics is in general all about ratios and if we see a less than successful architectural endeavour, we will often remark that the 'scale isn't right', the building is jutting out of its surroundings, it is not in tune with it, just as a bad dancer or a musician might be. A contrast, a ratio which adds emphasis, is quite a different matter though. That too is ever-present in the human perception. Kind actions will stand out more in war times, bravery will be most noted when surrounded by cowardice, and truth will out amongst lies. Yellow will appear most intense on a background of blue and all portrait painters since the Renaissance times know that green is the best backdrop for the human face. If we want to clearly express an idea, we must exaggerate it slightly, and if we really want our words to be noted, we will do best to be silent awhile before uttering them.

Similar results can also be achieved in the temporal sphere. The speed of actions in the natural world is likewise limited by the possible speeds of chemical reactions and other signal carriers. One of the most remarkable achievements of modern physics, the discovery of the continuous electromagnetic wave spectrum, ranging from kilometre radio wave length, to ultra short, heat, light, ultraviolet, to hard radiation, does not in any way correspond to our sensory experience. Our eyesight can only register a very small segment of this spectrum, less than an octave, although within that range it is able to distinguish with great detail, especially when it comes to mixed signals. It is said of the Eskimos that they distinguish over thirty words to describe white, just as a printer or a textile worker differentiates between hundreds of shades. When it comes to acoustic or pressure waves, our 'frequency zone' is considerably wider (some ten octaves), although not everyone is able to tell the absolute pitch of a tone. Usually, we register the relationship between pitches, that is to say intervals. Faster frequencies (ultrasound) are not at all audible to the human ear, while lower regular frequencies are perceived first as droning, buzzing etc., those within the limit of 0.5–3.0 Hz as rhythms. These bear an obvious correlation to the biological rhythms of our body, especially to those which we are able to perceive, such as the pulse, the rhythm of our breath or walking. Also, we are very sensitive to the slightest irregularities, tensions, or tendencies, which make rhythms rich with a multitude of expressive content. A slower rhythm is usually no longer perceived as a rhythm, and if we speak of the rhythm of days or years, it is in a wider metaphorical sense.

So, temporal scale can fundamentally alter our outlook. Where a young person may not see any change, for an old person everything has changed tremendously, and continues to do so. The daily movements of prices on the stock-market look like utter chaos, and yet we can read into them more long-term trends and tendencies. The historian follows a course of events which may look like a confusing blur. It was Fernand Braudel who pointed to *longue durée* (English *long term*), to important changes which are only visible from a greater distance. The art historian moves between styles which do not return and which enable him to say what belongs to a certain style and what is an anachronism or a fraud. Arnold Toynbee studied the rise and fall of entire civilisations in the timescale of hundreds or thousands of years. The sociologist cannot overlook irreversible changes in human societies and cultures which are not merely random fluctuations but which start from somewhere and lead into another direction. The biologist cannot overlook the evolution of living organisms, the geologist works with a clear sequence of periods and for cosmology the entire universe manifests itself as an enormous event, in which not only the stars and the galaxies, but physical laws themselves, develop and evolve.

With the exception of the mathematical subjects, which time does not touch, everything is in motion for contemporary science and it is only a question of time measurement how this motion will reveal itself to us. If seen from close up, it will be entirely chaotic, like Brown's movement of molecules, through the alternation of events which make some sort of sense, but which may return and repeat themselves, to the clear manifestation of long-term and irreversible change, which will carry us somewhere else. Indeed it seems – and not only to cosmologists – that this motion is growing ever faster.

Questions:

- Explain the difference between counting and measuring. What unit do we use when counting eggs and when measuring a piece of cloth?
- Could we say that the scale only exists in the eye of the beholder? What arguments could you use for and against?
- What is the point in distinguishing between the 'objective' and 'subjective'? Try to give some examples.

- Ratios play an important part in society, too – standard of living or poverty, equality, justice.
- Is it at all meaningful to say that 'everything is relative'? How and why?
- Why are we so fond of small-scale models, what is their appeal?
- When and why do we employ 'enlarging' and 'shrinking' in our thought processes?

16. Likeness and Imitation

When a painter paints a portrait, he strives to 'capture the likeness'. That is why a portrait is sometimes referred to as a 'likeness'. The painter's aim is to try to paint something which looks like the person, not create an imitation intended to confuse people. Antique dealers sell imitations of rustic furniture in order to fool customers, branded goods are replaced with cheap imitations, the products of money forgerers – all of these serve a single purpose, to produce something which looks the same but is in fact something different, and cheaper. It would be sheer nonsense however, to try and commit an imitation of a person to paper or canvas. For one thing, a piece of paper is flat, a drawing is often in black and white, and besides, each person looks different at different moments. Photographers are aware of this, which is why they either have to take one snapshot after another in the hope that one of them will turn out all right, or else leave a person sitting on the stool until their mind is quite void, and in their passport picture, they end up looking like a melancholic, or at best as someone faintly devious. And although we know full well that it is actually nonsense, we keep protesting that we don't look 'anything like' that photo. A good painter, on the other hand, can engage his subject in a conversation, or let them listen to music, or look out of the window, and he will come to capture the 'likeness' gradually.

The confusion of terms between likeness and imitation is probably down to Plato. For it was he who reproached painters with trying to imitate imitations, and his opinion of them was accordingly low. What he had in mind was that visible things are already mere imitations of eternal patterns and ideas, so the artist is replicating them for a second time. He was, however, most likely mistaken in this belief, as we have seen. An artist is not a counterfeiter, an artist does not imitate, he creates a likeness. Not by 'copying' the person and tracing every line and wrinkle, but by suggesting their expression. A good painter will manage this even without putting in much detail. In a way, the post-classical sculptors perhaps deserved all they got from Plato, for the late Ancient Greek art chiefly did just imitate and sought perfection in detailed correspondence. It is not quite clear how Plato imagined the relationship between, say, the idea of a horse and its imitation, a horse. Let us just mention that the Greek word for *likeness* is *eidos*, and it has a close connection to the word *idea*. Both are derived from the word *eidon*, I saw.

Let us try another approach now. We routinely say umpteen times a day that one thing resembles another. If somebody complains about the way things are at work or at school, we will console him by telling him that we are in quite a similar situation. Resemblance appears to be a broad and important category, without which we would not be able to think or speak. It is a correlation between two or more ideas, notions, phenomena, or things, which are in some way similar or related, one resembles the other. But how does it work? How can we tell if two objects resemble each other? What is the scientific view?

We have learned about similar triangles in mathematics, but that analogy is of no use here, for the similar triangles are actually all the same, only increased or decreased in size. That does not seem to be a true resemblance though, to be like something is different from being partly the same. Other disciplines do not recognise similarity as a scientific term, although resemblance is applied. Primates who bear the closest resemblance to humans are referred to as anthropoids, derived from the Greek *anthropo-eides*, i.e., looking like humans. Similarly in botany, there are whole families bearing a 'resemblance', such as lilies or roses. An experienced botanist will immediately recognise them, often even if seeing the particular species for the first time. A layman or a child will recognise them too, the difference being that for them, the resemblance may be misleading. A number of people who pick wild mushrooms have managed to poison themselves by the white variant of the death cap mushroom because it looks like an edible field mushroom, in that both these species are white and of a similar shape. A more seasoned mushroom-picker will make no such mistake, as to his experienced eye the resemblance is less prominent, and the silky sheen of the cap, typical of the *amanita* family, as well as the colour hue, will rule the field mushroom out. To the inexperienced, science offers a helping hand – if you are unsure as to what mushroom you have found, pick up a reliable mushroom guide and compare the particular characteristics. Does it have a ring? What colour are the gills? Does it have a volva?

In more intricate cases, the less visible attributes may have to be taken into account, e.g., the size, shape, and colour of the spores has to be examined under a microscope. If you had to do all this while walking through a wood, trying to collect mushrooms for your risotto, you would not get very far. But if you want to avoid poisoning yourself you need to acquire experience – from other mushroom pickers, from experts, or with a guidebook and a magnifying glass in hand. A living mushroom picker can be defined as one who has not made a mistake yet.

And just as an experienced botanist or an ornithologist would in their respective fields, the mushroom picker will no longer identify various mushrooms based on their individual characteristics listed in a guide, they will become recognisable on the basis of their 'likeness'. Many competent mushroom pickers may not even know what the gills or pores are, but they will have a clear image of the likeness of, say, a fly agaric, a bolete, or a field mushroom. Likewise in other areas, good musicians recognise whether they are listening to Janáček or Mozart after a few notes. They will know it even if they have never heard that particular piece, or if it is performed on a piano or by a choir, rather than by a string quartet, or whether it has been transposed, has a different rhythm etc. A butcher will take a look at a chunk of meat and know it is beef or lamb or pork. How can he tell? Unlike a mushroom picker, or a botanist, musicians and butchers do not have a manual at their disposal, where they could verify the similarity step by step, based on clearly distinguishable characteristics. They have to learn from experience. In Latin, intelligence means the ability to discern and distinguish.

When you get your intelligence tested, you will be shown an array of seemingly unconnected pictures or a sequence of symbols, and it will be your task to find 'something' in them. It can be some sort of regularity, a pattern, a similarity. And of course you must find it quickly. That can never be achieved by any kind of methodical technique of exclusion, trial and error. You must be able to really look and see, to find similarities and resemblances. This ability is developed through any demanding cerebral activity, and especially by engaging in a diversity of topics. Thus a person who has learned a foreign language acquires more than just the ability to communicate with a German or a French speaker. He or she gains the ability to compare – what we say in a certain way, others see differently. He or she learns to distinguish and see further connections and resemblances.

Since childhood, we have been learning to recognise others – family and friends, people we know and those we should beware of. We rarely make a mistake and if we do, we feel it is hardly our fault, because surely that person has a real double! On the other hand, when a European person looks at Chinese or Vietnamese faces, they all seem alike to begin with. Only once you get to know them better will they become distinguishable from the rest. It is the same with animals – I might see a herd of sheep, which to me all look identical, while the shepherd can tell them apart, or at the least those with a tendency to stray, lag behind, or fight with the others. When a newborn baby is brought home from the maternity hospital, all the family will gather round and argue over whom the baby looks like. They cannot agree, as each individual probably recognises likeness according to different criteria.

Likeness, then, is something which helps us recognise who is who and what is what. It is not being the same or identical. We never say that we recognised a five-pound note, unless perhaps it has been scribbled on. But we may, after twenty years, recognise a friend who has put on weight, acquired a beard and lost all his hair. How could we have done that? No pocket guide would be of any use here, as so many of his original characteristics are gone. But the 'likeness' did remain, and we immediately saw it. Just as the old servant recognised Odysseus, when he returned home after twenty years, greatly aged, bedraggled and dirty, and not actually wanting to be recognised. We may say to a friend who says or does something surprising: 'I don't recognise you,' or 'that's not you' – and it is not to say that we cannot recognise them because they had a haircut or shaved off their moustache.

Many have derided Plato's notion of ideas, for the most part with some justification. But having summed up the way in which we recognise people or things, we arrived at a list of characteristics that in fact do bear a strong resemblance to 'ideas'. Namely, recognition happens at first glance, guided by something which does not change, something which people cannot get rid of even if they want to, something which is somehow integral and unique, and we are often unable to analyse it and separate the individual traits. Might it be that the much-ridiculed 'idea' is really the foundation of our ability to recognise, that it governs the way in which we organise our perceptions and experiences, and distinguish and arrange things and events? Might it be that which we know and remember, which we talk and reminisce about? Only that it is not given beforehand and since eternity, rather it is something we each have to re-create? Perhaps Plato was not so far off the mark then, and where he did go wrong was in attributing too much autonomy and efficiency to his ideas, thinking that they exist 'somewhere' independently and form or create by themselves this world that we inhabit.

But are images really exclusive to us humans? What about a dandelion, which can grow more or fewer leaves, or bloom when it is convenient, while still remaining a dandelion? For sure, there is the seed with its genetic code, which will ensure that a dandelion will grow from it, and not a hawkweed. But the shared genetic code cannot govern everything – each dandelion is different, and yet it 'knows' how to be a dandelion, how to cope with adversity and to realise its image, 'idea', or 'nature', regardless of whether it is under our observation or not. As if it were itself guided by this idea of a dandelion. If this is so, we may have to significantly rethink a number of our concepts. Philosophy and science alike strive to gain knowledge – and knowing how we distinguish things is surely a part of that.

Likeness and resemblance have always played a major part in human life, in religion, culture and civilisation. That is why they have often been attributed properties which they in fact probably do not possess. Thus the whole domain of magic, a certain technique to directly control the world according to our wishes, is based on resemblance. If you want to harm somebody, you might make a wax figure bearing their likeness, before proceeding to prick it with pins. A root shaped like the male genitalia is surely going to cure impotence. A knight with a lion painted on his shield will emerge victorious from every battle. At times, such actions happen to be beneficial – as some ethnographers maintain, tilling the soil originally simulated sexual intercourse with the earth, with the crooked plough representing, or rather imitating, the penis. The overemphasis on resemblance, typical of the primitive peoples, and young children, has led European science to the other extreme – ignore resemblance, likeness, approximation, we are after bare facts, exact numbers, and precise answers. That has certainly proved a grand and hugely successful programme. But fortunately, it has not quite managed to do away with the notion of resemblance and likeness. The resemblances and similarities we see around us every day need to be critiqued – we need to form hypotheses, carry out experiments and exact measuring. But without similarities, there would not be anything for us to critique. If a scientist wants to learn about something, he must first learn to distinguish it from everything else. If a doctor is to treat a patient, he must first recognise what is wrong with them. The first step doctors take to establish a diagnosis is to create an 'image' of the ailment. If doctors spoke Ancient Greek, they would call it '*eidos*', 'idea'.

Some – often very important – matters are not appropriate to be directly spoken of, or it may be risky, or quite impossible. Then we frequently seek refuge in allegories or parables to talk about them. It is not at all easy to criticise the ways of a totalitarian regime, we can come up with an antithesis to each particular statement or thesis, which may eventually lead to a very learned and complicated analysis, comprehensible to few, and interesting to even fewer. George Orwell's *Animal Farm*, on the other hand, sums it up perfectly and pithily, so that everybody will understand it, while enjoying a good story at the same time. Naturally, this requires the reader to have some knowledge or experience of the subject. But given that, you will immediately understand which particular dictator is hidden in the figure of the pig Napoleon, that the dogs which he breeds in the attic are the secret police, and that the old horse who is eventually taken to the slaughterhouse, is just some good and honest soul who has swallowed the ideology hook, line, and sinker. Parables are even more effective, as they are more direct and no key is required to know what is what. Here, the resemblance to something we all know is plainly obvious. When Jesus speaks of the prodigal son (Luke 15, 11), or the minas (Luke 19, 11), everybody is likely to understand, but most importantly, they will hear something which would otherwise be very difficult to express. For a parable does not just present an isolated 'idea', it shows it in a real-life situation, which makes it so much more persuasive.

Human children, as well as the young of animals, first become involved in the world by playing. Children frequently engage in pretend games, playing house, pretending to be adults and to talk like them. We have learned the majority of the most important things, those we learned 'at our mother's knee' so to speak, through imitating – we saw somebody else do something and tried to copy them. And children are very competent in distinguishing between what needs to be faithfully imitated and done precisely in the way the grown-ups do it, and what things are just props, easily replaceable on the basis of some vague resemblance; thus a shoe becomes a boat or a car, a box is turned into a house, a bed, or whatever is called for. That is why children are often better able to play with very basic objects, while expensive sophisticated toys may be perfect miniature imitations, but will bore them much quicker, as they demand too little of children's ability to see the resemblance.

This kind of imitation, which is not designed to deceive anybody, which, on the contrary, wants to teach us something, make something relevant, or 'be something' for a while, is sometimes referred to by the Greek word *mimesis*. We all remember it from childhood, or from a drama performance, where it is obvious and explicit. We have learned to write, ride a bike, use a saw in the correct manner, or play the piano.

But most of all, we have acquired human behaviour in the same way, imitating our parents, friends or teachers. Moralists sometimes fret about today's youth being completely out of control, and they call for better morals and manners to be enforced. But such things cannot just be learned, not even described or expressed; they must be imitated and copied. Thus human society is shaped through imitation and mimesis. Retrospectively, someone can examine it, describe the 'unwritten rules', but we, who are shaping it, have never heard of rules, we have merely observed other people's behaviour and then went on to imitate it. Just as we have learned our 'mother tongue' perfectly, without the help of rules, so we have learned 'mother', or perhaps 'father' behaviour, and that is what we will always consider the norm.

Questions:

- Try to characterise the 'likeness' of a table, a fork, a plate, a cat. In what way does it resemble a definition, and how does it differ?
- Can you distinguish when a statue or a painting is a mere imitation, and when it is a work of art?
- Resemblances and similarities play an important part in language in general, in poetical language in particular. What makes a metaphor, good, pregnant, beautiful?
- Some living organisms sometimes imitate others, the hoverfly looks like a wasp, a praying mantis resembles a dry twig, one species of mushrooms imitates the smell of rotting flesh. Why is that?
- Why has science so little trust in resemblance? And why can we not do without it in life?

17. Life

When we were discussing things, various 'things/non-things' kept cropping up. We cannot hold fog, or a puddle, or a speck of dust in our hands, they may not have a definite shape, or a function, as things they leave a lot to be desired. On the other hand, there are also 'things' which we would never refer to by that word, for we know them to be more that mere things – a pine tree, an ant, or an elephant, these are animate, they are alive. What does it mean to 'be alive'?

Biologists will tell you about the main attributes – metabolism, responsiveness to stimuli, mortality and the ability to reproduce. Each one more wondrous than the next. Metabolism keeps the organism alive, i.e., it provides free energy and creates a sort of enclave, where the second law of thermodynamics does not apply. Unlike inanimate things, which are always more or less dilapidating, a living organism grows. It grows by utilising its environment, taking from it what it needs and discarding what it does not. No tree will ever grow sky-high though; organisms, too, have a limited life span – they come into being, they grow, they age and they die. But while an organism is alive, it looks after itself and is even able to 'fix' itself, to grow a scar over a wound for example. That is an ability over which a technician can only turn green with envy. Science-fiction writers do not tend to be technicians, so they may naively imagine that an inanimate robot could last for eternity. But in reality, even the most accomplished mechanisms, such as those on satellites for example, will not last over ten years without needing humans to repair them. A house that no-one cares for becomes a ruin within a few years.

This is not the case with living beings. If a dog is hurt, it will lick the wound without needing to be told. Whereas a dirty car has to be washed, a cat will lick itself clean. Living things are constantly caring for themselves and of course for their young. With some animals, this care can extend to more than their own body. The common snail carries its shell (which children call its 'house') on its neck, enlarging it gradually so it can fit inside in dry or cold weather or in the event of danger. No mechanism can be a match for this tiny piece of soft tissue with no brain. If an ant-hill is damaged by storm – or by a mischievous child – the ants will immediately swarm out and in a few hours everything will be as it was.

The other side of this non-indolence, or interest in one's own life, is responsiveness – an animal feels hunger or pain, a living organism is perceptive to its environment and is able to adapt to it. To be able to run away from danger, an animal must become aware of it in time. To be able to obtain food, an animal has to see it, smell it, and hear it. Because an organism is sustained by its environment, it can never be completely separated from it and is in a state of constant exchange with it, both metabolical and informational. Within its limitations, it not only consumes food, but also seeks it out, gathers it, hunts or grows it. This is where the great divide comes in, between bacteria at the mercy of its environment, a plant which can grow tall, creep on the ground or twine and climb on a support, and an animal, able to roam freely. The degree of abilities, movement in particular, goes hand in hand with the need for perception – a plant does not need eyesight, nevertheless a convolvulus or a sunflower will without fail turn their flowers to wherever the sun is at the moment. That is why Aristotle, who attributed a soul to all living things, distinguishes a 'vegetative' soul in plants, a 'sensuous' soul in animals, and a 'rational' soul in humans.

Science insists on using more reserved language, and speaks of 'irritability'. That is, however, such a gross understatement, a term appropriate perhaps for a worm, but higher animals, vertebrates and mammals, are capable of immeasurably more. They are not only able to smell, see, and hear, they actually have to form an image of their surroundings as a whole, a sort of orientation, a world in which they can navigate. They must have an idea of movement and time – or they would never be able to catch any prey. Bees are even able to communicate the direction and distance of their pasture ground. And the abilities of migrating birds, which probably use stars to guide their orientation, those are even beyond our own imagination. Can all of that really be summed up as mere 'irritability'?

Living organisms possess another ability, both awe-inspiring and terrifying, and that is their ability to reproduce. If you bring home a bit of mud, it is no big deal; you can clean it by and by. But woe betide should you accidentally bring home a living thing, a moth, a cockroach, or a flea. You will not get rid of them 'by and by'. Where there was one, there will soon be five, a thousand, a whole army of them. The obsolete belief that fleas breed out of grease and dirt may be untenable and ridiculous, but it does very accurately express the human experience of the virulence of living organisms, especially those that we are not too keen on. So we put a plant pot filled with rich soil on the windowsill. We keep watering it for a week or two, and lo and behold, tiny green leaves appear. But do not get ahead of yourself, it is not what you have sown, it is a weed. Where did it come from? You return from your holidays and there is a forgotten piece of bread on the table, grown furry with mould in your absence. A sugary solution will ferment and milk will turn sour without any further assistance. For all natural environments are teeming with yeast cultures, mould, weeds, and fleas, just waiting for a good opportunity, it would seem. It is extremely difficult and expensive to bring these all-pervading life forms under control and to create a sterile environment such as a hospital.

But back to philosophy. Reproduction is the living organisms' brilliant solution of the problem of existence or duration. A piece of rock will last a long time, but even the hardest one will erode in time. An individual living organism may live but for a short time, for days, months, or years at the most, but during that time, it will create progeny. They will be all new and fresh, and there may be thousands of them. The generational cycle keeps alive a species, a tribe, progeny. If there is a dry period, or it is cold, a few individuals may be clinging on to life hidden somewhere in a crevice. But let the sun come out or rain and there will be multitudes. A puddle appears, and within weeks, it is teeming with life. It will dry out again in summer – where does all the life in it disappear?

Plants and animals rely on their environment to survive, and if the conditions are unfavourable, they will perish. But in the meantime they will have managed to produce seeds, lay eggs, create spores – and these can lie in wait for better times. A plant seed can idle in dry conditions for years, and then start growing after the first rainfall. When the plant matures and creates new generations, it will wither and die. You could say that living organisms pass life on in a way similar to Chinese whispers. However the structure of even the simplest cell is incredibly complicated and has been perfecting itself for billions of years, and then all this precious experience has to be passed on, quickly, reliably, with astonishing precision. For this purpose life has equipped organisms with a recipe book, known to scientists as the genome. The genome is in reality a code, consisting of a sequence of four 'letters', chemical components, the same for all organisms, which the cell will pass on to its 'filial' cell in a matter of seconds. It will then start building the corresponding body following the same recipe as its 'mother'. If it is a primitive organism, such as a bacteria, the new cell will build up the body of a bacteria. If it is a higher organism, it will be a specialised cell, a building block in the body of a higher organism – a neuron, a muscle tissue cell, a hair cell. While all these cells look completely different, they in fact share the same 'family recipe', the genome.

What has all this to do with philosophy? The verb 'to be' may be ever-present in our speech, there always 'is' something somewhere, but it is as if it carried hardly any meaning. Perhaps we should just say 'I home', instead of 'I am home'; that is how Russian does it. That something 'is', is such a banal, everyday fact that we scarcely pay it any attention. But there can be a huge difference between 'being' and 'being'. Thus a table 'is' in the dining room, always in the same place, unless somebody moves it, it may become a bit scratched, chipped and rickety as time goes on, eventually it will be thrown out and cease to exist. We can always rely on it 'being' where we put it, 'being' always the same, if you had a good look at it, you know all there is to know about it. It does not pay any attention to its surroundings, and when it gets spilt with coffee, or soup, it bears it very stoically. It 'is', and that is that.

We have seen that organisms 'are' in quite a different way. First of all, they are never wholly 'here'. If a botanist wants to draw a plant, he must draw at least two pictures, which you will, in reality, never see at the same time – a flowering plant and a ripe fruit, the seed. It is even more complicated with insects – the egg, the larva, the pupa, the butterfly – each stage looks completely different and yet, it is all the same common white and none of its phases would be here without the others. Because it is originating, growing and ageing, a living organism has its 'personal history' and whatever we see right now is just a flash section of its being. A tree which you plant today will have changed beyond recognition in a few years; it will have grown. But there is another crucial thing – a living organism is 'for itself'. It feeds itself, defends itself, looks for light, path and prey. It reproduces and grows. It has its own goals (although it is possibly unaware of them and quite likely does not think about them), which it strives towards and endeavours to reach.

Life, however, means yet another amazing thing – organisms change and develop. The study of cellular morphology and genetics discovered that all living organisms are actually related and, on the most basic level, similar. All life forms are built of (similar) cells and all cells from (similar) chemicals, incredibly complicated as they are. The human body consists of 10^{14} cells. A cell contains some 10,000 different proteins, each consisting of several hundred amino acids arranged in a certain order. However, all living organisms are built from just twenty different amino acids and only an insignificant fraction (10^{-500}) of all the existing proteins. That cannot be a coincidence. It seems to indicate that all life has the same origin, roots, from which all its different forms developed in the three billion years since life developed on Earth. How did it come about?

We have seen the passing on of life, the 'tradition' being ensured by the genetic code, the genotype. Amazingly precise molecular mechanisms supervise its being copied exactly. But even then, something changes from time to time, an error occurs. With such a complicated system, an error usually means death. But very rarely, it happens that an organism with a changed code can survive, and is possibly even better equipped for survival and reproduction. Current biology sees such changes as random – and how else could it see them after all, since they cannot be necessary, and science does not allow for any third option? It is however certain that random mutations can only very slowly lead to evolution, and at a great risk – one step forward and a million steps to the side, up a blind alley. Could it be done better, more quickly, and above all, more safely?

The answer is yes, but it takes more than a single organism – there have to be two. New forms can be created through the combination of two well-established ones. Two different (and similar) genotypes will crossbreed, creating a combination, a compromise between the two of them. The risk of total failure will be radically reduced – if you extract from two articles, the resulting text is much more likely to make sense than if you were just randomly swapping letters. Besides, new combinations can be tried in each generation. That is the biological sense behind sexual reproduction – each new individual is created by a combination of two different ones.

Reproduction is not, as we have seen, merely one of the functions of living organisms, it is the foundation of their existence, their duration in passing life on. That is why all organisms pay it tremendous attention and invest a lot of effort in it. Even single-cell organisms have a genotype and undergo the complicated process of cell division, lower plants produce millions of spores, higher plants flower and produce seeds. Sexual reproduction introduces a new element into the existence of living organisms – if you want to exist, to continue, there must be two of you. How to go about it? While gymnosperm plants and grasses leave it to 'chance', that is to say to the wind – clouds of pollen seeds are carried by the wind, one of a million hopefully landing where it should, on a female reproductive cell of a plant of the same species. To shelter this precious cell, plants have developed the ovule, style, and stigma, designed to catch the pollen seed and transport it inside, to the egg. In a corn cob, each egg has its own 'wiring', carefully packaged together with the eggs. Higher plants have come up with an even more ingenious scheme, insect pollination. All it takes is to attract the insects by scent and a colourful display, lay on some refreshments, and success is virtually guaranteed – the pollen seed will quickly and accurately reach its destination.

But the process of reproduction does not end with pollination. A bean plant or wheat provides their seeds with a 'starter pack' of nutrients – just as birds equip their eggs. And for them not to be robbed of it, they will pack it in a firm shell as with a nut. The ripe seed has to be transported to a suitable location. Some plants leave this to chance, producing thousands of seeds and letting them drop to the ground. Other plants take care that their progeny 'see a bit of the world', they equip their seeds with parachutes and wings, they catapult them from their pods, as the touch-me-not or impatiens does, or fit them with hooks like the burdock, or again, rely on animals to do the work. They entice birds with sweet and colourful berries and let them transport the seeds in their digestive systems. The animal will then 'sow' them somewhere far from the mother plant, fertilising them at the same time. Plants are thus able to compensate for their own lack of mobility, while in a way demonstrating how the inability to move hinders them. But life has equipped all organisms with the ability of perception, and sexuality has taught them to rely on others; in the realm of life, various organisms are connected, depend on one another, live at others' expense or with their assistance, whether it be voluntary or enforced. Living organisms form communities and we, too, are a part of this one big mysterious community that is life on Earth.

Is all this 'being' not quite a different existence from that of a pebble or a penknife? Being with specific goals, in interaction with the environment, passing on life and nurturing the young, sexual relationships, and cohabitation with other organisms. Being, in which we can see ourselves as if reflected in a mirror, being which we can understand. An elephant, a mosquito, or a fly agaric, really do not seem to be 'things' in the sense we came to understand things in our kitchen back home. We may be able to say of them that they 'are', just as we say it about ourselves, but we must be aware that it means something quite different from a book being on the table, where we left it last night.

Questions:

- Try to describe, using examples, the 'being' of an inanimate object, a living organism, a human being.
- How is the ability in living organisms to move connected to perception?
- What is the correlation in different organisms, between the level of care for the young and the number of seeds, eggs and babies?
- How would you describe the nurturing of the young in a viviparous vertebrate and mammal?
- How does human sexuality differ from that of plants and animals?
- What is a community? How is it connected to human society?

18. Nature

When we went to the countryside as children, we were struck by how different it was from ' home', in the city. It was peaceful greenery, there were no people or tarmacked roads, there was nobody tidying up and no switches to turn on after it got dark. But this notion of 'nature' as an opposite probably did not develop in this way – lumberjacks and seafarers, who are surrounded by it all year round, have never tended to speak of it; they have no reason to do so. The experience of a city dweller was first described in the Epic of Gilgamesh, some five thousand years ago – nature as something wild, beautiful, and dangerous, lying beyond the city walls of Uruk. One does not speak when out in the wild; you must be always on your guard, on the lookout for things lurking everywhere. Humans are no longer at home when surrounded by nature, and the more we rely on human institutions, the more acutely we feel this.

This separation and alienation from nature, which perhaps appeals to us but which we are not a part of, has been felt by humans ever since they started living in houses, or at least since they settled in the artificial environment of towns and cities. In short, ever since they started living in an environment, which is mostly man-made. Up until not very long ago, people simply could not avoid encounters with 'nature' and only in the 20th century did it become possible to be acquainted with woodland only through a TV screen. The way people relate to nature, as the older counterpart of humanity, is twofold. Romantics have always looked to nature for everything they lack 'at home', admiring its beauty and power, and if it was not for the few practical details, such as running water, heating and a warm bed, they would rather make their home there. The pragmatists, on the other hand, do not venture out into nature without having an ulterior motive – there are a lot of good and useful things to be had from it, and what is more, they are free.

Both of these attitudes are to be found in science, too. The pragmatic approach can be coyly masked as a purely material, objective, and impartial interest, which will usually let the mask slip by constantly having an eye on what else could there be worth having. Our times will make history by being the first period when nature is also important as a place where you can dump anything without charge. That, too, shows that the balance of power is shifting. Time was when nature was powerful and sacred, awe-inspiring and the humans had no chance against it. The Ancient Greeks made a distinction between what is 'natural', that is to say eternal and unchangeable, and that which is devised and determined by humans. Even at the dawn of the modern age, nature still seemed infinite and inexhaustible; just two hundred years ago, a drought usually meant famine, and the Romantics in the early 19th century were the first ones to suggest that nature should be in some way spared and protected. About a hundred years ago, scientists became worried that some beautiful animal species were on the brink of extinction, and nowadays, we all know what we should and should not do because poor old nature is not doing so well.* But it would cost us some of our comforts and luxuries, and some money, too, so that, with the exception of a few enthusiasts, we are not too keen to embark on it. We just keep our fingers crossed that it will sort itself out somehow, although this seems to be a mistaken hope – nature's defeat in the war declared against it by Francis Bacon has been so rapid and comprehensive as to place the victor in immediate danger. After all, despite all the achievements of science and technology, we all continue to eat only things grown by nature, and we obtain our heat and energy from sources stored up over millions of years.

How could all this have happened and, within the time-scale of nature and the Earth itself, in such a short time? As the human race started to firmly establish itself after the last Ice Age, nature began to lose some of its sacred power. Some three thousand years ago, the Jewish Bible took a significant step, repeated not much later by the Ancient Greek thinkers – they stripped nature of its divine aura. Ever since then, nature has become an object, a thing. In the Middle Ages, 'natural' meant that which there is no need to ponder over, that which is normal and common. The science of the Renaissance took away the illusion that Man and the Earth are the centre of the universe, with everything revolving around them. It made up for the loss by handing the earth over

---

*   'Humans are an example of nature's unique patience.' (Christian Morgenstern)

for man to plunder, like prey and property. The Renaissance referred to the words of the Bible, according to which the Creator gave Man the Earth to rule over. They concealed the fact that the same Bible adds (just a few lines down) that God put Man in the garden 'to till it and guard it'. Both Bacon and Descartes overlooked the fact that if Earth becomes man's property, it will become a collective property – with the corresponding results.

Modern philosophy opposed the human mind to material nature, as merely an extended thing. The subjugation of nature became the project of science. In conditions of warfare, no intimacy is allowed and we only learn to see a certain aspect of our opponents, namely how best to catch them. At the same time, however, other sciences were completing their inventory of everything that lived on the Earth – a project which had commenced in the Middle Ages. When Carl Linné completed it in the 18th century, it conveyed anything but the image of an 'extended thing', or an adversary. Suddenly, another, perhaps more modest and more Aristotelian science emerged, which did not promise to conquer the world, but which attempted to see what existed – and it turned out that there was a great deal of it. The endeavour to classify this amazing wealth of animate and inanimate nature alike lead to the discovery of various structural similarities, which were just a step away from developing a real notion of relatedness and evolution. This idea was in turn in keeping with the Enlightenment idea of progress and was also supported by the discovery of geological layering and fossils, so that it became widely spread among the 19th century naturalists.

In those times, science was nowhere near as specialised as it is today, and it was not separated from thinking in general, and philosophy in particular; so new ideas spread easily between the individual disciplines. Thinkers such as Vico, Buffon, or Kant played an important part in it, and Goethe, for example, was among other things a noted naturalist and a supporter of evolution. Eventually there emerged the daring and revolutionary idea that man, too, is a part of nature; and Darwin accompanied this with his liberal exposition that only those life forms which are best equipped for life will survive (*survival of the fittest*). That was the beginning of a turning point, which is culminating at the present time. Just as the balance of power between man and 'nature' has altered, so too has the way we regard nature. This is, no doubt, connected to the shift in the prestige of the respective scientific disciplines – in the last decades, the sciences of life and living organisms seem to have replaced physics at the helm of scientific development.

The current view of the world also blurs the classical distinction between animate and inanimate nature. A rock or a crystal is just as 'natural' and almost as 'alive' as a lizard, and probably more 'alive' than a battery-reared chicken. On the other hand, it is sometimes difficult for us today to consider chemical substances as part of 'nature', and chemistry as a natural science. Our grandfathers would shake their heads in disbelief over this. On the other hand, it seems that we feel more acutely the difference between 'natural' and 'artificial', which technology constantly attempts to cover up – plastic materials try to look like leather, laminated photographic foil imitates wood, and even meat and fruit undergo such procedures that we can scarcely refer to them as 'natural'. In short, the scarcer real natural things become, the more we appreciate them. Furniture made from ordinary knotted spruce is more expensive than artificial mahogany or oak, tiny shrivelled apples are the most expensive, as they are sourced locally and grown naturally. To be precise, it is their 'natural' look that commends these things.

This is very much in keeping with our basic description of 'nature' as the world 'out there', not created by people, and where we are no longer at home. Brightly polished and utterly flavourless red apples are only to be found on supermarket shelves, while sloe berries and crab apples are to be found in the countryside. The border between natural and artificial is shifting, inconspicuously. The ever-rarer sound of a real musical instrument now seems to us something 'natural', compared to electronic noise. And architects feel the need to stress the 'natural' light, the 'sunlight', and the collocation 'artificial light' becomes used less and less, as the adjective in it is becoming redundant. And the word 'artificial' in general, which originally had something to do with art, has very little in common with it now, and suggests rather something which is a substitute, something cheap and of questionable quality.

The ruthless exploitation of this 'extended thing' may continue in business and technology, and we may all take part in it, but few of us can fully identify with it and feel 'righteous' about it. Most people feel some shame about it somewhere in the depths of their soul, although this shame will rarely come to the surface, and if so, it is often in the form of frantic and desperate outbursts, such as demonstrations against beef burgers and the suchlike.* But even a gesture like that is a sign of something. At the same time, a growing number of people view nature as an irreplaceable source, not of 'resources', but of shapes, forms and beauty, a source of

---

* 'Everybody wants to get back to nature but nobody wants to walk.' (Anonymous graffiti)

inspiration for new ideas, a treasure trove of millions of years' worth of genetic 'wisdom'. In addition our new attitude towards animals, despite all of its strange and ridiculous features, is a sign of something more profound. Darwin's disciples believed that man is 'merely' a part of nature. Nowadays, we can hardly fathom how our ancestors could have found this notion offensive. On the contrary, we see in it a wonderful opportunity to deepen our understanding of nature, not as something alien, but as a bigger picture, of which we ourselves are also a part. Even though we do not live in it, we can understand it from within, based on our own human experience, which is also a part of nature. We have already mentioned that science still objects to this consequence of Darwinist revolution, rejecting a number of new approaches to nature as signs of 'anthropomorphism'. But within the current conception of the relationship between man and nature, 'anthropomorphism' cannot be a transgression against purely scientific methods, only a consequence of the fact that man originates in nature, and in so many ways still belongs in it.

Despair over the way man has damaged nature, and continues to damage it, is becoming more widespread, especially in the developed world. This is certainly better and more hopeful than the dull apathy of pure consumerism. But as grown-up people, we cannot settle for a feeling of revulsion, which inevitably reflects also various motives of personal frustration and so on. We bear responsibility for the mess we have made and so we have to search for solutions. The idea that we should turn back the clock and lead an idyllic 'natural' life is a dangerous illusion, for it was our 'more natural' ancestors who endeavoured to make the world what it is today. That is why it is also dangerous to mechanically oppose man and nature, 'nature' and 'culture'. For, whether we like it or not, every possible route forward will be a 'civilisational' route, one planned and guided by humans. It is, therefore, of great importance who these people are and where they will take us. Human civilisation will have to tighten its belt and gradually learn to live with restrictions. And it is up to us to come up with an idea of how to do this, as there is no-one in the world today who knows how.

Questions:

- Have you ever visited a natural area 'unspoilt' by humans? Where would you look for it?
- Would you see a crop field as damage to nature? A castle park? A beautiful city? A garden suburb? Why?

- Where do you see the limits of growth of today's civilisation? Why?
- What is the most harmful aspect of our civilisation with regard to nature? Consider what you would potentially be able to live without and could you somehow replace it?
- Imagine you are politicians. How would you explain to the voters the necessity of restrictions, while still managing to persuade them to vote for you?
- What could we, as philosophers, do to make this task easier for these good politicians?

19. Necessity and Chance

When we were talking about certain knowledge, we juxtaposed scientific evidence and detective work. Both are connected by the need to assert a certain point of view whatever it may take, supported only by arguments, but arguments so forceful, that nobody can contradict them and we must accept them, willingly or otherwise. The investigator and the scientist do not seek to persuade, but to compel acceptance. It is fairly obvious why a detective might need this – his goal is to get the culprit behind bars and in order to do so must overcome his resistance. But why does a scientist need such a method?

As long as the aim of science was to explain the cause of things and to understand what we see and distinguish real knowledge from superficial impressions and opinions, it did not need to make such strict demands of its method. Aristotle's concept of cause corresponds to this – a cause is that which has somehow 'caused' or contributed toward the particular thing, and there are always several such causes. Aristotle names four. So for example, a builder has 'caused' a house, there is also the brickworks which made the bricks, the idea of what the house should look like, and also a person's need for the house in order to live there. Thus the creation of the house is explained in a reasonably satisfactory manner; and this also provides a blueprint, should I too require a house. But as soon as modern science became involved in the construction of the world, something quite different came into play. When a technician calculates the load-bearing strength of a bridge, he is not attempting to explain why the bridge did not collapse; he must guarantee that it *will* not collapse. It is his task to design a bridge which not only *can* last but *must* last. Therefore its strength must be proved not only to the technician's friends and to satisfy curiosity; it must also be proved against the earth's gravitational pull and other wily adversaries. Karl Marx put it very succinctly when he said that up till now, philosophers were merely explaining the world, whereas now their task was to change it.

That is why modern science had no use for Aristotle's theory of causes. It needed something else – a necessary cause, and preferably a single one. Every science from time to time speaks of causes in the same way we speak of them in our everyday life. But only those scientific disciplines which managed to find the necessary causes were of any use in the building of the modern world, in the conquering and subjugation of nature. Those sciences which managed this feat have ever since been anxious to preserve their power and are suspicious of any signs of multiple possibilities and the suchlike. Some disciplines have *a priori* been excluded from the race – for example, what can history discover that would be determined by necessary causes? Some other disciplines have only managed by employing statistics. For example, behaviourist psychology or quantitative sociology deal with matters that are hopelessly 'undetermined', but they have succeeded in finding statistical methods and questions, to which they find almost determined answers. That is to say answers with a certain degree of probability, which then apply with a rock-solid certainty. For example, nobody can calculate when exactly a person will be born or will die, but demographers are able to forecast with astonishing accuracy how many people there will be in ten or twenty years. From the viewpoint of such a stern science, the only connections in the world are those determined by necessary causes – or nothing, i.e., 'chance'.

Chance is one of the few everyday words which have enjoyed a successful career in science. In everyday speech, it means something which happened without us planning or expecting it: 'it was a chance meeting.' If we think it through, it could mean two things – either there was no cause, or we do not know of any. But these are two quite different things. My not being aware of any cause might be obvious, but it does not tell us anything remarkable. However, to prove that there actually is no cause would be a thankless task. The possibility will always remain that we have overlooked something. If I wanted to prove to you that I have a real English penny in my possession, I would simply reach into the box where it is kept and that would be that. But if I wanted to prove that I do *not* have one, it would be an exhausting task for both of us, lasting several days – and there would always be a lingering doubt over whether we really did look everywhere.

This uncertainty as to what exactly 'chance' means does not really matter in everyday life, for, after all, there, everything is somehow uncertain and imprecise. Besides, 'chance' does not affirm much more than denying an intention or design. To a detective, who wants to investigate the suspicious circumstances surrounding the death of a well-known banker, it will bring nothing but defeat – he did not uncover anything, it was just an unfortunate coincidence. But the exclusion of a conscious intention can also bring deliverance. If you hit a streak of bad luck, you have been given a parking ticket, then lose your wallet and come home to receive a court summons, it could easily leave you feeling paranoid – somebody is surely out to get you. They are not visible (which makes it even worse) but they must be fairly influential and well-connected people. If you find yourself in such a state of mind, it will be a relief to find out that it was all just a coincidence.

Conflicts between people should be considered by an impartial and disinterested judge. But there are occasions when that is not possible, where everyone concerned is partial and has some sort of interest in the matter. Then we often call upon chance to fulfil the role of the 'impartial' judge, as a substitute justice – after all, chance, too, is blind. When people cannot agree and a vote does not yield a decisive result, then the decision is made by drawing lots. Similarly in various games, where the vision of large sums of money drains small sums out of people's pockets, in lotteries and at roulette wheels, it is chance which decides the winner. Here, though, something is at stake, so the randomness of this kind of chance must be ensured. Nobody can see the numbers (in the old days, it used to be a blind person drawing the numbers) and a notary is present, symbolising the state's role in overseeing the whole activity and certifying the authenticity of chance.

Statistics, which can achieve nigh-impossible feats, has assigned a new function to chance. If a mayor wishes to find out what the electorate thinks of him, he could perhaps ask them. But if there are too many of them, he cannot ask them all. If he asked those whom he happens to meet, the information he receives would be distorted – if he went to a pub, he would encounter mostly men, if he went down the street during working hours, he would meet mostly work-shy people, and so on. But if he follows the rules and selects a truly random sample, the answer will not be far from the truth. Experience has shown that several hundred carefully selected answers closely approximate the result of asking every single person. Here, however, the randomness of the selection is very scientific, and also a trade secret of the companies which provide such surveys. The same goes for the mass production of, say, light bulbs, where it is not each individual bulb which gets tested, but items whose numbers correspond to a table of random numbers. It is very difficult to compile such a table, and for the same reason – by definition, random numbers should not follow any pattern, there must not be any correlation between them, each one of them must be quite 'unexpected', like the winning lottery numbers.

Paradoxically, it would then appear that apart from the necessary cause, which best serves the purposes of science, it is also possible to reasonably employ pure and utterly random chance. Why? Well, it is quite 'blind' and if something happens completely by chance, we can be sure that there is no other hidden causality and we can rely on it to be that way. All other states 'between' necessity and blind chance contain a factor which can never be predicted and which in humans we call the freedom of choice – the possibility of doing something one way or another. From the outside, the result would appear random too (unforeseeable, that is) but in a much more radical sense. With truly random results, we may presume that they are not governed by any causality, so they may be fairly evenly distributed – flies will sit on a sheet of paper randomly, and their bodily traces will be more or less evenly distributed all over the sheet. Free decisions, on the other hand, will almost certainly not be random; they will be governed by criteria or preferences – unfortunately, nobody knows in advance what they might be. So if there was a piece of honey smeared on a wet sheet of paper, invisible to the naked eye, the traces of flies' bodies will create a visible image, no longer evenly distributed or random, but surprisingly clearly defined, presenting us with quite a puzzle. Chance has been replaced with something representing a value (honey), creating an opportunity for choice.

The existence of value, and the possibility of choosing in accordance with it, therefore definitively prevent any meaningful prediction of behaviour. For it is not 'necessary' like a cause, neither is it completely 'random', but it means that an element of consciousness (be it very elementary, like that of our flies) has to be factored in, making not random, but conscious decisions. It would be a gross error to suppose that decisions are made randomly in the mathematical sense, i.e., 'without a cause'. They are influenced by a number of various affiliations, influences and reasons and a choice must be made from amongst these. The vast sums of money that businesses pour into market research and advertising bear witness to the difficulty of predicting and influencing such choices. Proper scientific prognosis is really not possible here.

This sufficiently explains why sciences which focus on more or less certain prediction, and therefore the controlling of reality, are not only suspicious of anything between necessity and chance, but that they disregard it entirely. That 'in between', which we could anthropomorphically call the area of free choice, governed by preferences and values, is by its very nature unacceptable from the point of view of scientific method, as the postulate of causality does not apply here, not even in its weakened form of 'chance', where the absence of causes is guaranteed. That is then the true, and quite legitimate, reason why the strict, exact (or 'hard') sciences cannot allow anything like that in their domain. Any sensible scientist should, however, clearly understand that this is a case of methodological simplification, which is all very well until we start presenting it as the whole reality. And in this grey zone of free choice, there are many dark forces at large, such as fashion, personal predilection and convictions. Their effect is, on the one hand, extremely powerful, and on the other completely unpredictable. That is why the powers that be do not care for them much either, and try to curtail them somehow – usually without much success. And a good thing for us too, as this is the domain in which we live all our waking lives, do our shopping and play our games, shout at each other, love each other and raise our children.

Questions:

- The oldest form of necessity is the belief in fate. Can we still encounter this nowadays? When and where?
- What concept of reality is the idea of a single necessary cause rooted in?
- What does the idea of causality look like in various sciences? What about your field of study?
- How can you tell if a sequence of numbers is truly random?
- Under what circumstances will we start looking for the cause of something we have been observing? When would there be no sense in it?
- What would we do if we wanted to act in an entirely random manner?
- How is it that group behaviour (e.g., people moving across a town square) may look random, although every member of the group is following some kind of goal, and therefore not behaving randomly?

20. Technique and Technology

'Such technique!' a TV sports commentator gushes admiringly, as a figure skater suddenly lifts off the ground, gracefully spins round her own axis three times and lands again assuredly, smiling at the spectators as if it was the easiest thing in the world – and on ice, to boot. Technique is acquired skill (*techné* in Greek), an ability to do useful things, which most of us are not able to do. Originally, the word was mentioned in connection with trades and crafts, although the Ancient Greeks considered even sculptors and painters as craftsmen, as they produced material objects. The aim of a craft or technique is to make, or at least demonstrate, something which is useful to people, or something one could make a living out of; one must concentrate on the end result so there is not much scope for thinking about the hows and whys. For these reasons philosophers have tended to be scornful of technique and technology, although it has also been suggested that the real reason was their lack of talent in that particular area; the only exceptions being Socrates, who is said to have been a stonemason, and Baruch Spinoza, who was a lens grinder.

Technology began to separate from craft when it became necessary to manufacture things so complicated that an apprentice could not simply learn from the master. The necessity arose for things which cannot be made by one person alone. Dozens of skilled craftsmen were involved in the construction of ancient and medieval temples, cathedrals and bridges, so there had to be somebody to oversee their work, the builder, or the *archi-tectón*, the chief carpenter in Greek. He would prepare the plans; a simple 'idea of a house' would not suffice. But to draw plans was in these days not a simple matter – there was nothing to draw on. Greek builders would proceed as follows: they would first build the temple's underpinning wall, precisely measured, smooth and slightly convex, so that the temple would appear longer in perspective. The smoothed surface would be whitewashed or painted with clay pigment, and then the plans of columns, column capitals, and architraves would be drawn into it, for the stonemasons to use. The builders were able to employ a number of ingenious geometrical tricks. For example, the columns of ancient temples are slightly convex or barrel-shaped, with a hundred-metre radius. How to draw a plan for such a column? Quite easily – the drawing would be carried out in a 1:1 scale horizontally, and in 1:10 scale vertically. In this way, the radius of the bulge could be easily drawn using a string. Medieval architects had it easier in this respect – they had parchment and paper at their disposal, and plans for stonemasons were drawn on metal sheets. On the other hand, they were required to deliver more complicated and complex forms, and also the technical aspect of building a cathedral, with its ribbed arches and supporting pillars, is immeasurably more complicated.

The medieval builder, and even Leonardo da Vinci himself, was an artist, a craftsman and a technician rolled into one. It was technology that was the first to break away from art. Art lays emphasis on the person's originality and creativity, and since the Renaissance on his personality too. Technology, on the other hand, is a collective business; it is concerned with organising and planning the co-operation of many people, each of whom is only able to carry out a part of the task. People learn techniques and crafts from others because the main objective is to create something useful, so the individual creativity of a craftsman or a technician remains somewhat hidden. It is too remote from the natural world, which we all understand, so that a layperson will not perceive it and only specialists in the given field can appreciate it. After all, we do not so much require a tradesman or a technician to figure out where the sink should be, or the switch, but to meticulously install them where we tell them. We do, however, have to rely on their meticulousness, as we are not ourselves able to judge what is 'good' in this case. That is why we need a specialist.

The great creative minds who invented new techniques do not usually come under the heading of crafts and technology. We call them inventors, scientists, artists, although they were frequently mere amateurs. They made a huge contribution to technological progress, and in some areas, such as watch making, they were responsible for most of the significant breakthroughs. Unlike an artist, whose every sculpture is new and different, a craftsman or a technician has to repeatedly deliver the same results, hence the emphasis on reliability and equilibrium. A good technician, craftsman, or tradesman, will first and foremost never mess up the task, or cheat anyone. For it is usually their job to do things which their customers have little understanding of and they rely on them to deliver.* That is why doctors take the Hippocratic Oath, pledging not to poison their clients, or to shorten their lives.

The modern age has brought with it new areas, as well as new problems. It was necessary to build ever-bigger ships, deeper mines, more complicated fortresses, bridges, and dams. Complex machinery began to emerge, which, while designed by a scientist, had to be made by someone else, who had to possess the necessary skills to make them, but also possess a clear understanding of their function. There was a shortage of skilled labour for mass production and it was necessary to organise production so that the quality was more and more dependent on the master craftsman and the technicians, and less so on the ordinary workmen. Thus factories were created and the division of labour was advanced further, the position of technical foremen in textile factories was created, in metal works and elsewhere. More sophisticated tools, and later machines, were invented. In the 17th century, the first technical schools began to appear, the very first ones devoted to the building of bridges and forts. The incredible advance of technology, however, only started with the invention of the steam engine and steam-powered manufacturing in the 19th century. Then, technology finally broke away from craft, and began to converge with science, and also with economics.

In the history of human spiritual efforts, technology always gets mentioned last, if at all. The reason is largely, as we have mentioned, the layperson's inability to evaluate and appreciate a technician's work. At times, we may be astonished at the results, extol the 'miracles of technology', but we become accustomed to them in the course of time, and take them for granted. Anybody who wants to gain even the slightest understanding of the modern age cannot bypass technology. It is unforgivable for philosophers to criticise technology without a smidgen of understanding for the subject. Nobody would dare to adopt such an attitude to art or science. Let us try and use a trivial example to suggest what genius in technology looks like. The sewing machine used to be a part of every household and surely we have all seen one. There is nothing to it – until it occurs to you to build one yourself. There are a number of activities which we can easily imagine being performed by

---

* 'Avaricious people like to ascribe to themselves abilities which can be pretended: they call themselves clairvoyants, wise men and healers.' (Aristotle)

a machine. However, sewing is perhaps not one of them. A seamstress perforates the fabric with the needle in the right spot, passes it form one hand to the other and has a feel for tightening the stitches just right. Can that be mechanised at all? A machine may have several advantages over human handiwork – it works faster, it is more precise and reliable, it can apply greater power. But you cannot expect it to have the 'feel' a seamstress has for her work. The movement of passing the needle between the hands is only easy for a human seamstress, who is guided by her attention or intention, and for whom it is a most natural thing to focus attention on something she can see, pick up and hold, provided it is within her reach. A machine on the other hand, cannot see anything and it can only repeat the movement it has been set up to perform. It is blind. That is why even in the most automated productions, the menial task of feeding the materials in and taking away the finished products is still left to humans. A machine simply cannot do these things, or only at the cost of unbelievable complexity.

You or I might then very well give a negative answer to the question whether sewing can be mechanised: just how can it be done? The key to the success here is a principle which actually strongly resembles that which Plato speaks of in connection with true knowledge – true reality is usually the exact opposite of what it seems to be. In technology, this principle tells us that a machine can do many things, and it is in the vast majority of cases bound to do them in quite a different way that a human would. A milling machine does not imitate the movement of a file, a washing machine does not imitate what a washerwoman does, a car does not have four legs, nor does an aeroplane flap its wings like a bird. The mechanisation of a given activity must then be sparked by an idea; it cannot be based on the way we ourselves perform it. The two crucial ideas, which enabled the construction of the sewing machine, are a mark of true genius – to replace the movement of passing the needle through the fabric by the use of two threads, which then bind in each stitch, and moving the needle's eye to its point. After it has gone through the fabric, the thread will gather and create a loop, through which the bobbin shuttle will pass with the other thread, creating a stitch. If you have never witnessed this delightful trick, you should take the effort to see it; an old Singer machine would be the most suitable, but a diagram will do in its absence.*

---

* You can find an animation on Wikipedia and elsewhere on the internet.

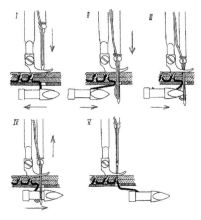

Fig. 4 The stages of the boat shuttle in lockstitch. **Phase 1** – the shuttle retreats quickly, the needle pierces the fabric, the thread take-up lever descends and the feed dog descends below the needle plate: **Phase 2** – the shuttle completes its backward movement, the needle reaches the bottom dead centre (BDC), the take-up lever finishes feeding the upper thread and the feed dog is submerged beneath the needle plate, moving along a track to the point where it will emerge again: **Phase 3** – the shuttle's nib enters a loop created by the movement of the needle completes the loop and the feed dog completes its backward movement below the needle plate: **Phase 4** – the shuttle continues its forward movement through the loop in the upper thread, the needle again descends to the BDC, this time accompanied by the take-up lever, and the feed dog begins to emerge from under the needle plate: **Phase 5** – the shuttle goes through the loop and continues towards its turning point (it pulls the lower thread forward and tightens both threads together), the needle emerges from the fabric, the take-up lever completes the stitch that is created and the feed dog moves the fabric along.

True technology, then, is just as creative, intellectual, or (if you will) spiritual an activity as philosophy, art, or science. It simply operates in a different environment and is governed by different criteria. If philosophy concerns itself with that which can be understood, and science with that which can be known, technology concerns itself with that which can be done. We could broadly say that philosophy systematically deepens and develops our understanding of the world, science extends our knowledge of it, and technology creates and organises our world. That is, the man-made world which we now live in. We have said of 'genuine' technology, science, and art, that they are creative and spiritual disciplines. On the other hand, philosophy, science, or art can be a mere means to earn a living. And this is doubly true for technology, and with the gravest consequences. A bad artist may dull our aesthetic taste and a bad philosopher may muddle our brains. But a bad technician, who has never come up with or proved anything, will have a tendency to 'manage' everything.

We have already spoken about technology becoming separated from craft once it became necessary to organise the work of many people while constructing a cathedral, a fort, or a bridge. Modern-age mass production brought the realisation that skilled craftsmen are few and far between, and the search soon began to find ways of achieving quick and reliable production without them. At that moment, the factory worker and the technician were borne out of the division of labour. The worker became a person who did not need to have many skills; he only needed to carry out someone else's instructions. That 'someone else' – the engineer, the technician – had to deliver a detailed procedure of what was to be done, and to draw a plan, describe it and take steps to make it happen. He could not rely on the worker's diligence; he had to introduce effective control. And that is only a step away from the 'rationalised' production as introduced by Henry Ford or the Czech shoe manufacturer Baťa, where each worker carries out only a few simple operations. And what the worker loses in practical freedom and responsibility for his own work, he is compensated for by comfort, wages, and holidays. The world thus becomes polarised into two areas, the area of work, or rather employment, where no free time or freedom is allowed, and the area of 'free time', in which nothing is done.

After this separation from craft, technology threw itself into the arms of science, which was just at that time searching for an ally in its project of subjugating 'nature', that is to say, the world. The theories which scientists constructed and the experiments which they carried out in their laboratories were then practically utilised by technology, which in turn provided scientists with more and more sophisticated equipment, and more and more frequently also with practical problems requiring solutions. Technology ceased to be simply the means of searching for various ways to do what is needed, and it became a search for the limit of possibilities. Science ceased to embody the examination of how things are in the world, and it became a problem-solver. Since the 19th century, however, both areas have come under pressure from economics, which decrees what we can afford, what we should spend our money on, what is beneficial and in what quantities. Again, that belongs to another chapter.

Technology supplies us with things which we can use without actually understanding how they work – they are too complicated and we cannot see what is inside. Sometimes, they can even frighten us. Not just the horrendous killing machines, the missiles, bombs, and rockets, but even those which faithfully serve us in our homes – what if they one day rose and rebelled against us? They are fast, strong, sophisticated, and they work ever more independently of us. They make life easier but also rob us of work. Man is no match for them any more. Take chess, for example. We have already become accustomed to the fact that even the strongest man in the world cannot stop a locomotive engine with his bare hands, and the fastest man in the world cannot catch up with a car. But a machine beating a human being at chess – is that not monstrous? And yet it is almost the same thing. Chess is a peculiar game with a finite (albeit vast) number of possible combinations and each situation can be fairly precisely analysed. Unlike the human, who also relies on intuition, the machine is at each step able to go through millions of options and choose the best one. So chess, too, is played in quite a different way by the machine and by the human. The machine can beat us not because it is more 'clever' (a machine can be neither clever nor stupid), but because it has speed and precision on its side. All its 'cleverness' has been factored in by those who made it, who also have to check it over from time to time, and perhaps change the batteries. A machine can never rise up against mankind because it has no identity of its own. When a person is killed by a car, it will not be the car that will stand trial, but the driver – or possibly a negligent manufacturer. It is always man against man, it is man who sends jets and tanks against his fellow men. It can of course happen that a bomb which has been devised to kill others will kill its maker too. The bomb does not care; it is a machine.

We have said that technology comes in where it is necessary to organise co-operation of people with various, usually highly specialised skills. Typically, there is no one person who would understand a whole project with all its individual segments. This, however, creates the danger that no one person will bear responsibility for the whole – 'I am just doing what I was told to do, the rest of it is none of my business.' Whose business is it then? As modern people, we live in two strictly separated roles. In one of these, we are specialised to do what others require of us, what we have an understanding of, but because it is only that which we do, we cannot be held responsible for the whole. On the other hand, in our 'free time', we use an ever greater number of things which we do not understand in the slightest. We also deny any responsibility connected to what these things might cause to the world – it's none of my business if there are CFCs in the fridge, or if my car pumps poison into the air.

I don't understand any of it, I have just read the instruction manual and I behave accordingly. The fact that in either of these roles we do not feel responsible for what we may be causing is the root of the ecological problems of today's world in the broadest sense. However, we are also aware that without technology and the way it distributes and organises work, we would not be able to survive anymore. How can we survive without giving it up?

Questions:

- Try to describe an instance of technical genius (a few ideas: knitting needles, the flush of a toilet, a bow, a safety lock, a bell).
- Where do you see the boundaries between technology and craft, between technology and science?
- Why could technology in Europe not fully develop until the Modern Age?
- What do we mean when we say that something is only a 'technical question'?
- Why do we need to specialise? What advantages and dangers does that bring with it?
- What responsibility should be expected of a specialist, and of a user of technology? Could this be somehow enforced?
- Try to consider the responsibility of the specialist who constructed the furnaces at Auschwitz.
- Organisation and planning are a necessary part of technology. What impact does this have on our freedom at work, in our civilian life? Can anything be done about it?

21. Society, Institutions and State

A child enters the world among people, but family is not yet a society. Parents must look after the child, whereas the child is not required to do anything at all. In the family unit all the members belong together (no matter how frequently they may fall out with each other), they all have their own separate roles and they act as guarantors to each other in the outside world; if a child breaks something, the parents will have to pay for it. Until the end of the 19th century, the family performed a far more fundamental function than it does today. 'Family' also meant an economic unit and it secured most of the things that were necessary to life: my great-grandmother said that money was only needed at home for salt and taxes. A person without a livelihood was hardly in a position to start a family, and a person with no family had to live off of relatives or even strangers; such people were called hinds. Only with the coming of industry was it possible for such people to earn their own living as independent people. To begin with, this only applied to men but from the early 20th century independent women could also earn their livelihood in this manner. It is often said nowadays that the family is in crisis; and indeed how could it be otherwise, when it has lost so many vitally important functions. Many families do collapse, but is it not rather a minor miracle that so many of them hold together, when in fact there is nothing compelling them to do so?

As a child grows, it is given ever more responsibilities (in the old days children were also expected to help in the fields). The child also begins to leave the family and go out among other people's children, to nursery school, primary school – in short, into society. Society only begins where people do not belong to each other 'by nature', where they are tied by no 'natural' bonds and where they are (at least in some sense) equal. Society begins at the point where people do not only have to obey the will of another person, but also the law. This is why the Ancient Greeks differentiated so strictly between the private sphere, in which we work and earn our daily bread, and society, to which belong only free and property-owning men, where public affairs, war, peace and politics are debated. In Greek the word *idios* means 'one's own' and the Greek word for a person who only looked after his own affairs was *idiotes*. The fact that this word became such a common term of abuse bears witness to the contempt the Greeks felt for such people. Incidentally, for Aristotle the word 'free' meant the same as 'wealthy' – a man who depends on others for his living cannot be free. As recently as two hundred years ago only moneyed people could vote in the USA; and the idea that women also belong in a free society was only acknowledged in the majority of societies in the 20th century.

Among strangers, in society, a child learns to observe various types of personality and learns to seek reliable friends and defend itself against fraudsters. In this roundabout way, through other people, the child learns to know itself and its possibilities. It learns to live among others and to choose from among them. A child cannot choose its family and in the family circle is usually surrounded by people somewhat similar to it. Only in school does the child encounter the full variety of human personalities, opinions and backgrounds. There the child learns to choose its friends and to get along with others. In order to achieve this, the child must learn to adapt; it learns that many people find it difficult to tolerate the things that seem normal in the child's home environment, and *vice versa*. And so school and the wider society enforce, often quite brutally, certain types of behaviour which are a prerequisite for living in that society. In school and in society at large people of very different backgrounds, beliefs and behaviour come together. They must all learn to live together and resolve their conflicts so as not to endanger social peace. This extremely important process is called *socialisation*. Some children have severe difficulties with this, especially in cases where they come from very different backgrounds, for example ethnic minorities, and they do not understand each other.

A society which enforces only the indispensable rules, but which otherwise places as few obstacles as possible in the way of human contact, is regarded today as an inevitable condition for human life. There are several reasons for this. First of all, these societies (at least in some conditions) have proven themselves to be very viable; not only do they prosper, but they are also the most intellectually productive. Secondly, we believe that rich and free intercourse between people overall does more good than bad; the coming together of people for useful and beneficial purposes is more significant than the crimes of the mafia.* And finally, we would find it difficult to imagine a society built on any other principles. We all regard it as unacceptable and unfair that some people should have privileges and advantages. However we should not overlook the fact that the aim of such an 'open' society is not isolated and 'sovereign' individuals who live only for themselves, but rather the free affiliation of people at every possible level and for every possible and admissible aim. Only such a society can be called 'civic'.

The tragic experiences of the 20th century demonstrated to us, at the expense of awful casualties, that society cannot be allowed to expel anyone who has not disobeyed the accepted rules. This is a very difficult and uncomfortable principle, but after the tragedies of the Jews in Nazi Germany and the 'class enemies' of the communist bloc we know that we simply cannot do without such a principle. Or, more precisely, we do not in any case want to do without it. There are laws which delimit our freedom, and every decision to restrict it must be made on a purely individual basis, on the grounds of what the person concerned has done or not done and for what he or she bears responsibility. This must be done on the basis of laws known to everyone, and the decision-making process must not be swayed by majority opinion. The majority must never be given the right to expel someone from society merely by virtue of their greater numbers; imagine the passengers on an overcrowded life-boat voting to decide who will be thrown overboard. This principle has primacy in modern societies and must be adhered to with pedantic precision. This is why minorities play such a major role in contemporary debates about society; because they are a reliable indicator of how far a given society is able to restrict itself through rules that do not only apply to the majority, but to everyone equally.

In the family circle there can, at least theoretically, be no debate about who should obey who; this is set in advance in the form of authority. But in society at large, conflicts and disputes are common and the question arises who shall settle them. In cases where two people are unable to agree or convince the other there is naturally a tendency for them to resort to force. This is extremely dangerous for any society, as it will set a precedent for others to resort to violence, leading to an escalation of violence that is impossible to stop. The relatives of a murdered man will seek revenge and killing can escalate into a chain reaction. Some

---

* 'Good spreads itself more than evil.' (Thomas Aquinas)

tribes which have been unable to resolve this problem live on the verge of being wiped out because of these family vendettas. The issue was only settled when it was established that man cannot obtain justice by himself, that it is the concern of a third party – a judge. The existence of laws and unbiased judges are therefore the basic characteristics of society. As the Roman lawyers said, 'where there is society, there is law.'

Of course, if these laws and judges are to be effective, everyone must be governed by them. That this is to the benefit of the society as a whole, and therefore each of its members, is however a weak argument against an angry opponent. Therefore laws and judges must also have recourse to some kind of authority and legitimacy; and because their job is to restrict the use of force, this recourse cannot be the mere threat of force. For this reason social authority was, to begin with, always religious; the laws and judges were established by God (or gods) and for that reason we must subordinate ourselves to them. In the course of time other sources of legitimacy were discovered. According to these, we obey the laws and judges because we ourselves have chosen them. We call such societies 'autonomous'. It is interesting that traces of this transition to 'autonomy' are captured not only in the Bible but also e.g., in the chronicle of Cosmas of Prague (who died in 1125). Another necessary buttress of law and the judiciary is that it is *just* – that is, it corresponds to a certain human conception of how things ought to be. This is where the just avengers in western films draw their legitimacy from – but let us be careful here. This naive conception that we all surely know where justice lies has also led to the lynching of people who have in some way offended others – perhaps simply by being different from them. The simplest model of justice is equality – everyone is treated the same, an eye for an eye and so on. But this is by no means the only model. Most societies have acknowledged various exceptions or privileges which confer advantages to the rich and powerful (who are more socially 'valuable') or on the contrary, have tried to compensate for natural handicaps. The Bible, for example, contains laws affording special protection to widows, orphans and foreigners.*

Laws which (nearly) everyone freely acknowledges are therefore a fundamental and indispensable condition of all societies. Disputes are settled by a third party, who is not biased towards either side. Judges, however, have no real power of their own, and can only intervene when asked (by at least one side of the dispute) to do so. In more densely

---

* 'It is always the weakest who seek law and equality; the strongest have no need of them'. (Aristotle)

populated areas, and in wealthier societies, there also arises the problem of common defence against external enemies, robbers and so on. Here it is necessary to act quickly, decisively and effectively; mere case-by-case agreement is insufficient. It is again in the Bible (in the Book of Judges) that we find a detailed account of the reasons why settled societies wished to have a stable ruler with his own power and army. The author himself is not at all in favour of such an arrangement, which makes his account, on the whole, more convincing. The modern idea, that government was created by the richest in order to subjugate others, is probably not historically accurate. That almost nobody has ever become a ruler other than through their own action, and that such action is seldom gentle, is another matter.

We said a while ago that the greatest threat to a society is violence. But of course, all power must be able to use certain means of compulsion, including force. Is there really any difference between power and force? Where does the difference lie? This is not an easy question, made even more difficult by the distortion of communists, who claimed that power is distinguished from violence simply by being organised and class-driven. If this ever was the case, then it was not power but violence. The difference between the two may at first glance appear to be insignificant, but in reality it matters a great deal. Power is different from violence mostly because it is limited in various ways. The point here is not that its means are limited but that it limits itself in its use of them. So power does not rely on force but on a certain legitimacy, which cannot be enforced by violence. For this reason it can only use forceful means of compulsion after it has exhausted all peaceful measures. There are clear rules governing the use of force. When a policeman recites an incantation to a man he has just arrested, reminding him of his rights, it might seem like a ridiculous formality. But in reality he has demonstrated in so doing that he is an agent of power, and not of violence. A mafia boss would not waste his time with such things.

The positions of judge and ruler probably start out as individual commissions: the power of a specific person. This is naturally connected with that person's abilities and talents. A capable and energetic ruler could bring great benefits to his society, but this made the problems that arose on his death all the greater. The next great step forward happened when these functions took the form of settled institutions and offices with rules governing selection. That one person, and not another, has a certain authority within an institution is not explained with reference to that person's unique abilities and advantages; rather, that this person was legitimately installed and authorised in that position. This is clearly expressed in the sarcastic Czech saying that to whom God has given an official position, He will also give wisdom. Even if God does not provide the wisdom, the person holding the office does so legitimately. And, strangely enough, the experience of several centuries teaches us that sometimes the wisdom also arrives – eventually. The office of judge or ruler is handed on to the oldest son, lots are drawn, or finally, there is a vote. It may come as a surprise to see how often lots were drawn in ancient societies. However in these societies the drawing of lots was not understood as an expression of chance, but of a super-human, divine will, which is the surest criterion. It is certainly the case that the establishment of institutionalised (that is, impersonal) judicial and governmental power is within itself fundamental and indispensable, while the means of selecting and appointing people to office can vary greatly.

It seems to us today that it is only fair that our governments are elected. But if we want to consider it philosophically, we must ask why. In addition to such poetic phrases as 'all power comes from the people' and 'man is born free' there is perhaps a two-part answer. It is based either on faith in human abilities, namely the ability of the majority to distinguish and choose the best people, or alternatively on the more sceptical claim that whoever the majority vote for, they get what they deserve and are therefore in no position to complain. The practical result is more or less the same in both cases, but only the first of them is an argument in favour of democratic elections. Another frequently-heard argument claims that elections enable anyone to get into power. However, an unbiased view of reality tells a different story. This argument might apply to small, harmonious societies, but in mass societies the road to electoral success is complicated and costs a great deal of money; so only those to whom it matters greatly and who are willing to dedicate all their strength to it (to say nothing of money) have a realistic chance of achieving power. Elections, therefore, remain a free choice, but a choice from a severely limited number of options.

In a mass society, where people do not know each other, a decisive role in the outcome of elections is played by advertising and campaigning, in which the candidates attempt to convince the voter that they are the best choice. This gives a great advantage to eloquent, quick-witted and (of course) wealthy people, and creates the very serious problem of political demagogy. This reality renders practically impossible systems of direct democracy, in which citizens make decisions on everything themselves. With the exception of questions that affect everyone, and about which everyone has some opinion, the path is wide open to demagogues. Responsibility is also effectively lost in direct and secret decision-making: who is to blame if a referendum decision turns out to be wrong? Opponents of democracy sometimes use the paradoxical argument that hereditary succession, or the drawing of lots, leads to a situation where ordinary people come to power, and not only those who desperately want it.

An even more serious problem occurs in connection with the electoral cycle. From the perspective of our own lives, four years may seem like a fairly long time, but from the viewpoint of the problems of the world and society it is all too short. There is not enough time to carry out any far-reaching changes or reforms in a four-year period. Those who wish to be elected must accommodate the wishes of the people, which are for the most part selfish; and so even the best government has barely two years to carry out essential and unpopular changes. And so democracy, while no doubt characterised by extraordinary stability, nonetheless becomes a government of short-term goals, while long-term needs tend to go by the wayside. This is one of the reasons why long-term concerns are not entrusted to elected governments but to institutions which are independent of them – such as central banks, constitutional courts, NGOs and quangos.

In compact societies, where everyone knows each other, the exercise of social authority, and the selection of the people who are to perform it, is relatively straightforward. Everyone then lives under the constant control of those neighbours. This is the reason why classical authors were convinced that a free society is only possible on a small scale – and throughout history this has always been the case. It was only in the modern age (and through great intellectual effort) that the principles were created which made it more or less possible for a free society to exist in the large scale that was made necessary by contemporary political and economic conditions – that is, in the scale of tens or hundreds of millions of people. One of the most effective of these new principles was the idea of *federalism* and *regionalism*. This emerged from the discovery that different types of decisions need to be made on different scales. A village may decide how to tax dogs, a district may decide which roads or schools to build, whereas the pollution of rivers is a matter for the entire country and often beyond. A well-organised society should therefore not attempt to make all decisions uniformly or insist on an 'everywhere or nowhere' approach; rather, it should allow, and even encourage, different decisions to be taken at different levels. Indeed, in the EU the principle of subsidiarity is established – this principle means that all decision-making should be undertaken by the smallest possible social unit, which, for practical reasons, is in a position to do the job well.

The operation of modern society is ever more complex and we continue to depend upon each other ever more. The time is long past when a village could be said to be self-sufficient, and today this is no longer even true for states. The significance of borders is becoming ever weaker (at least in peacetime) and the influences and dependencies which cross national borders continue to increase. Economy, finance, science and technology are rapidly globalizing, as well as terrorism, crime, drugs or pollution. For this reason it is no longer possible to insist upon the absolute sovereignty of states. A bad government or a dictator in one country can threaten all the countries surrounding it; and the dangerous running of a power plant, for example, can be a direct threat to a neighbouring country – especially if the plant is located close to the border, as they tend to be. It is therefore legitimate, in serious matters, for states to be concerned about what is happening next door, and they cannot be said to be 'meddling in the internal affairs of another country'. After all, what today is purely an internal affair?

However the democratic will of the citizenry is organised, there remains the serious question – who in fact are these citizens? The ancient ideal, that it should be the 'better' (Greek *aristoi*) and more responsible people fell down because nobody could determine who these people were. Is it then everyone who lives in a given territory? Hardly. It should certainly only be those whom we could expect to hold some sort of opinion – so not small children or the mentally ill. As we have seen, decisions are only free when they are guided by reason and by responsibility for their consequences. This is particularly important in connection with political decisions; here we are not dealing with issues that can be safely predicted and decided upon scientifically. We would not consider a decision about how to build a bridge as a political decision. Only decisions about where to build it, and perhaps who to appoint to build it, could be called political. When the majority elect a bad government, everyone suffers. In the days when the population of a village had no certainty that they would be able to save any of their property after a war or other catastrophe, the assessment of a free citizen came from the (rather justified) opinion that those who have the most property risk the most – and they should therefore have the greatest say. In the modern era this assumption is no longer valid and so the right to vote is no longer conditional on property or on how much tax one pays, as was the case only a hundred years ago.

If the votes of all citizens have the same weight, they should only be free votes. If a wealthy man could bring a hundred of his underlings to the polling station and then force them all to vote the same way, or get his opponents drunk and then lock them in a coal-shed, as in Dickens' *Pickwick Papers*, it would surely not be a free and fair election. For this reason, poor people and women were traditionally barred from voting; for the same reason we must now insist that their human rights are respected. Only if all citizens are free, only if they can freely express their opinions and freely congregate, can their votes be decisive. The theory of democratic elections assumes that people remember what the winning party promised in the previous election, that they can compare this with the reality and that they will accordingly renew that party's mandate or remove them from power. If this assumption were not valid, if elections were to be decided by 'campaigns' (i.e., advertising) they would no longer be democratic elections. It is, therefore, one of the most important tasks of the mass media to remind us what has happened and what has not happened, so that we can make our minds up according to the reality and not on the basis of catchy slogans. The freedom of the press is therefore also a necessary condition of democracy, which we should, according to Heraclitus, defend just as we would the city walls.

Questions:

- Consider the differences between the way people behave at home and in public. Are there any rational reasons for these differences?
- Describe the ways in which human societies have gradually become more organised.
- Explain the difference between power and violence.
- Give some examples of public rules and laws which are the same in all societies and some which are different from one society to the next.
- How is law related to justice? Can one exist without the other? Can they both blend into each other?
- How do social restrictions (rules, laws, morality) relate to freedom?
- Why do we need settled institutions? Give some examples. In what way are we restricted by institutions?
- How can we prevent the abuse of power? What do we need most in order to prevent it?

22. Values and Money

We have seen that human action is not strictly determined by necessary causes, like the movement of balls on a billiard table, but neither is it entirely random, like Browns' movement of molecules. The field of possible action is always limited by given conditions, within the borders of which it is governed by the clash of forces, which repel a person from one thing and pull him towards something else. There are undesirable and fearsome things which people take care to keep their distance from, such as hunger, danger and uncertainty. And then there are other things, that so attract a person that he will climb over mountains – and sometimes even over corpses – to attain them. Amongst these desirable things are (of course) property, power, fame and honour, but also beauty and purity. These may not be things in themselves but they render attractive things that otherwise would not be. And finally, there are the purely human values, such as honesty and love. People observe these values, the positive and the negative, they choose between them, they select and combine them; this is the concrete form of human freedom. This is why the influence of values becomes manifest only when people are free.

A stone falls only where it must fall, and if it is not to fall straight down but rather onto, say, a railway truck, then some kind of trough must be built for it. An animal will either run where it must, that is, between the railings and fences, or where it wants to go – to find better food, water or a mate. The shepherd or animal tamer can choose in each individual case between 'the carrot and the stick' – to compel the animal to do what he wants it to do, either by forcing it (with a whip, stick or electric shock) or by tempting it with something. Both methods work, but in different ways. You can get a horse to run by using a whip, but to get it somewhere specific, say into an enclosure, is much harder and is a job for more than one cattle-rancher. Fences and enclosures work, but must be free of holes. At first sight, using temptation and attraction is less reliable. A well-fed animal does not respond to clover. But when it does respond, you can make it go exactly where you need it to go. People can also be herded into enclosures; they can be pushed along like balls on a billiard table, by what philosophers have called a force from behind – *a tergo* in Latin. Speaking cynically, however, this is not an effective use of their specific potential. People do a much better job of chasing themselves. It is sufficient to show them something they like, and they will run after it cheerfully all by themselves; they are free, after all.

That to which people gladly and willingly run, and which renders things (or even people) desirable, attractive, precious and dear, is what we call *values*. Plato would perhaps say that a value is that which things share with the idea of the good. From this it would seem that a value is always a value *for someone*, and rarely a value for everyone. That is why a small child is unlikely to get excited about owning stocks in a prestigious company, or an old person about an integrated motorcycle helmet. But as soon as a person responds to a certain value, it becomes a powerful force, which is almost impossible to resist. As soon as he has glimpsed it, he will follow it. He must first, however, know how to get there; what he must do, where to start, so that he can get to the value, or at least approach it. This is why people do not normally speak and think about values *per se*. They always see them as being related with some thing, or some person. This can be very easily exploited, and abused.

It is natural for a young man, who is harassed constantly at home and at school, who has to stand in line and who feels crushed like a sardine in the tram, to long for freedom; he just doesn't know how to attain it. Until one day he sees a poster of a sun-tanned cowboy with his lasso, relaxing on a boulder and looking calmly into the distance. He is not hurrying anywhere, he is not needed anywhere; he is his own master. It is the very essence of freedom. It just so happens that the cowboy is smoking a cigarette. Have you guessed yet? The writing on the billboard will help you to decipher what you have to do in order to be just as content as that Arizona cattle-rancher. By sheer coincidence, it is Marlboro. Or take another example. An investment fund is an extremely uninteresting thing; nobody would pay it any attention. But on a poster you see the face of actor who you like. He has lent his face, his smile, and even the values you associate with him, to that fund. And suddenly it is no longer just a boring investment fund – and you have become interested in it.

The connection between values and advertising is not coincidental. Nobody understands better than advertising agencies how our values really influence us. Of course they will not reveal this to us, because that is a trade secret; but they demonstrate it superbly. And those who want to learn something about human values should make a study of their work. Advertising agencies know, first of all, that values operate at first sight, without conscious reflection, and that they operate through things or people; through faces. Because they appeal to us in this manner, they can be freely, indeed arbitrarily, associated with anything – with cigarettes, for example. This association need not have any rational basis because it operates in a part of our mind that does not respond to rational criticism. A person who is taken in by an advert never asks why. He simply knows it. And it was just what he is wanted. This is why clever advertisers can choose whichever value they want. They do not choose it because it is somehow connected to the thing being advertised, but on the basis of whether it will appeal to the group of people that they are trying to address. Adverts can project values onto objects which up until then had lacked any such values. So, for example, chocolate bars are aimed mostly at sweet-toothed children and older ladies; there is certainly nothing manly about them. That is why it is necessary to show a muscle-bound athlete with a javelin on the poster, no matter how slight the connection with the chocolate bar may be. The chocolate bar itself is not changed one bit by this, it remains what it always was, but sweet-toothed grown men are no longer ashamed to buy it. As for beer – it is well known that the consumption of beer tends to promote girth and it most certainly is not an aphrodisiac. This is why it is appropriate to ease the anxieties of beer drinkers by associating beer with ('decent') erotic images. The fact that emancipated women are outraged by this association does not matter; they are not the people that the brewers are aiming at.

Sceptical philosophers have often doubted whether any such thing as 'values' actually exists. Behaviourists try to demonstrate that people act according to conditioned reflexes. According to behaviourists, people chase after the things they need, and not after 'values'. And advertisers secretly chuckle at all this, because they know very well how things really are. If people only ever chased after the things they really needed, there would be no need for advertising and it could never have come into existence. This is why genuinely necessary things almost never appear in advertising. Bread, for example, is something that people need *per se*, it cannot be replaced by anything and for well-fed people it holds no interest. Only those who have slept and have been fed, and who are not cold, start looking around them for what else there might be. They try to find what they do not yet have. They are looking for values.

A young woman who goes from shop to shop, looking at beautiful dresses in the windows, may have the feeling that she has found just such a value. The longer she has to try to find it, the more valuable it will be for her, until she finally buys it. Then she will take it home and put it on, and for a while she will be happy – she has got what she was looking for. In time she will get used to it, it will come to seem more ordinary to her, and again she will go looking. She has not found *it* yet. Either it will seem to her that this dress was not the right one, and will start looking for a better one, or perhaps she will reach the conclusion that she was really looking for something else (Plato would say she was looking for beauty, which the dress somehow had a share of) and that it cannot be gained simply by putting a piece of clothing or jewellery on one's body. But those who have been going in search of beauty for some time understand it better and better and it may happen that one day they will realise that they will have to do something about themselves. They will realise that they are searching for a value *per se*, not only in objects. And that is probably the crux of the matter.

In the modern age values have been much meditated over, but people have for the most part imagined them like the dress we have just mentioned; as some beautiful thing which exists somewhere and which is just waiting for us to find it. But it has always turned out that when people finally reach the place, although there may be something there, it is not a value: like with the dress. It becomes clear that values are 'somewhere else', a long way in front of us. This conception of values as things which can be found lying somewhere, complete and ready for us, however, leads to even direr consequences. We have already discussed obedience; that is certainly a valuable quality. But it depends on when and where, to whom one is obedient and for what reason. Obedience is a value, as long as it costs something to the person who is obedient. At a time when everyone is quietly obedient, then perhaps disobedience is a value. This is why Nietzsche says we should 'create' our own values. Does that mean I can make a value out of any old thing? Certainly not. But I do have to seek it out, go after it and persevere in my search. And I should do all this by myself. A man who sets himself on fire for the truth does not prove by doing so that something is or is not true; but he proves that the truth is a value for him. And it is only these kinds of values that we can truly honour; not those that cost no effort at all.

When one is free – that is, not living in a state of constantly being chased and constantly having to do something or other – then one begins to pay ever more regard to values. However, there are a great many and varied values, there are the illusory and short-lived values as well as the genuine values, and one must choose from between them. Values attach themselves to objects and it is through objects that they present themselves to us. Every creative person, every artist, scientist, athlete, writer, politician or teacher works with values and brings them into the world in their own way, in order to help the rest of us see them clearer. Every good technician and artisan who creates something tries to ensure that the things they create are as much as possible within the reach of everyone. This is how the real wealth of societies comes into existence. To make something, on which there is the signature of a value, is not something everyone can do, and even those who can do not, for the most part, make such things for themselves alone. People must exchange things between themselves as best as they can, and a well-ordered society is one which ensures that everyone can do what they are best at doing. But then how do we decide what to exchange for what? How to tell who has cheated who, and who has given their work away too cheaply? This ancient human problem has, for now, been solved by two ingenious institutions of freedom – markets and money.

Whenever something is exchanged for something else, two judgements come up against each other: that of the person who makes or sells the object, and that of the person who wants it. Who should settle this? Is a pair of shoes worth an egg or a whole hen? Is a lecture on ancient Egypt worth a kilo of meat? Is a house in the town worth a cow, or two cows, or ten? Who is supposed to know this, especially when we have seen that the worth of something is not the same for any two people? A hungry man will favour bread, while one who has been well fed may prefer a ticket to a concert. When two men are exchanging things, the man who is knowledgeable, experienced and self-confident will have an enormous advantage. He will praise his or her goods and tell the other man about all the people he has sold this item too in the past and for how much, and finally he will smile and say: 'I'll make a special price just for you'. If he is really good at this, you will consider him the kindest soul and greatest philanthropist under the sun – regardless of the fact that he may have ripped you off atrociously. He is able to do this because he is alone with you, the inexperienced novice. And so the defence against this kind of dishonesty is simple. All that is needed is for all those who want to sell something to line up alongside one another, to display their goods and to state clearly how much they want for them. As long as they are all guaranteed safety, access to the public and a level playing field, then we get one of the most beautiful examples of concrete freedom – the market.

For some people the word *market* is a synonym for something brutal, materialistic and barbaric. And yet markets are founded on a range of civic virtues and represent, as we have seen, a highly effective means of defending weaker, inexperienced people against cheats. It is a defence so perfect that many cheats, both big and small, has been unable to make their peace with it and have done everything in their power to avoid the open market. The smaller-scale cheats try to at least limit the functioning of the market by agreeing prices amongst themselves and not letting in anyone who sells for less, thus creating what is called a cartel. The larger-scale ones do everything in their power to ensure that they can sell their goods in a different location from the competition and to win us over with advertising – in short, everything to avoid genuine competition. And the largest of them all try to destroy the opposition and secure a monopoly for themselves. But this is the exact opposite of a market.

Exchanges between people were made very much easier by the introduction of an abstract and symbolic, but nonetheless lasting and universal measurement of value. It appears that the first of these were precious objects, which would not spoil and which were countable and even divisible. The Slavonic verb *platit* (to pay) apparently stems from the word *plátno* (canvas) as this was once used as a means of payment; it clearly had some worth, it did not rot or fade, and it could be divided up into smaller pieces. In some places shells or stones were used, but mostly it was precious metals that became established as a form of payment. They are rare and beautiful, they do not rust, you can fit plenty of them into your pocket and all that is needed is to weigh them. In order to prevent fraud, cities and rulers started to put stamps on these small pieces of metal as a guarantee, and thus were created the first coins. In the course of time it became clear that if the ruler and the state were reliable, the pieces of metal were not so important in themselves; what mattered was the guarantee. During the revolutions of two hundred years ago, states did not have enough silver and their money was needed for the army, so it came about that money was made out of paper. When the wars were over, states were bankrupt and people were unwilling to accept paper money. Governments understood that people would only be satisfied with paper money if they could be sure that it would remain valid; and so began currency policy. Our banknotes may well contain references to gold, but in fact money today is purely symbolic and contractual, depending for its validity on our (more or less voluntary) trust in banks and the state. Most money does not even appear in its paper form today, being stored electronically.

Money originally started out as a means of simplifying exchanges. But it was not long before its other benefits came to the fore. For example, unlike most other useful things, it does not go off, it lasts as long as you want it to, it can be easily transported from place to place and just as easily stored. Unlike bread, which we can only eat, money can buy you not only food, but beer, shoes or a motorcycle. For this reason it is better, in normal circumstances, when the currency is performing normally, to have money than almost any other supplies. This state of affairs supports the tendency to delay consumption, in other words saving on immediate operating expenses and investing with a view to the long term. And this in turn greatly supports long-term economic stability, which in its turn leads to political stability. And so, from a means of exchange money has become the most common form of property, a universal measure of value and, finally, a miraculously successful engine of economic development. And yet we know nothing at all about precisely why and how it functions.* It is surely in part down to the aforementioned universality of money, and also its portability, which bankers refer to with the eloquent term *liquidity*.

We have seen that in our modern society values are measured by money; a value represented by money is called a price. This of course greatly simplifies all human exchanges, but it does a great violence to the multifaceted world of values. As we know, a value is a value *for someone*, whereas a 'value' represented by money is a kind of abstract mean, which expresses nothing other than the relative scarcity of the goods or services on offer, the relation of its desirability to its availability: the more desirable it is, the more expensive it will be, the more readily available the cheaper. Centuries ago, an unknown folk economist said that 'salt is above gold';** in other words, that usefulness need not have any connection with value, in the sense of scarceness. Salt is essential to life; it is not, however, scarce. This is why it is much cheaper than gold, which we can do just as well without. Those things which are most essential to life, provided they are not scarce, have no price at all – clean air and water are free, at least they used to be. It is only now, when these things have become scarcer, that

---

* 'Practically everyone loves money.' (Aristotle)
** A well-known Czech fairy tale.

we buy, for example, water in bottles. Our grandmothers would not have believed such a thing possible.

In societies where exchange plays as great a role as it does today, the successful mechanism of prices and money has become more and more widely established. More and more objects and activities have become goods to be purchased for a price. So we pay not just for books and concerts, for museum and lecture tickets, we pay for good (and sometimes even bad) advice, we pay someone to entertain us, and so on and so forth. But we also sell our own 'manpower', that is, our time – and that is nothing less than a piece of our life, a piece of ourselves. An hour of my work costs, let us say, ten Euros; I myself could cost (taking into account my used condition) about a million. The more I sell of myself, of my life, the more money I earn. But if I sell my whole life, what use will all that money be to me? And yet the human need to simplify life by concentrating on a single main goal continues to drive a great many people to sell greater and greater parts of their lives, that is, to do work which they do not enjoy doing. The English writer G. K. Chesterton once wrote: 'It is cheap to own a slave. It is cheaper still to become a slave.'

The universal use of money to measure values has the inevitable effect of flattening and averaging out these values, and of comparing things that cannot be compared, and in the end can lead to absurd consequences. So for example the work of a mother who raises a child has no 'price' in monetary terms. The same holds for a great many other activities which we carry out in the 'inner circle' of the family – activities for which we do not expect to be paid. According to most economists there are more of these types of activities than there are activities which are bought and sold in the marketplace.

Money as a universal measure of value enables modern societies to function, but if these societies are to be maintained, some limits must be put on it. In a free society you are allowed to produce and sell almost everything – except money itself. If everyone could print their own banknotes, money would cease to function. If people could bribe the police and 'buy' a jury's verdict, society would collapse. As human beings, we must also be able to say what things we do not want to measure with money, and which values have such great importance to us that we would prefer to give them away for free. For that matter, we have never bought, and never will buy, the things that we value most in our own lives – life itself, health, happiness, love, children – so it is as if they had no price at all.

In a free society, which cannot bring about the necessary co-ordination of the actions of its members by force, but rather by the attraction of values (meaning mostly money), money comes to represent a certain power: big money especially. Naturally a wealthy man has a certain influence, nobody wants to mess around with him and many people are dependent upon him. At first sight this seems simply immoral. But before we allow ourselves to get too upset about it, we should first know what other options there are. Of course money means power – but that also means that this power can be divided and measured out, so that everyone gets at least some of it. Yes, some will have more and some less, but if there were no money then things would surely be like they were in distant authoritarian societies: all or nothing. A ruler, lord or chief would alone decide who gets what and who doesn't. Instead, thanks to money, it is shared out and each of us knows how much we can get. So almost everyone has enough for a bicycle, most people have enough for a small car, some perhaps a Mercedes and occasionally someone has enough for a private jet.

So money thoroughly measures out our power. But for money itself to exist, there must be a power within the society which guarantees the money, and which cannot be bought by that money. If we could all print our own money, nobody would be willing to accept it. If political power within a state were to become goods to be purchased, there would be nobody to guarantee the money and people could no longer have faith in it. If people could bribe the police and the courts, if they could buy a town-mayor or a minister, then the society would go down the drains and its money with it. This is why every society must make the most urgent effort to keep money and political power separate – if this is at all possible. Those dangerous places where they could rub up against each other are what we call 'conflicts of interest' and lawmakers and the courts must be on their guard at such places. When a finance minister who has been withdrawn from his post becomes a director of a bank, or when an elected official offers rewards to the voters, this is a cause for alarm – are we not bargaining with political power and the state? Universal voting rights, an independent and critical press, the guarantee of civil rights and of course some minimal standard of living – these things are a society's best defence against the power of property and money. Existence, or to put it more precisely, the effectiveness of money, depends on trustworthy power, just government and civic peace. The whole magic of freedom, money and the market consists in these precious and untradeable things – peoples' trust in each other and in the world in which they live.

Questions:

- What do we express with the word *value*? How is it connected with *evaluation*?
- Everyone who makes a decision is evaluating: where do our value preferences come from? To what extent can we influence it?
- Give examples of times when our evaluation changes. How and why?
- To decide means to choose between values where we cannot have both of them. Give some examples of this 'conflict of values'.
- How do our own personal values become common ones? What role do money and the market play in this process?
- In what way does money depend on trust? And how is this connected with inflation, interest, savings, investment and so on?
- Describe different abuses of money and demonstrate how they erode society.
- Analyse a current case of conflict of interest.

23. Custom and Society

We have shown in the preceding chapters that human action can be free only when it is not arbitrary. Only when it really matters whether I do this or that can I choose. When there is nothing at stake and we are indifferent to everything, there can only be crushing boredom and a lingering sense of futility. Strangely enough, there is no risk of this wherever people find themselves in genuinely bad circumstances: in concentration camps, in dire poverty or under oppression. In these circumstances, there is always something that needs to be done – and in this way people can win for themselves small amounts of freedom, even if this freedom comes at a great cost. On the other hand, boredom and futility are an ever-present threat wherever people lack nothing.

We have seen that free action is always governed by something. It is governed by what attracts me, what matters to me as a person, what my goals are and what I want to work towards: in short, my values. But of course, the attraction of values does not operate in a vacuum, or on a wide open plain, but rather within the realm of possible action, which contains within it a great many limitations. It is full of well-beaten paths, along which everyone walks, but also full of impassable thickets, which nobody wants to enter, and there are a great many warning signs saying 'No Entry'.

One could say that social custom, or manners, in the widest and most modest sense of the word, is a kind of topography to the realm of possible action (and inaction), a summary of the rules of human operation. Morality as 'manners', as a summary of all that 'one does and does not do' – and also *how* one does or does not do it – is first and foremost an extremely useful tool. Thanks to this tool, we are able to attend to all the things we have to take care of every day without a great deal of thought – indeed, often while thinking about something more interesting. For example, we usually do not think too much about the fact that we wash and dress ourselves every morning, that we put our shoes on or that we go somewhere for lunch. Thanks to custom and manners we can buy ready-made clothes and shoes, because we all wear more or less the same things. We even buy food in standard shapes and sizes. Without expending much thought we can greet our neighbour with learned formula (imagine if you had to think of something meaningful to say every time!), we can go out on to the street and wait for a tram. We can do all of this calmly, in the comforting certainty that this is 'how it is done', that all decent people do it this way because that is how we have been taught.

However superficial it may seem, this indispensable, pleasing and comforting harmony in everyday action has a further important function. It is precisely this harmony which holds a society together and differentiates it from other societies. The idea of homeland is not necessarily bound up with a certain place, but there are some people who manage to take it with them even if they move somewhere else; we feel at home wherever people behave in the manner to which we ourselves are accustomed. A large, national society has, in addition, a common language, which does not just mean vocabulary and grammar, but a certain manner of speech common to one's compatriots.

Where does this huge and invisible apparatus, this human 'software' come from? Animals possess something similar to it. Thanks to Konrad Lorenz we now know that there is nothing trivial about this animal 'instinct'. So, for example, predators and birds of prey, in addition to teeth and claws, are also by nature equipped with a particular custom or manner which prevents them from killing weaker members of their own species. If a small dog lies down and puts up its legs, a larger dog will never bite it. Is this just instinct? But then where do we get our human 'social instinct' from? Most likely from the same place that we learn everything useful from – namely, at home, in the kitchen or the children's bedroom, where we simply copied what we saw without a great deal of discussion or analysis; and those things that we did not want to copy, we had to be taught. Everyone learns the common social custom in a similar manner, like they learn to speak and think: from parents and siblings, and later from teachers and classmates.

Because basic social customs are so important to all societies, whether large or small, these societies must also be able to enforce them. If a society is unable to do this, it will fall apart. The same is true of animal societies, about whose customs we now know a great deal. Large societies which have their own state, and with it the necessary enforcement apparatus – laws, courts, police – enforce the most important 'customs' in this external manner. But that for which there exists a tariff in the criminal code no longer belongs to the realm of possible free action, and therefore not even to 'custom' or 'manners'. The connection between manners and freedom can be clearly illustrated by traffic laws. Minor traffic offences are attended to by the police and are punishable by a fine – and for that reason, very few people are ashamed of committing them. Even as children we sensed that there was a difference between taking pears from an abandoned orchard (when such things still existed) and being bold enough to climb over the fence of a protected garden, which entailed a certain amount of danger. It is morally worse to beat up a defenceless man than to overcome an armed warrior. In short, all violent or physical forms of defence tend to weaken moral defences. This is why Baruch Spinoza wrote, three hundred years ago, that he who seeks to prescribe everything with laws will in the end destroy morality. Indeed, all justification undermines the foundations of morality: if an action is sound, healthy or financially advantageous, there is little reason to call it moral.

How, then, is a genuine (that is, free) custom maintained, how can it be enforced? Primarily it is through the action of parents and elders. However, there are those who did not quite manage this as children, and they then have difficulties in adult life, or in a foreign environment where a different custom is the norm. When I was an apprentice in a goldsmith's workshop, there was an unusually strict custom in force. Each of us had perhaps a kilo of gold lying around freely on the desktop, and only mutual trust and custom could protect it, so there was a powerful reason for this custom. One day a foreign trade-union delegation arrived and forgot to greet us. This is a sensitive area in Czech society, and so there immediately sounded a thirty-strong chorus of booing. This was in the early 1950s and the delegation was accompanied by a local Party bigwig so this did not go unnoticed, but in the end no great trouble came of it; for once the working class was victorious.

Let us notice another important thing. Custom, as we have learned it, mostly deals with small things, almost formalities. So for example nobody really knows why we hold forks with our left hand or why we do not shake hands cross-wise. These customs perhaps originate in superstitions which have been kept up because they are pleasant, and perhaps in an embarrassing moment where everyone in a room is shaking hands it is appropriate to make light of this theme while demonstrating that we know how it should be done. This is, incidentally, why customs and manners cannot be described, and if anyone has ever attempted to do so, perhaps in the form of social catechisms, the result is usually no more than a light comedy of manners. And yet it is from the observance of these formalities that we can judge whether we can trust a person in more serious matters – like in the goldsmith's workshop. Put simply, this common correspondence in behaviour is what creates society as a community of mutual help, solidarity and trust, without which we simply could not live. Of course, this natural simplification is open to abuse; cheats and fraudsters know this very well, and if they betray themselves at all, it is precisely through exaggerated courtesy or 'manners'.

The word *courtesy* comes from *court*, where a large part of our customs and manners originate. Our ancestors imitated these customs because they liked them; not slurping at the dinner table may entail a degree of self-sacrifice but others will most likely appreciate it. Perhaps it is because the French court was more visible that even French masons on the scaffolding use at least a napkin while eating. And perhaps it is because there was no royal court in America that Americans have no equivalent for *bon appétit*. So custom is not merely a bothersome prohibiting of things; it can, for example, have remarkable aesthetic effects; it can be an elegant game which we play together every day and it can be the source of the feeling that one 'takes good care of oneself'. And this can be an extremely serious matter. For example, in the Second World War it was repeatedly demonstrated that the chances of survival for POWs who stopped shaving were minimal.

We should definitely not get the impression that custom and manners only concern themselves with silly details. We have already seen that a person's behaviour in such small details enables us to judge whether we can rely on that person in serious matters. Is this mere superstition? Perhaps not. The foundation of manners and 'good behaviour' is a certain concern for others and the will to restrict one's own freedom. A person to whom these things have become self-evident is (or at least can become) a free person, for he or she has understood that freedom is not the same as licentiousness. It is therefore ill-advised to distinguish too much between what is fundamental to custom and manners and what is merely decorative. The Czech philosopher Václav Bělohradský has emphasised the importance of 'scruples' – a form of self-restraint whose existence we cannot quite justify. Yet there is something repellent about a person who has got rid of them – a person without scruples.

Social custom as a whole is the result of common experience and nobody can ever say for sure how important each part is. It is the whole which matters.

We have up to now been speaking of custom as something settled, which is handed on from generation to generation. And yet, in the same unseen way as it arises from human experience, so custom also changes. Those things that a society ceases to assert for itself, decay and crumble, and they are maintained only for show because in reality nobody is troubled by them anymore. Exhausted customs, which no longer contain anything that people can understand, are especially irritating to young people. And the more desperately their elders fight to maintain them (without themselves knowing why) the more irritating the customs become. Eventually someone will find the courage to visibly breach the custom. People wishing to attempt this require not only courage but also a vivid imagination. But if their novelty appeals to others, then within a few years it could itself become the norm and then it will be those who do not wish to jump on the bandwagon who require courage. And so it was that several years ago, young men – possibly out of spite – asserted their right to grow their hair long and perhaps even wear earrings. In a stagnant society, where nothing other than custom is acknowledged, it is impossible to breathe freely. But when protest becomes too fashionable the society *per se* is threatened.

Social custom in most societies – ancient and modern – is centred on a few common themes: hairstyle and facial hair; clothing; dining and table etiquette; behaviour toward other people, especially one's elders; and relations between the sexes. If you have ever read any books on ethnology or travel, you will know that peace and stability in any society – from the poorest bush tribes to the most fashionable cities – have always depended on these same themes. And it is precisely these themes that various forms of social revolt have aimed at – from Romanticism to the skinhead movement. It is also apparent that they have very little to do with morality in the narrow sense of the word – of which more later.

The accepted rules of behaviour change continually – albeit slowly. They may resist external interference (even in the communist period, 'comrade' as a form of address never became truly established) but they can distinguish very sensitively between what is meant seriously and what is merely maintained through habit. So we may feel rightly disgusted by some behaviour, whereas we may regard other misdemeanours as 'gentlemanly' and even secretly admire them. For example, in some countries, especially southern, traditionally Catholic countries, the prevailing morality has never been troubled by petty theft; and elsewhere, crude behaviour and rudeness are greeted with remarkable tolerance, and even regarded as a sign of manliness. In Lutheran countries, even today, we can see how highly obedience is valued, without any qualification or exception (which is, incidentally, a serious flaw in Kant's otherwise brilliant ethics). Another very interesting area is the varying evaluation of faithfulness and unfaithfulness in marriage. In times when the lives of most people depended on the stability of the family, unfaithfulness was unforgivable. Modern societies are, perhaps, too lenient on this subject, because the damage done to those affected by it, especially children, does not seem to be taken very seriously.

It seems to be the case in modern societies that custom and manners as a whole are tending to erode and fade away. This, however, means that the society itself will also fade, to the extent that it will collapse. In a collapsing society, which is unable to defend and assert its customs through the normal channels, there will always arise groups who seek to replace them with something else: skinheads, for example. These people do not, however, seek to establish custom or manners, but rather, to 'sort this place out,' so to speak. What this means for young people who do not know the difference between 'order' and fear, is that they want to scare people. But a society which is unable to deal with even minor, everyday disorder, has no chance against people like this. And here and there one even encounters adults who foolishly believe that 'there might be something to this'. Such people are gravely mistaken, however. Fear creates only more fear, or anger; but it can never create good manners – that is, a practical and everyday community of free people.

Questions:

- Try to express the difference between values and manners.
- In our contemporary society, what is demanded, what is regarded as a 'gentleman's' misdemeanour, and what is completely tolerated?
- Could you compare the custom in your own society with that of another?
- Describe the manners that surround eating. Why are they so important?
- Describe the relationship of a society to its custom.
- How do custom and manners develop? Give some examples.

24. Morality and Ethics

Those of you who have devoted some thought to the subject of morality may have become somewhat impatient by now: 'What kind of morality is this?' Morality is surely something much more profound and serious than mere politeness or custom, which even animals have. It is therefore high time that we took a closer look at the roots of true human morality, which is indeed much more than custom and social norm, although it is related to them.

Morality in the true sense of the word only begins where one does not make decisions based on what everyone else is doing, but on what one considers to be right. 'For wherever a man's place is, the place he has chosen, there he ought to remain in the hour of danger; he should not think of death or anything, but of disgrace,' says Socrates in Plato's *Apology*, his defence against the Athenians, who have just sentenced him to death for corrupting their morals. The biblical Book of Exodus puts it even more bluntly: 'Thou shalt not follow the multitude to do evil. Neither shalt thou speak in a cause to decline after many to wrest judgement.' Suddenly, it is quite the opposite – moral behaviour is not that which is in accordance with everyone else, but that which can stand up to the 'multitude'. How is this possible?

Here, we have to start to think very carefully, so as not to jump to premature conclusions. Socrates' action is not moral because he is standing up to the other Athenians. He himself clearly explains that he is not doing so out of 'self-importance', merely to provoke them. He acts in this way because he feels bound to something which the other Athenians apparently cannot see. If they could, they would surely act in the same way as him. Moral behaviour is not merely swimming against the tide no matter what. It is behaviour which is not dictated by the opinion of the majority, but by something else. It is also true, however, that it will become most pronounced in conflict, when it is in opposition. While Socrates gets on with his fellow citizens, it is not obvious what their respective motivations are.

While manners and custom allow the distinction between the well-bred and the ill-bred, morality makes a much more serious distinction – between what is right and what is wrong. That is why the social norm requires us to do something and not to do something else, but it does not ask why. With morality, this question is unavoidable. Let us consider the most important rule of any moral code, 'thou shalt not kill'. Would we be able to answer the question 'why'? Some possible answers could be:

1. Because then you yourself could get killed;
2. Because it is not allowed and you would be punished.
3. Because life – especially that of another human being – is not yours to take; you were both given it.

The first answer, the pragmatic one, is potent and effective. It refers to experience. Its weakness is that a person can decide either not to kill or to arrange sufficient personal security so that he is not also killed. That, after all, seems to be the solution favoured by the most powerful killers, whether they act privately or are commissioned by the state. The second one is the answer of the law in a nutshell – it puts actions into connection with external responsibility and punishment. That is what is taught in schools and that is what the state is based on. And the job of the state, in turn, is to ensure that it is effectively enforced – it has courts, police and prisons to that end. This answer is also the closest to the custom we spoke of last time – thou shalt not kill because it is not allowed. Similarly to the first answer, it could however only lead to the killer taking good care not to be caught and punished. That is what all detective stories are about. There remains the third answer, one which is not based on fear. There is no way we can escape from it, as it appeals directly to our conscience, our inner being. But it is based on something which is to be found in religion, and which we perhaps do not all share. The Swiss humanist Albert Schweitzer called it 'reverence for life'. He considered it to be something indisputable and did not try to prove it by arguments, but rather through his actions.

As soon as we started to justify moral behaviour, to come up with answers to the question 'why', we entered the realm of philosophical ethics. Philosophers' answers to the question why one should not steal and kill fall roughly into two categories. Some philosophers try to base morals on the regard one has for oneself, others base it on the relationship one has to other people. Within the first category, we can find for example the ethics of the Stoics, which points out that only virtue can guarantee a contented life without upsets and disappointments, which are, on the other hand, a result of unchecked emotions. The Epicureans, too, who primarily sought after a contented life, were of the opinion that it can only be achieved through exercising a modicum of self-control. To paint a balanced picture, let us add that for the Ancients, virtue is not anything fastidious or effete; rather, it is bravery that ranks first among virtues. The idea that most misdeeds and crimes are caused by passion ('hotheadedness' in modern terms), which it is necessary to subdue by reason, is typical of the ancient ethics. It would seem that our times are more sceptical of the potential of reason, having had the experience that the worst atrocities are those which had been calculated and carried out with a cool head, without emotion – as was the case with the extermination camps.

A classic of modern ethics is surely Immanuel Kant, who based it on the postulate of equality – one should act in such a way that his actions could become a universal law for others. That is very close to the biblical 'Do not do to others what would anger you if done to you by others'. The New Testament puts it in a positive way: 'Do unto others as you would have them do unto you.' Nevertheless, there is one significant difference – the biblical rule requires one to recognise that what he or she wants (or does not want), everybody else may want (or not want). Kant's rule, on the other hand, requires one to think for all humanity, which it is hardly possible to do, and it also contains the danger of us unwittingly transferring to others our ideas of the norms of correct behaviour, or possibly demanding them. From here, it is only a short step to the widespread but false idea (against which Kant himself warns us) that morality gives one the right to demand something of others. Unlike custom, and unlike the law, which can and must make such claims, thus curtailing human freedom from the outside, morality operates in the realm of freedom and is based solely on the voluntary self-restriction of each individual. But the fact that I restrict myself gives me no right to restrict others. That is why moral commands tend to be formulated in the 2nd person singular – they do not say 'one must not steal', but 'thou shalt not steal'. They speak to me directly and oblige each of us individually; they do not address 'mankind'.

Among strongly individualistic societies and classes, among the nobility or the samurai, officers, and among the upper classes in general, the notion of honour plays an important role. One acts in a way which will not detract from one's honour – one does not take advantage of those weaker than oneself, one does not tell lies and will live up to one's promises no matter what. Such people attribute everything they have done to themselves, and act always in the knowledge that they cannot disown their actions. Socrates says that a man who has killed will to the rest of his days live with a murderer – with himself. One must therefore act in a way so as not to feel remorse in future. That is certainly easier said than done, but it is a strong ethical motive. For example, nowadays, when many moral imperatives have lost their power, we still consider keeping one's word as a necessary prerequisite of a 'decent person', of a partner or a friend. This is closely connected to Heidegger's idea that it is man's mission to try to see and shape his life as a story, as one whole right to the end, to the very moment of death.

One of the Ten Commandments has an interesting reasoning behind it: 'Honour thy father and thy mother; that the days may be long upon the land which the Lord thy God giveth thee.' The connection is obvious – you will achieve a long life and happiness with the help of your children, so it is best if you yourself behave that way towards your own parents. It is an order though, not just an explanation of a factual connection. What it says is a reason, but one aiming to the future – if you want to achieve something, you have to make an investment first. But there is more to it than that. The commandment expands the horizon beyond our own life span – your life is connected to your parents and your children, not just in the biological sense, but also as a mutual pledge. There are people who feel this pledge very keenly, and who devote themselves to creating a legacy which they themselves took over, and which they want to pass on. That is why children, family, and nation are the natural way in which moral rules, or rather the concern and care for a good life, reach beyond the individual. It is here that the concern for the distant future enters our thoughts, which will not affect us in person, as well as the hope for what we ourselves will not live to see. Only because man thinks of his progeny can he undertake such laborious projects as building a house or planting an orchard. It is for a reason that precisely these three things, children, houses and trees, often occur together in various proverbial sayings.

The German sociologist Max Weber showed that, especially in public actions, it is necessary to distinguish between the 'ethics of opinion', which makes decisions on the basis of already established principles only, and the 'ethics of responsibility', which also takes into account the anticipated consequences of each action. So when the accusation was levied against Winston Churchill for extraditing Russian POWs to Stalin's Russia or against the first Czechoslovak president Masaryk for sanctioning the army to fire at demonstrating workers, one should take into account what options were available to them as responsible politicians, and what consequences these might have led to. The same goes for the decisions made by a military leader or a flight captain – in short everybody who has to make decisions about other people's lives, and who is not responsible for his or her life alone. The difference is obvious at first sight. To risk one's own life can be a sign of bravery and heroism; to risk other people's lives is in itself problematic, even if it may be, under certain circumstances, such as war, necessary.

Classical systems of ethics try to find rules which would apply to everyone and under any circumstances. But in reality this is an overly strong 'methodological simplification', and it can lead to somewhat absurd results – an informer might claim he was just telling the truth, for example, or a coward could say that he wanted to avoid violence. This is why in today's world the picture presented by dramatic tragedy, displaying as it does the conflict between values and morals, is so much closer to us. *Antigone* and *Hamlet* clearly show that moral behaviour is always performed within a certain situation, which itself partly determines what is moral and honest and what is not.

A person's actions are always carried out with an intention, a goal one has in mind. The Utilitarians therefore turned Kant's idea on its head – it is not the decisions you make that matter, but rather the goal that you achieve. John Stuart Mill expressed this in his famous quote that what matters is 'the greatest possible good for the greatest number of individuals'. That sounds fairly convincing at first, but there are several problems with it. The expected good will materialize at some unspecified time in the future, so one must make decisions based solely on estimates and expectations. Evaluation is only possible in retrospect. Furthermore, it is not even clear what we should understand by the term 'good' – is it more food, more cars, more money – or is it also clean air, a clean environment, or firm friendship? It is also unclear how the 'good' of many people could be measured against each other and added up. Is it permissible for a society to rid itself of an inconvenient individual in order for peace to prevail in the land?

Even the best result imaginable cannot justify a bad deed, and it cannot therefore be the decisive factor in what one should or should not do. Bravery, even if it fails in its aim, is surely distinguishable from cowardice, and even a very successful liar will still remain a liar. Up until now, we have overlooked something which is fundamental to moral behaviour. Unlike mere reacting, which we ascribe to animals and rash people, a person who acts is characterised by being able to keep a distance from his impulses. Man does not merely react, but follows a certain goal, choosing to take according steps. The aim and goal of such a person is however not obvious from the outside, something a good strategist or player will take good care to maintain. A chess player offering a gambit has not neglected the pawn, but rather has set up a trap for his opponent. It is too bad for the opponent if he or she fails to notice. And so from the very nature of human behaviour, and the possibility of putting distance between one's goals and one's immediate actions, arises the possibility of trickery, deceit and lies. From the viewpoint of ethics, such a possibility is hardly neutral.

There are, therefore, also schools of thought within ethics which do not derive the moral evaluation of a deed from the evaluation of their goals, but chiefly from the honesty and truthfulness of the person performing the deed; they therefore see pretence and lies as the root of all evil. The most famous of these is surely Nietzsche's ethics. Also very instructive in this respect is the biblical story of David and Nathan (2S 11-12). King David takes a fancy to the wife of a man who has gone to war. He spends a night with her and the woman falls pregnant. King David then tries in vain to cover up his actions. When all fails, however, he ensures that the woman's husband is killed in the war and then marries her himself. But then the prophet Nathan confronts the king and reproaches him for his deplorable deeds – not only adultery and murder, but most of all his premeditated lie. And in this hopeless situation, the king indeed confesses that the blame is entirely his. He cannot undo his deed, but he no longer lies to himself. According to the author of the story, this has an unprecedented effect – he is forgiven by the Lord, and, in turn, by the whole Hebraic tradition. Can we then imagine that honesty and truthfulness towards oneself could somehow provide absolution from serious misdeeds? What sort of ethics would that be?

We have spoken here of values in a much broader sense than tends to be common in ethics. We have, however, also demonstrated that there are considerable differences between values; some can be measured by money, whereas with others we would resist such an approach, and with some it would simply not be possible. As the Beatles song says, 'money can't buy me love.' And honesty and generosity are certainly perceived as values, although they may actually damage the economic interests of the person we ascribe them to. Even the frequently heard argument that honesty is profitable in the long run is not entirely convincing. As the English economist John Maynard Keynes ironically put it, 'in the long run, we are all dead'. It is obvious that a society cannot exist without these 'unprofitable' or rather 'non-utilitarian' values, and especially not without people who will, without too much thought, be guided by them in their everyday lives. It was traditionally said of such people that they were 'honourable', as people believed that such action 'honoured' them. If we stay in the realm of rational ethics, is there an explanation for this?

While it is important that people look after those things that are in some way beneficial to them, it is in fact natural and not something to be surprised by. What about those activities whose aim is not personal gain? The easiest to understand are those which one undertakes to take care of one's progeny. Some even connect them to our hereditary equipment, genes, with the interest in maintaining a genetic line, and so on. That said, the human instinctive apparatus is, even in such things as the care of our young, very weak and uncertain. Moreover, people are able to take care of severely disabled offspring, who do not offer any future in the biological sense and who often are not a source of much happiness to the parents. People do, however, sometimes act for the good of the whole community, risking life, sacrificing themselves. Heroism has always been held in high regard, and not just in wartime. But the pinnacle of behaviour has always been seen in those people whose actions could not be explained away or understood; such people used to be called saints. They were esteemed because there was always something purely personal and creative in their actions, which could not be acquired or imitated; there was something noble and beautiful, which was difficult to describe, other than it grows into something which goes beyond any one individual. Man is, unlike other creatures, certainly endowed with special possibilities and abilities; that in itself, however, does not give any grounds for a privileged position in the world. That can only be justified by acting not only in our own interest, but by somehow thinking and acting on behalf of others, including nature and the whole world. And for example, the demand of unconditional regard for each human life cannot be justified by anything else but the fact that man alone possesses the ability to perceive that which exceeds him. And that is not only a prerogative of religion. Friedrich Nietzsche was certainly no lover of religion, but when he wrote that 'man is something that must be overcome', and that 'man is a rope stretched between the animal and the Superman' (*der Übermensch*), he meant more or less the same thing.

Throughout human history, the ethical systems based on religion are the ones that have probably had the most impact. This is because they do not stem from the notion of the autonomous human subject, the independent and rational individual, who is indebted to no one, but from the notion of human dependency, which is probably closer to reality. A baby is certainly not born 'independent', and even fully-grown adults usually receive more than they give. The 'balance sheet' between me and the world can never be even. Economists also know this, and they refer to those things that we get for free, such as the soil and the resources within it, or air and water, as 'externalities'. But even in Christianity itself, twofold ethics can be found – one is based primarily on fear of (eternal) punishment, and is therefore not ethics in the true sense of the word; the other, much rarer, appeals to thankfulness – through good actions people repay, in a very imperfect way, what they been given beforehand without any effort on their part – life, good health, happiness, friends, children. The words of Jesus, such as 'freely you have received; freely give', or the parable of debt forgiveness (Mathew 18: 23) provide, to those who are willing to accept them, perhaps the best foundations of ethics. This is mostly because they so well encompass the free nature of truly ethical behaviour, as they are not based on fear, but on thankfulness and love. Nevertheless, it is the task of the philosopher to point out that these are internal and supremely fragile things, which are best not talked about, and if so, then with the utmost tact.

Questions:

- Explain the difference between a social custom (norm), morality, and ethics.
- A person learns the societal norms from childhood; is it the same with morality?
- What is morality based on? Where does its authority stem from?
- How can a moral claim be justified? Compare various options.
- What is virtue?
- Why is it difficult to speak (or write) of moral greatness?

25. Law

It seems that some fundamental notion of justice is part of being human; small children have a strong sense of it, and all human societies depend on it. But when we look closer at it, we realise that justice can take different forms in different situations. Wherever something is being divided up or shared out, this should be guided by *distributive justice*; gains and burdens should be dealt out fairly and proportionately. But what does this mean? When a bar of chocolate is being handed out to children, they should all get the same amount. But in other cases, the fair thing to do would be to give one of the children more, perhaps as a reward, or because the child is ill. A person who works harder, or has more skills, should earn higher pay; and on the other hand, the state should support people who are in any way handicapped. The tax system, rewards for work and benefits for those who are unwell or faring badly should be governed by this kind of justice. Those responsible for deciding these things need to weigh carefully the principle of equality, the principle of merit and the need to even out inequalities. Distributive justice is therefore complicated and will always be the subject of disputes. If it were understood only as strict equality, this could lead to conflict with individual freedom. Societies and states ought to treat each of their members equally, but by no means everything in life ought to be entrusted to society and the state. In civic matters people should be 'equal', but this must never be taken to mean that they should all be the same.

A different situation arises whenever a person is owed something by someone else. That which has been borrowed should be returned, that which has been broken should be mended and that which has been eaten should be paid for. This corresponds to the notion of *retributive justice*, as it exists in both civil and criminal law. In the most straightforward cases, this seems to be no more than a continuation of the idea of equality.

A person who has borrowed money from someone else should return it. However, what if that person stole the money? Here it is no longer enough to return it. The person has committed a criminal act, which calls for punishment. In addition, many criminal acts cannot be made good; if a murderer is sent to prison, it is of no help to his victim. It is the state (in the form of the public prosecutor) which carries out criminal proceedings against the accused, and punishment alone is on the agenda. The victim plays no part in the proceedings, except perhaps as a witness, and if the victim seeks compensation, he or she must go through other channels.

The idea that criminals should be punished mainly by working towards some form of reparation (perhaps merely symbolic) is only recently starting to be considered. The commonly-used justification for the punishment of criminals is that it acts firstly as a deterrent to others, secondly that it has an educational function for the criminal, and finally that it performs a defensive function for the society at large; a criminal who is behind bars cannot hurt us. Despite this it would seem that the ancient mythical idea of mending the order of the world, disrupted by crime, still to this day has an influence on our notions of just punishment. After all, unpunished crimes are seen as a wrong not only by their victims, but by law-abiding people everywhere. As an ancient Indian law states: 'A crime which is punished falls on the perpetrator. A crime which is unpunished falls on the ruler, the judge and on everyone else.'

We have already seen that the assertion of justice can lead to dangerous procedures. If a person takes something away from me, I consider it my right to pay that person back. However, it is very unlikely that my assailant will consider this as just. Here we have two ways of seeing the same event, and it is very unlikely that they will be in agreement. This becomes even more difficult if someone takes another person's life. Then the fight for justice is most likely taken up by the victim's relatives, and the number of people involved becomes ever greater. The Bible illustrates probably the first attempt at preventing the escalation of killing. In the story of Cain (Genesis 4) a strict and highly surprising prohibition against killing the murderer is enforced. Similar measures have been found among primitive tribes but have most likely been unsuccessful, as they are hard to reconcile with the notion of justice. It is probably for this reason that these measures were soon replaced by a much better idea – namely, that victims of conflicts between people should not try to attain justice on their own, but rather this task is taken over by the society at large, in the form of an appointed judge. To begin with, these judges drew their legitimacy from exceptional personal abilities, closeness to the gods, age or wisdom.

This simple fact – that in a given society, victims do not exact justice directly against their assailants, but rather through a third person, a judge – is probably the most important prerequisite for the development of organised society, government and law. Judges are historically 'older' than rulers – and, it would seem, more important. It should come as no surprise that in the early days the position of judge was closely bound up with religion – from where else could they draw their authority? It is only in a society where something like a judge exists, that a form of government can emerge which is more than mere force – and which can change into an institution, surviving the passing of individual chiefs or rulers, and establishing procedures by which power can change hands. In Europe this process occurred almost a thousand years ago, and we can follow it step by step in ancient chronicles.*

As soon as the social authority consolidated, it could lent legitimacy and efficiency to the decisions of judges. A sense of justice is the best guarantee of stability and peace within a society – and it has always been known that these, in their turn, provide the conditions for prosperity. It is only natural that governments have frequently sought to bring the courts under their control and to curtail their independence. The relatively freer societies have been more or less successful in preventing this, and it was the French thinker Baron de Montesquieu who expressed this as the principle of the separation of powers: the legislature, the executive and the judiciary. Judges have a significant position in society, and considerable *de facto* power. From the beginning, therefore, ways have been sought to guide their decisions and prevent arbitrary verdicts. In small, homogenous societies, established on a common religious foundation, this kind of safeguard was provided by the notion of divine justice, to which even judges were bound. With the emergence of large, urban societies, however, in which people came from different backgrounds and a single religious identity was lacking, other ways had to be found.

There are essentially two ways of doing this. In the first, judges are bound by previous verdicts and cannot contradict them. This is the basis of *common law*, which has given rise to the legal systems of England and the USA. The second, more radical approach attempts to formulate, in advance, mandatory rules to govern verdicts and justice. The laws, which

---

* For an example from Czech history, read the early chapters of Cosmas' Chronicles (circa 1100).

apply equally to everyone, are public knowledge and the judge is charged only with their interpretation and application in individual disputes.* This is basis of Roman law, and of the legal systems of Continental Europe. Naturally, neither of these methods is applied in their pure form today. The English system gives wider powers to judges and permits a better understanding of the specific features of each individual case; however, the rules by which judges are bound (namely, the entire history of previous cases) are extremely extensive, and inaccessible to the layman. Because of their more wide-ranging powers, judges are elected in the USA. The continental system gives the citizen a better chance to become acquainted with the rules he or she will have to follow; however, because the laws are universal, their application often leads to outcomes that we consider unjust. For this reason, the laws do not, for example, set specific punishments, but only within certain bounds; they also frequently permit extenuating circumstances or grounds for leniency. The problem of judicial independence from state power is also more difficult to resolve in this system.

We have seen that, over time, certain moral laws have crossed over into the area of law, so that now obedience to them is enforced by state power. This applies mainly to the gravest rules, the breaking of which is a threat to peace in the wider society: the prohibition of murder, theft and violence. These are not all, however. It has become clear that even very serious rules cannot be effectively enforced by the external authority of the state. The best example of this is lying. Lying is certainly something which threatens society; but to prove a person guilty of lying is a very difficult task. Contemporary law, therefore, only touches on lying in a few exceptional circumstances (perjury, fraud, slander etc.), as it would be impossible to effectively enforce any such prohibition in other areas. Throughout history, attempts have been made to persecute every single lapse in morals.** These experiences have however shown that this is only possible at the cost of intolerable intrusions into individual liberty, and by instituting almost totalitarian conditions. The repressive power of the state, aimed at the establishment of the rule of law and the maintenance of peace within society, encompasses the police, courts and the criminal justice system. The strength of this apparatus has grown tremendously in the modern era, and can represent a grave danger to citizens if it is

---

* According to Plato, it is the law and not humans who should govern a good society.

** For example in the so called Four Articles of Prague (1419) the Czech Hussite movement required that all 'deadly sins' be publicly punished. Something similar was attempted later by Savonarola in Florence and by Calvin in Geneva.

abused. Such abuse can come from two sides; from citizens and from the state. In addition to the separation of powers and the independence of the judiciary, therefore, modern societies also need to have effective defences against such abuse. The most frequent form of abuse by citizens is false allegation. If a man is accused of committing a very serious crime, such as murder, the society will be tempted to isolate or otherwise damage him – to be on the safe side. His enemies could take advantage of this and, rather than hurting him directly, could create suspicion around him and therefore cause the state to intervene and hurt him. Citizens are protected against this possibility – which is not merely theoretical – by the principle of the presumption of innocence. Until guilt is proven, the defendant must be regarded as innocent. This principle may severely impair the effective prosecution of criminals, but it is absolutely essential to the defence of society. Whenever it has been abolished, for example in totalitarian regimes, widespread abuse has immediately followed.

Even more dangerous, however, is the abuse of repressive power by the state itself. The most important defence against this, alongside political plurality and a free press, is the principle of human rights. This principle is one of the most significant restraints on the power of the state over its citizens; and this is the reason why undemocratic states hesitate to acknowledge it. In contrast to the ancient notion that everything that citizens possess, including their rights, comes as a 'privilege'* from the chief, or state, to whom unconditional obedience is required, the principle of human rights declares an entirely different relationship. The real holder of rights is first and foremost the individual, who may forego some of his rights for the greater good of the state – for example, the right of self-defence and the right to exact justice – but who holds onto other rights which may never be foregone. These rights can only be taken away on an individual basis, by the verdict of a court, in front of which the individual had the right to defend himself. These fundamental rights (the origin of which has been interpreted in different ways by different theories of human rights) are not given to the individual by the state, but rather are part of the individual's being and can never be reduced, even by the state. Such rights include personal freedom, freedom of expression, freedom of movement, freedom of assembly, protection of privacy and the secrecy of the postal service, among others.

Societies which gained this arrangement for themselves – often at great human cost – were in a position to treat it with due respect.

---

* Literally exception from the law.

Contemporary societies have simply inherited it, without a great deal of activity on their part, and others have arrived at it suddenly and without preparation (like the societies of the former Communist bloc). The true meaning of human rights is often misunderstood and underestimated for this very reason. One of the most frequently heard objections against human rights is that they provide things which are not essential to bare survival, but which will not help people if they have nothing to live on. What good is freedom to a person who has nothing to eat? This is certainly a serious objection, despite its abuse by totalitarian propaganda; only a society in which people are not starving can really be free. This is the reason why the European codification of human rights contains a range of other, *social* rights, which are of a different character. They refer to people having the right to work (not the same as being given a job), to be fairly paid for their work, to have some free time, to be seen by a doctor, or to have access to education. For political reasons, however, the question of who should provide all of these necessities – and who is going to pay for them – is usually avoided. The naive answer – that the state should provide them all – would involve equipping the state with such wide-ranging powers that it would no longer be a state of free people. For example, if the state were responsible for securing employment for all its citizens (as described by communist propaganda) it would have to introduce compulsory labour, invent 'jobs' and tax all economic activity so severely that it would end up having to close its borders. Social rights are of course essential for the protection of the weaker members of free societies, but if it were to be seen as an individually enforceable subjective right, it could lead to the exact opposite. These rights represent a commitment on the part of society to ensure that none of its members go without these essentials. But they are nothing more than that. On the other hand, genuine individual freedom is not so much a 'right' of each individual person, but rather a guarantee that state power will not be abused.

So, law and justice are prerequisites for good societies. As St. Augustine once wrote, 'kingdoms without justice are mere robberies'. Their broader connections can be seen in language; for example, the Czech word *právo* means both *law* and *right*. The words *právo* and *s-prave-dlnost* (justice) are related to the adjective *pravý* (genuine, real) which originally meant 'straight'. Ancient tribal societies placed great emphasis on the role of the right hand in performing a whole range of important actions; only then were they 'correct' (s-*právný* in Czech). The meaning of 'right' as the opposite of 'false' stems from this. The same root is shared by the verb *praviti* (to pronounce), which originally referred to judicial sentences to resolve disputes and establish law. What is wrong has to be corrected (*na-pravit*), and finally there is *pravda* (the truth) as the third which resolves doubts and conflicts. This truth gains its validity not through the will of political rulers but through being 'right' (*pravý*) in itself.

Questions:

- Did you ever suffer an injustice in your childhood – at school, or later on? What do you think of it now?
- What do you imagine as justice in exams, for example entrance exams to a school or university?
- Theft is punishable by law. Can you imagine a case when this could be unjust?
- Consider the role played in a trial by the prosecutor, the defendant and the judge. How do they each contribute to the enforcement of law?
- On the court buildings, Justice is portrayed as blindfolded and holding scales in one hand and a sword in the other. What does this signify?
- What is the point of punishment? Can death be used as a punishment? If so, why? If not, why not?

26. Text and Interpretation

Speech is, as we have seen, a tool of thought, but is first and foremost a means of communication between people. By speaking, we interact with each other, we express our wishes, feelings, and impressions; we communicate what we think and what we know. Language and speech forms the broadest kind of community, to which we all belong. To be excluded from it ('I'm not speaking to him') is unusual, and it can affect a person quite considerably. Ordinary speech, which is not used to express any groundbreaking ideas, forms the basis of human interactions ('We had a good chat'), opportunities to express fondness or displeasure ('I'm going to tell it to him straight!'). In speech, we can play games ('But you won't get the better of me!'). Speech is used to establish and maintain relations of subordination and superiority ('Did you hear me or not?'), authority ('Don't you dare talk to me like that!'), as well as deference and love. With speech, we can demand, implore, we can pressurise, persuade and intimidate. We can 'give somebody a piece of our mind', we can 'give them a good talking to', or we can have a ' heart to heart'. Whenever we are 'lost for words', perhaps at a funeral, this is an expression of hopelessness. We feel a lack of something; although sometimes words can be at least substituted by music.

Dialogue is, then, the basic mode of speech – speech flowing back and forth between me and you. A dialogue is always in the present, in the here and now, and accompanied by gestures, facial expressions and pauses. In a real dialogue, which in many aspects resembles a game,* the speakers take turns, react to each other's ideas, and develop the topic in various directions. Neither knows beforehand where their conversation might lead to ('We got sidetracked'), nor when it will finish. A genuine,

---

* Since Ludwig Wittgenstein 'language games' have become an important field of study both in linguistics (pragmatics) and philosophy.

open dialogue between two equals is a demanding and difficult affair, because it requires willingness to listen, the ability to understand, and sometimes even accept other people's point of view. That is why dialogue can so easily degenerate. A talkative person will usurp the conversation, while others simply listen and say nothing. It may be difficult to develop the topic of the dialogue, so it falters. Or it may happen that people meet who are too preoccupied with their own interests and worries, so that they all just talk at each other, their thoughts do not converge, and the dialogue is turned into a monologue, or a series of unrelated monologues.

The basic limitations of dialogue rest in its temporal nature; it can only include those who are present (or on the phone). That is why it requires a good deal of quick-wittedness and concentration, and it puts at a disadvantage those who are less quick-witted and who perhaps only come up with the right wording once the topic has moved on to something else. Dialogues are also time-consuming, and a general manager of a business cannot deal with every issue by having separate conversations with each of his employees. That is why we cannot, especially in larger communities, do without speeches, lectures, sermons and monologues, where a single designated person imparts to a multitude what he or she thinks they should hear. Once the monologue is over, questions and discussions may follow, in order to somewhat mitigate the disadvantages of a monologue; on other occasions it is not possible or convenient to do so. Some speakers do not relish this; Sigmund Freud, for example, is reported to have told his listeners at the beginning of his lectures that there would be no discussion afterwards.

Monologue is fundamentally different from conversation in that it is much less time-bound. A speech or a lecture tends to be prepared in advance, it can be repeated at any time, and it is all the creation of a single person. This person can afford to carefully think it over, research whatever is needed, check the reference books and documents; he can rehearse the speech, or even pre-record it. So, while a lecture is delivered in the present moment, it could have been written years in advance. This slowly moves speech further away from its original environment, that of conversation. A lecture which is delivered 'live' can however still be enhanced by gestures; the speaker can take into account the reactions of the audience, and react or even improvise accordingly. That is something which a recorded lecture can no longer do. On the other hand, it can 'take place' without the speaker's physical presence, and if it is broadcast on the radio or TV, it is not even restricted to one location – we can all listen to it separately in our own homes.

Long before recording technology was invented, people discovered that speech could be recorded in writing. As 'preserved' speech, which can be reconstituted – that is to say, *read* – thousands of years later, it offers rather different possibilities for communication. Written speech may last, but with many limitations. First of all, it continues its life without its author, who, once the text has been 'handed over' has no further input into who might come across his or her words, what context they will be read in and how they will be interpreted by different people.[*] The author cannot accompany his writing with a gesture, has no say in who will read it, what attitude they will adopt towards it, or what mood they might be in while they are reading it. It has become a text and it lives an autonomous life – unless it dies away. On the other hand, the author of a written text possesses many more possibilities to hone his message, to make sure and doubly sure that he is really saying what he wanted to say. Instead of gestures and intonation, the author can use punctuation, small and capital letters, different fonts, or possibly diagrams and illustrations. The ornamental and metric language of poetry, too, has a different effect when written and when spoken, and some poetic forms (such as acrostic) will only become really apparent in the written form.

The writing is only the first stage, and the purpose of a text will only be fulfilled when it is read. So how does this 'preserve' become speech and how does it achieve meaning? This happens in very different ways. One extreme is a confidential letter or a love letter, which often allows us to say more than we would dare to say eye to eye. When Franz Kafka wanted to express himself sincerely to his father, he had to write to him. At the same time, there is a great danger of misuse here – the letter could fall into the hands of a person who it was not intended for. That is why the secrecy of the postal service ranks among the most basic human rights – a letter is a part of my private sphere. At the other end of the spectrum, there are texts which intrude and impose themselves on everyone - flyers, slogans, and adverts. They are not addressed to one person in particular; they are addressed to anyone. Apart from intrusive texts which aim to

---

[*] 'That is a truly terrifying property which writing shares with painting. For paintings seem to brim with life, but if you ask a question of them, they will maintain their silence. It is the same with written expositions – you would think there is some thinking behind them, but ask them a question, and they will always point to the same thing. They will be lying around in the homes of those who understand them, just as of those who do not have a clue; the text cannot know who it is to speak to or not. And when it is not treated nicely, when it is unfairly tarnished, it always needs its author to come to the rescue, for it is not able to defend or help itself.' (Plato, *Phaedrus*)

grab our attention, there are other, stark messages, which express power, symbolically on the pedestals of memorials, and practically in decrees, summons and laws. There are texts which impart some information, ranging from newspaper articles to scientific literature, and there are others, which only confirm what has already happened or been said. From birth certificates to death certificates, and ID cards, passports, school reports, diplomas and all manner of documents, step by step, our real life is accompanied by that other life, in the paper world of text, which is the basis of our all-powerful bureaucracy. A person queuing up in an office is in the process of attempting to have his or her existence recognised in the other world, at the other side of the office counter.

All these are texts, at a glance often undistinguishable from one another. While they live within their individual contexts, while they fulfil their functions, nobody is likely to get them confused. But once their original world disappears, the majority of its accompanying texts will disappear with it. Only a few will remain here and there, in an archive, somewhere in an attic, buried in a chest under the ground, and they will turn up at some point, like the proverbial message in a bottle. Such texts, devoid of their original function, become material for historians. These historians can now embark on the adventure of deciphering, reading, and interpreting: a process known as hermeneutics. Unlike live speech, which is always personally accompanied by its author, and living texts, circulating among people possessing understanding and knowledge of how to deal with them, these really are bare texts, shipwrecked texts, so to speak. So what can be done with them? Can they be somehow 'resuscitated', made to speak again? What can be read in them and how? The very first, dramatic part of the deciphering process can bring great surprises. For example, to our eyes, cuneiform writing looks deeply mysterious, almost sacred. How must the first experts to have deciphered them felt, when they realised that most of these texts are bills, reports, and other traces of the ancient 'paper world' of bureaucracy? The story of Cretan linear B writing is even more dramatic. Only small fragments have survived, and the first of them to be successfully deciphered contained an itinerary of the dishes in the royal kitchen, including 'five tripods, one of them with a leg broken off '. The understanding of a text can be hindered not only by its being very ancient, or in an unknown language or script. Sometimes all it takes is for the text to be unusually frank – many had originally considered Hitler's *Mein Kampf* as pure gibberish, for they simply could not imagine it being meant seriously. Within ten years of being published, it became a gruesome reality.

Hermeneutics, the art of textual interpretation, was established in ancient times for the purposes of understanding legal and religious texts. Nowadays, it belongs among the foundations of the study of history, philosophy and the humanities in general. In the natural sciences, which have left such a strong imprint on our times, the demand for impartial examination of reality has proved successful – the scientist is to suppress all his personal, individual interest, and simply strive to record the facts accurately. So is it possible for a historian to do something similar? Hans-Georg Gadamer, the German philosopher and a classic author on modern hermeneutics, maintains that it is and is not. If a historian wants to come close to the true aim of any scientist, that is to say truthfulness, he or she must first of all realise that a text is not a bare fact, but a preserved speech, which needs to be interpreted. Besides, not even scientists (let alone philosophers) can be quite impartial in their approach to any given text – if that were the case, what would even make them notice that particular text, and select it for examination? However, if one openly embraces this involvement, it offers the best available means of beginning to uncover the meaning of the text. For the meaning cannot be gleaned without using this preliminary understanding (*Vorverständnis*), with which one first picks it up, as a starting point. The requirement of truthfulness will however lead to the need for a continuous reassessment of this preliminary understanding and involvement, as one progresses further in understanding of the text. And it should always be at the forefront of one's thoughts that any understanding has been and still is only 'preliminary', that is requiring critique, cross-checking and possibly correction. Thus, one can make the journey from the original interest, which was purely personal (and therefore 'subjective'), to the true understanding of the text, however ideologically remote one may find it. The only difference is that if there is some live tradition connecting us to the text, this journey to understanding will be significantly shorter and safer than with those for which we are only armed with the most general, somehow 'panhuman' preliminary understanding.

If a text really is just preserved speech, all that is necessary to obtain understanding of it is to renew the context in which it had been created. For the context can dramatically influence the meaning of the text. Thus the slogan 'To each what they deserve' may represent a reasonable legal rule, but it acquired quite a different meaning as it was written above the gate of a concentration camp. A text itself may be written in such a way as to make its meaning obscure; it can be a puzzle, a cipher, or an allegory, which requires the reader to think about it. With very ancient and significant texts, old commentaries may be helpful – those who wrote them were closer to the text than we are. But with texts which are difficult to understand, fragmentary or sacred, people have always tried to gain not just a superficial understanding, but to get at some more profound meaning. They have always tried to uncover other, allegorical and hidden meanings, which would somehow be relevant to their own situation and the questions of their lives. Then it is also more difficult to distinguish to what extent we have really found these in the text, or to what extent we are ourselves projecting them into it.

Questions:

- Explain the difference between a dialogue, a monologue, and a text.
- Think of all the knowledge that is required for the understanding of a newspaper article! Can you think of all the things which you would have to explain to your great-grandfather in order for him to understand it too? And what about a foreigner? Or a Martian?
- What constitutes the context of a letter, an instruction manual, and a scientific book?
- Look at this quote (from *Love's Labour's Lost*): "He hath never fed of the dainties that are bred in a book; he hath not eat paper, as it were; he hath not drunk ink"? What sort of person is Shakespeare seeking to describe here?
- What do we mean by saying that we 'can't make head or tail' of a text? That it 'does not make sense'?
- Why do we need to rely on various certificates, invoices, contracts, permits and documents? Under what conditions would it be possible to do without them?

27. The City

Almost all of us live in towns and cities, and not only in this country; one of the characteristics of rich, or 'developed', societies is that some 80% of their population live in urban areas. Whether we detest cities, whether we are ashamed of them, or love them, they represent our natural environment, where we know our way around and where we feel at home. And yet it was not so long ago that things were quite different: right up until the 20th century, our ancestors were for the most part country people.

The city is an artificial world, one which people have created according to their dreams, ideas, and, of course, possibilities. Through city life, they have rid themselves of their dependency on nature; they can be dry when it is raining, they can have light at night, and they can be warm in winter. If the city was walled, they had no need to be afraid after dark. Cities have been around for at least six to eight thousand years. They were first built on the back of successful agriculture, as an expression of prosperity, overabundance. In those places where people just barely scraped a living, cities were never established, and whenever a society sank below that level of sustenance, its cities soon disappeared. The function of cities is to manage surplus – surplus population, goods, wealth and time – and the activities of the city are, from the viewpoint of bare survival, always something of a luxury: shopping, culture, education, industry, transport.* Life in the city is richer, more comfortable; that is why so many people are attracted to it. You can convince city people that the best symbol of the free life is the cowboy; western movies never show

---

*   'It is not permitted for the pupils of the wise to live in a city where any of these things are absent: a doctor, a barber, a spa, public toilets, running water, a river or stream, a synagogue, a teacher, a copyist, a voluntary treasurer, a criminal court.' (Moshe ben Maimon – Maimonides, 1135–1204)

him having to look after his cows all year round, in rain and mud, getting up before dawn to milk them, not even able to dream of any such thing as a holiday.

This is, on the other hand, what makes city life more dependent and vulnerable. Everything that city dwellers live off has to be brought in from elsewhere. If a war breaks out, it will be the city dwellers who starve first. And as a luxury, the existence of cities is dependent on long-term political stability, peace, and prosperity. As city life becomes ever more technically advanced, it also becomes increasingly vulnerable – nowadays if the power cuts out for a few hours the city is brought to its knees. The city is an incredibly complicated organism, in which everything is interdependent. It is extremely energy-hungry, and entirely dependent on functioning organisation.

Ancient cities were created out of surplus, which it was necessary to defend. The city's defence rested mainly on the deities and the temples devoted to them, on a strong ruler, and finally on the city walls. All of this required substantial investment and a great deal of time. First of all, there had to be a firm belief in future success, a willingness to invest in an uncertain future. Work on cathedrals and city walls dragged on for decades – all for the benefit of future generations. To ensure that such investments were fruitful, and to prevent people abandoning them, it was necessary for rulers to have a firm hand, and for him to be fortunate enough to enjoy periods of peace and prosperity. If the first investment came to fruition, others moved inside the city walls and space became ever scarcer. This is why old cities are so crowded and their streets so narrow. The density of population and the cramming of more and more people into small homes gave rise to other, hitherto unknown problems, such as the provision of fresh water supplies, the disposal of refuse, and outbreaks of fire and disease.

The fall of the Roman Empire went hand in hand with the disappearance of the ancient cites – in Rome itself, scarcely a tenth of the original population remained, and those who did struggled to make any kind of living. The Roman Forum would provide pasture for cows for the next thousand years. The magnificent ruins would nevertheless carry a reminder of the distant past, and once mediaeval life became relatively settled and prosperity returned, cities once more began to sprout up like mushrooms after rain. They were, however, of a different, much more secular, nature. While the name for 'city' in Romance languages (*civitas*) was derived from the name given to its inhabitants (the Latin *civis* originally meant 'neighbour'), the mediaeval town was simply a place for commerce, where markets were held (as shown in the etymology of the German *Stadt*, or *Marktflecken*, while the Russian *górod* and the English *town* emphasises the defensive walling of cities). Cities no longer had a primarily political role, to provide governance, order, and safety. They were established in an environment with a different form of political organisation – the feudal, territorial system. Only in Italy did cities retain their political sovereignty (including their own army, currency etc.).

The mediaeval city represents a sort of enclave where people are not bound to the soil. Partly in practical terms, as their livelihood at least partly constitutes of craft and commerce, and partly in legal terms; as they are exempted from serfdom, they can move freely, and are allowed more or less autonomous government. Towns were founded in various ways, which are still today discernible from their street plans. The oldest and most important Czech cities appeared spontaneously in favourable places, where there had been ancient merchants' routes and thriving trade. In due course, as they prospered, churches, town halls, and city walls were built. That is how Prague's Old Town, Olomouc and Znojmo were established. The second category is towns founded by decree, usually by the land's ruler. You can tell them immediately by their regular plan and spacious central squares. Some Czech examples are Plzeň, Budějovice, Jičín, and Vysoké Mýto. And the final type is mining towns, where silver was mined. Some were built hastily, such as Kutná Hora, when rumours of silver deposits spread through the surrounding areas; others, like Jihlava and Kolín were founded by mediaeval developers, who laid down the plans and often invited people from neighbouring Germany to populate the newly established town. These settlers would bring with them their own ready-made political organisation and laws.

Towns have played an important part in Czech history. They were a source of support for the king in power struggles against the nobility, and they grew in importance as barter was replaced by monetary trade. The mining towns helped the king maintain a monopoly over currency, which was only broken by the minting of the *Joachimsthaler* by the von Schliks of Jáchymov in the 16th century. It would be fair to say that it was the towns, and especially the colonial ones, which enabled the early and comprehensive centralisation of Přemyslid Bohemia, the crux of their power in the late Middle Ages. Another wave of urban expansion came in the 16th century, with the rise of trade; then, after the devastation of the Thirty Year War (1618–1648), the 18th century ushered in the era of industrialisation.

All over Europe, cities have been the cradle of democracy and a laboratory for social experimentation. It was here that the new manner of individualised and mobile life emerged, where one is continuously surrounded by a multitude of strangers and must learn to maintain a certain distance while acting in a polite and non-committal fashion. In such an environment, one is free to choose one's friends. While a farmer would lead a fairly solitary existence in the fields throughout the working week and Sunday would bring some welcome socialising, the city dweller looks forward to moments of privacy. While the farmer is dependent on his neighbours, who are always the same, the city dweller is dependent on his or her customers and on more or less anonymous services. The mobility of town people, who move house frequently, and can gain or lose fortunes very quickly, means that urban hierarchies are based strongly on personal success and abilities. That is also reflected in the changeable, elected municipal councils. Another feature of municipal self-rule was the guild system, and later various associations which would bring together people with a common aim. Towns gave rise to individualised and internalised religion, civic law, banking, and the secular education system. It is only in the city that everybody needs to be able to read and write, and only in the city that education becomes of practical value. Towns have become the natural base for the development of industry, and the rise of the modern transport system.

The things that we now take for granted in city life have evolved gradually, and some of them are in fact fairly recent. The streets of a medieval town were intended for pedestrians, here and there it was possible to ride a donkey; carriages and carts did not begin to frequently appear until the 16th century, hence the modern-day traffic difficulties in historic cities. In Paris, these were solved in mid 19th century in a brilliant, if rather brutal way, when Baron Haussmann had the maze of narrow and winding streets intersected with wide, straight boulevards. In Rome or Naples, nobody has to this day dared to try anything this audacious, so these cities have no central thoroughfares running through them. Street paving was first introduced in the 14th century, and spread very slowly; drinking water was up to the 16th century mainly drawn from individual wells. The supply of running water into houses became available in the 19th century, as were the overall city sewage system and street lighting. Towards the end of the 18th century, the strengthening state bureaucracy gave rise to tenement housing, and public transport was not introduced until the late 19th century. And such 'mod cons' as bathrooms, central heating, lifts, or telephones only appeared in the 20th century.

The role of the city was dramatically transformed by the expansion of industry. Thousands of the rural poor moved to cites to become factory workers – the livelihood they found there was hard, but still better than what they had in the country. It was enough for one person, and one did not need to have a family to make a living in the city. When country people moved to the tenements, they would often bring their country habits with them, and in the 19th century, people would still spend time in the tenement yards chatting and singing together, just as they would have done on the village green. The city lost its military importance and city walls were torn down. Huge, poor and ungainly working class suburbs appeared; in the Czech context, their creation meant that the Czech element finally gained numerical superiority over the German-speaking citizens, and eventually political control of the city. The radical increase of population necessitated costly public projects, such as waterworks, sewage, schools, hospitals, regulation of rivers, and new bridges. Industry required the supply of large volumes of resources and goods, with the railway being best suited for the task. That in turn offered the possibility to move about freely to the masses, with many moving and commuting to work.

The expansion of industry, and of the service sector in particular, in the 20th century, has brought a change in the relationship between town and country. While in the 19th century, a typical inhabitant of a small town would still own some fields or pastures to supplement the uncertain income gained from his occupation, in the 20th century, people from far and wide began to commute to the city to make their living. The dismantling of the city walls meant that space was no longer strictly limited, and leafy suburbs began to sprout up, offering a pleasant combination of town and country life. The growing area and decreased density of population, however, presented serious challenges to public services, from water, electricity and gas supplies to the public transport, which an expanding city cannot do without.

That is why, in the 20th century, large housing estates and commuter towns sprung up everywhere. Their function was purely to provide housing, without having much in the way of infrastructure and services, and large city agglomerations were formed, sometimes tens of kilometres long. The historic city centres were at the same time depopulated, as they only offered limited comfort at an inflated price, which only banks and businesses could easily afford. The growth of various megacities in the poor ('developing') countries is even more rapid and alarming, with millions of people trying to eke out a living at the fringes of urban civilisation. They live in shacks and find food among garbage, but it is still preferable to starving in the country. Thus, out of the 80 million population of Egypt, one fifth lives in the Cairo area today, mostly in dreadful circumstances. To a lesser extent, makeshift housing estates are to be found in any modern city, and they are the destination for the majority of the immigrant population. Such agglomerations then become a breeding ground for all kinds of crime and various extremists, and but for the occasional few acts of individual charity, the prospects of their inhabitants do not improve.

Cities then face vast problems, and an ever-growing number of people feel that this is not the way forward. But where does the way forward lie? Possibly in combining the advantages of the city and the country, the building of spacious suburbs, and expansion of the commuter belt. The provision of urban comfort, utilities, public transport, as well as health care, schools, and policing in such built-up areas is even more costly (in money and resources) than in the dense inner cities. Perhaps the underlying problem here is not 'the city' as such, but rather our demands of comfort and security, which the majority of us have come to take for granted. But for how many will they remain permanently available in future?

Questions

- What are the conditions for the creation of cities? Under what circumstances can people make a living there?
- In what ways is city life comfortable and varied?
- Have a look at the map of a city you know. Try to explain it, find various functions within it.
- What do we use as points of orientation in a city?
- How did the demands on transport in a city change with the rise of the motor car?
- How do you envisage an ideal city? How would you organise housing, shopping, and transport in it?

28. History

For a young child, there is always something happening – and it is happening here and now. That which is happening right now fully engages the child's attention, and he or she will have forgotten what was happening an hour ago. As we grow up, the sphere of our experience broadens, and at some point we have to start stringing our experiences into some sort of context, for example in the form of a curriculum vitae. From early on, we hear of events which happened to other people, then later we read about them, and we realise that the world did not begin with our birth. In this way, collective memory is created, the narrative of all that happened in the past. For many reasons, this is very valuable to us humans. First of all, it is a reservoir of beautiful stories, food for thought, and perhaps even a source of some enlightenment – although, as we know, 'the only thing we learn from history is that we learn nothing from history' (Hegel).

The true telling of collective memory is held together by the material context – the family, tribe, or community. The stories which it consists in share one trait – they are 'ours'. Otherwise they would disintegrate into an assortment of stories, or rather, they would never have formed a whole; they would be merely an assortment of stories. Such memory is never quite complete, it is not a full documentation – we have already touched on that. It will only contain things which have moved the listeners enough that they will remember them unaided. Human memory, as we already know, does not contain any experiences in their raw form; memories are already labelled, expressed, articulated. Thus, only 'beautiful' and gripping narratives, articulated by a great poet or storyteller, will 'make the grade' for collective memory. The poet's, narrator's, or listeners' focus is not really on 'history'; they do not aim to express those various details which a modern historian would find the most interesting. That is why such narratives, like Homer, or Livy, although not considered 'historical' in the modern sense of the word, are nevertheless the forerunners of contemporary historical writing. The Greek *historia* meant exactly that – knowledge or narration.

Despite the ancient storytellers' phenomenal feats of memory (they were able to memorise precisely the whole of the Homeric Epics, the equivalent of a fair-sized book) the possibilities of oral narration were nonetheless limited in content. As time went by, and with the rise of settled kingdoms based on agriculture, another 'social demand' was created, which could not be fully met by oral narration. The basic aim of any kingdom is to be stable and lasting, to offer the people a prospect of continual peace and prosperity, to convince them that the kingdom will be there for eternity. A very persuasive argument in such cases seems to be the ability to show that they have been established for a long, long time. This is in fact so persuasive that, to this day, many businesses or banks are keen to boast that they were 'established in 1757', and so on. Thus these two needs gave rise to the revolutionary invention of writing, a form of speech which will not fade.

Unlike oral narration, which would be created long after the related event happened, and was not intended primarily for future listeners, but for those present, writing enables a new kind of historical communication in the form of a chronicle. A chronicler does not endeavour to create a gripping story, such as that of Gilgamesh, Moses, or Ulysses; his task is to record what has just happened for the use of future generations. Unlike a poet, who may live to become famous, a chronicler will only be appreciated long after his death. From the literary point of view, a chronicle is a much more primitive form, but all the more valuable as a historical source. A chronicle is, as a rule, told by someone who has witnessed the events he relates, someone who was close to them and who has understood them as a contemporary would. These are great advantages. On the other hand, a chronicler does not record 'all that has happened', for that cannot be recorded, but rather what he considers of greatest importance, in the way he himself understood it, and to the extent that he is willing to relate it to future generations. Thus a chronicler, too, will paint his favourites in a better light than those he disagrees with, and he will skip or gloss over those things that do not fit his view of events. Very rarely do we come across chroniclers who have also included the misdeeds and misdemeanours of glorious heroes. These include several authors of the Jewish Bible (e.g., the Books of Samuel) or the Greek historian Thucydides.

Chronicles, then, record remarkable events which happened within their horizon, their own experience, and in the order in which they happened. Unlike a narrative, which is held together by the logic of the story, the plot and its *dénouement*, the chronicler's narrative is strung together by the passing of time. It is therefore only natural that the need arises to somehow label and record this flow of time – the need for an era. In the ancient empires, the timeline would usually start with the accession of a ruler, as the first and foremost purpose of the chronicle was to preserve his glory for eternity. But already in Ancient Greece the counting of years became separated from the political situation and was based instead on the Olympic games. The Romans would simplify this further by taking the founding of their city as the starting point, as that year signified the beginning of the civilised world. Before that, there was only barbarian chaos in which nothing worthy of note happened.

People who live close to nature, and who are entirely dependent on nature, see their life as determined by two major powers – the changing of the seasons, and fate. Fate is tortuous and unpredictable; the seasons, on the other hand, seed-time and harvest-time, come round repeatedly and regularly. A year which we have survived is a successful year, and our greatest hope is for the next year to finish that way too. The best we can hope for is that things will remain just as they were. Or rather, as things do change, for the next spring to be just like the last. Just as the heavenly bodies eternally move along the same trajectories, people wish for their society, cities, and empires to move along the same lines. As nature can be yearly reborn fresh and green, the society should rid itself of all the dirt of the last year and start afresh as in its very beginning. That is the aim of many ancient rituals and ceremonies, with mythical narratives providing a template which we seek to return to year in year out; and, finally, it is also the aim of the chronicler recording the successful fight of his ruler against fate.

Nevertheless, the world does change and periods of crisis, when these changes happen before our very eyes, bring the idea of change into sharp relief. As soon as man has the power to observe a period that is longer than the span of a human life, he cannot fail to see that change is irreversible, and that to attempt an eternal return to some sort of beginning is futile. This knowledge can initially lead to deep scepticism – the world is changing and this can only mean that it is in permanent decline, and that this decline will deepen every year. The golden age of timelessness is gone, it is behind us, and the further away we move from it, the less of it remains. The bronze era follows the silver, with only the iron era remaining. Individuals will react to this experience in their own way; take for example Parmenides or Heraclitus. Plato's *Laws* bear witness to such scepticism (the scepticism of an old man) and a desperate attempt to at least halt this decline. Reason, which is our strongest weapon, and philosophers, who can wield it, must find a way to save what can still be saved, and to slow down the continuous decline and decay.

So what has actually happened? The city dweller no longer lives surrounded by wild nature, nor with nature, so he or she will see the changes in the man-made world rather than the perpetual cycle of nature. Time ceases to be the perpetual return of the same thing, the same seasons following one after the other, prompting man to join in and be guided by them. The importance of nature's cycles – especially the annual cycle – gradually pales into insignificance, overshadowed by the changes in the human community. We can see that as far back as Thucydides, the pinnacle of Ancient Greek critical historiography, living in the urban world, where nature has little impact, as opposed to the plotting, partiality, and conflicts of people. If there is anything which does recur, it is the cycle of imprudence and excess, '*koros* – *hybris* – *até*, surfeit – insolence – ruin', which is, however, not in any way regular, and even less a sign of eternity. Four hundred years later, the emperor Augustus would grasp this change even more keenly than Plato, and he would attempt to counter it through much subtler means, namely a brilliant propaganda campaign. The most precious gems of Latin poetry, Ovid's *Metamorphoses* and *Fasti*, were created at the emperor's instigation. They endeavour to rekindle interest in traditional mythology and in the yearly cycle of festivities, the sacred image of nature and the basis of cyclical time. But people in cities already lived in another time, a time in which things are always happening.

This change in the perception of time would be felt by other urban civilisations, but only one would be able to see it through the other end of the telescope: late Judaism. For centuries, Jews had lived in the expectation of a great event, of deliverance and victory not through military might, but through divine intervention at some time in the future. The cycle of seasons, which represented true and perpetual reality for the Greeks, is but a superficial image, through which one can sense the advent of the much longed-for moment. The passing of time is thus not seen as being dragged away from that golden age of long ago; on the contrary, the great day is approaching. If anything is a cause for despair, it is the repetitive passing of years in unchanging subjugation and destitution, whereas changes are in fact a cause for hope. It is proof that the time is coming. The bigger the changes, the more impatient the expectation, as shown in apocalyptic literature, which aims to calculate in advance the date of the day of deliverance.

At this same critical juncture, the expectation that a saviour would come paved the way for Christianity. Christianity started at the borderline of the two cultures (Jewish and Hellenistic), but its centre would soon shift to the centre of the empire and of the world: to Rome. Here, too, the first idea of history would begin to form; an idea that would be entirely new in two ways. We have already mentioned that for the chronicler, history means the history of his ruler, and possibly his surroundings. History, as Christianity began to see it, concerns the whole world; it is for everybody. Secondly, this grand history becomes one dramatic story – that of God's dealings with people, from the creation and the fall, to the covenant with Israel, to deliverance through Jesus Christ, the founding of His church, and the expectation of the glorious ending, the second coming, the last judgement, and redemption. The despairing fable of the golden, silver, and iron eras, of endless decline, is replaced by a more dramatic and hopeful image of the history of salvation. The bottomless fall comes at the very beginning, and it is caused not by fate, but by man himself, for disobeying and disrupting the created order.* Everything which follows is a series of remedial steps, culminating in the death of Christ and his resurrection, after which it only remains to wait for this redemption to be openly manifested in the Last judgement.

It was only within the framework of Christianity that history could emerge in the sense that we understand it today, as a unified and continuous narrative, in which great events are played out. The character and form of this narrative nevertheless continues to be a subject of endless debate. For Christian thinkers, from St. Augustine to Bossuet** or Newton, it is indisputable that the narrative of the history of redemption is finite in time, and all the authors accept what they consider the chronology of the Hebrew Bible, that the world is about five thousand years old. The content of the story of the world is divine assistance to fallen man, bringing him step by step back to God. It was, however, characteristic of the Hebrew idea of history that it is a story with a known development, but it is open-ended, with an unknown outcome. Both the Hebrew and Christian faith rest on the reliance that the end will come and that it will be spectacular. However, the majority of people find the

---

*   See Genesis 2 and 3.

**   J.-B. Bossuet (1627–1704) was a French theologian, court preacher of the king Louis XIV.

idea of an open end too demanding and unsatisfactory. They cannot bear it for long. They want not only to believe, but to imagine how things will turn out, to see the ending with their own eyes. Out of this urgent need, apocalypticism was born in late Judaism, that is to say literature that attempts to uncover the mystery of the future. That is why the original biblical promise, which scrupulously avoided any concrete and definite image, became more articulated, acquiring shape and form as time went by. The more colourful and detailed, the better, and preferably complete with a date.

One very persistent idea is that the definite end of history is preceded by the coming of a 'thousand-year reign' of peace and justice, which both is and is not a part of history. Christianity and the whole of western civilisation have been grappling with this tendency for two thousand years. The idea that the final deliverance of the righteous and the final judgement of the world are just around the corner, that it will come within the next few years, has been recurring throughout the European cultural history, and each time it emerges, it releases an enormous amount of human energy. The anticipation of the end of the world before the year 1000 AD brought far-reaching reforms of the western church and state. The idea that the thousand-year kingdom could not come about because the city of Jerusalem was in the hands of infidels instigated the crusades. Dante wrote his *Divine Comedy* with the imminent end of the world in mind. In the Czech context, the policies of King Charles IV (+1378) were guided by the idea that foundations needed to be laid for the coming of the thousand-year kingdom, and in another way, this idea inspired the Hussite reformation: in 1420, the town of Tábor was founded as a gathering place for the faithful, in order for them to follow the biblical instruction to 'go up on the mountain' when the end of the world is nigh.

These movements, which are referred to as millennial (or *chiliastic*, derived from the Greek *chilias*, a thousand), have always ended up in disappointment and a sense of deflation. Their failure has considerably contributed to a dramatic change in the spiritual atmosphere, to the transition from the Middle Ages to the modern age. Millennial movements have nonetheless survived into the modern age, albeit in a different form, and usually in some sort of disguise. They are usually initiated in an environment which generally rejects, or simply is not familiar with the Hebrew and Christian ideals, and which is thus more and more forced to come to terms with the idea of a very wide span of history, if not infinity. Since the 18th century, science has been concerning itself with the question of the creation of the world, and the estimates of its age have been increasing ever since – at present (but only since the 1960s), it is estimated at some fourteen billion years, a million times more than Isaac Newton imagined. Modern science has also amassed a great wealth of knowledge of what has happened, and is happening, in all this time. Nowadays we know that the appearance of nature, which had been traditionally considered as fixed, or even eternal, only gained its present form a few million years ago, and that it had been preceded by a number of other forms, or 'eras'. The content of the historical narrative has thus become immensely enriched and broadened, which in turn offers new ways of how to understand its direction and meaning.

The idea of history as an open-ended narrative, but with a clear and defined content, a 'programme', or at least a direction, is fundamental to the 18th century Enlightenment. It places infinite faith in human reason and ever-improving knowledge, which leads humanity to ever better ways of running its affairs, against the dark ages of the past, full of ignorance, superstition, and bloody disputes over nothing. This new society, which has shaken off superstition, and which is based purely on reason (which is common to all people, accessible to all, and the same for everyone) must inevitably lead to the continuous improvement of the human condition, it must do away with the causes of quarrels, and make way for boundless progress. As much as the Enlightenment could never fully penetrate into practical life, and remained the preserve of the educated classes, it has sustained the people of Europe for a full two centuries, two centuries of amazing changes and undeniable successes. Despite all that, even the Enlightenment succumbed to millennialism – there were Enlightenment thinkers planning totally Utopian projects, and the famous French Encyclopaedia (1751–1772) is an expression of the conviction that the time is ripe to definitively sum up all the knowledge of the humankind, because the advance of worldly knowledge was very nearly at its end.

The first explicit and systematic alternative to the Christian narrative of the history of redemption was developed two hundred years ago by the German philosopher Georg Wilhelm Friedrich Hegel. His concept of history incorporates the main features of the Christian picture, but the story does not actually take place in the visible world, but rather in the sphere of the spirit, of which this world is the visible manifestation.[*] Even Hegel, however, was unable to tolerate the idea of open-ended

---

[*] 'Only the whole is true. The whole however, is only completed in development. It must be said of the absolute that it is fundamentally the result, that it is only at the end of that which in reality is.' (Hegel)

history, and succumbed to the temptation of millennialism – the end of history, the perfect expression of the spirit, is at hand, embodied in the modern civilian state, the Prussian Kingdom. While Hegel may have compromised the concrete form of his philosophy of history by including this idea, the idea of history as an entire narrative, in which things happen, became firmly rooted. It also encouraged the natural scientists, who subsequently extended it to pre-human nature (Lamarck, Darwin), and even to nature predating life on earth (Lyell). In this manner, despite the firm resistance of most natural scientists and historians, the historical framework was enhanced firstly by archaeology (the study of the unwritten evidence of ancient societies) and even the one thing that all modern thinkers, including Hegel, dismissed explicitly from the framework of history – namely, 'nature'.

The age of Enlightenment and Hegelian historicism is also an age of tremendous technical progress, which naturally increases man's power over people and the material means at the state's disposal. Therefore, the millennial excesses of this time will also be much more serious and terrifying than ever before. When the belief in Enlightenment and progress faltered in the early 20th century, it suddenly became obvious that progress and reason do not only unite humankind, but rather that they also provide new reasons for friction and new ways to inflict violence. Hand in hand with this new conflict, which grew into the First World War, new millennial projects appear, promising to solve human problems through technical means, and to bring history to a close within the foreseeable future. This is why these projects make so much play of the idea of the 'new order' or the 'new man', and question the importance of individual freedom, restricting it to the private sphere. The project of National Socialism, launched rashly on the back of Germany's shock at losing the war and the widespread disillusionment with the new economic situation, had to show its true colours fairly early on, and it will be remembered by history for the atrocities it committed. It is not at all a coincidence that its wrath turned mainly against Jews – for all its secularisation, it sensed in them the embodiment of the idea of history as an open-ended narrative. The project of Russian communism was better equipped intellectually, and therefore lasted longer. It won the support of many intellectuals worldwide, and, for a while, its fight against Nazism helped it cover up its true nature, which is an abuse of millennialism.*

---

* That is to say a protest against the unbearable burden of the open-ended narrative, which we should carry on bearing as free and responsible individuals.

Just like all the other forms of millennialism that preceded it, it eventually failed because it was unable to fulfil what it had promised.

In our times, then, we live under the shadow of various failed millennial projects, and it is no wonder that we view this idea of history as narrative with a degree of suspicion. The English philosopher Karl R. Popper expressed this scepticism in a savage attack on Plato and on Hegel – in his view the two main standard-bearers of historicism, and therefore also of the worst misfortunes of the 20th century.* After the experience of the war, such a reaction was quite understandable; but it cannot be defended in the long run. After all, modern man cannot evade the question of history. One cannot accept the stance of some professional historians, who consider 'history' as mere construction and who would gladly reduce it to a mosaic of precisely reconstructed stories, a sort of improved chronicle. The Hebrew and Christian belief in the historicity of the world was already incorporated by the Enlightenment, which was able to witness it in the world at first hand. We can hardly refute this view even now. We may perceive historical change differently, but it happens all around us. We have to look for a better defence against the ideological abuse of history.

It seems to me that we must above all else insist on the 'open-endedness' of the historical narrative, that is to say that while we see clear shifts in the world as well as in ourselves, which lead in a certain direction and are not just a sort of Brown's movement of individuals, there is however nothing that gives us the right to declare that we know 'where' this movement is leading to, and where it should finish. Whether we like these signs of historical change or not (and nowadays they are more rapid and more pronounced than ever before) we should observe them closely, and, of course, evaluate them, too. History certainly is not, as the Enlightenment saw it, a straight path leading automatically to a better future. The amazing development of communications, the merging and mixing of different cultures, the disappearance of local peculiarities and traditions, and the emergence of a global lifestyle with the same fashions, music, and similar ideas of happiness; all of this simply exists. It is not, however, the manifestation of some superhuman forces, but rather as a challenge to our thinking and behaviour, as to what we can do with the new possibilities, and what misuses we will be able to prevent.

---

*   Karl R. Popper, *Open society and its enemies*. First edited 1945.

Questions:

- Have you ever been in the role of 'historical witnesses', in that you witnessed an irreversible change happening in the world? When was it?
- Explain the difference between a story, a chronicle, and history.
- Nazism and communism would not have become so widespread had they not responded to some deep-seated human wishes and anxieties. What were these wishes and anxieties?
- How did the viewpoint of historians change when they were no longer limited to written documents? How has the whole discipline changed?
- In what ways do geological and biological evolution differ from the history of human societies?
- What implications would it have if we reject this difference?
- Which changes in the modern world do you consider as important and long-term tendencies? Why? Do they lead in a particular direction?

29. What Happens in History?

At the start of this book, we saw that people look for sense and meaning in everything they encounter – that is how the concept of constellations or of the figure of Europe in old maps came about. In history, too, as soon as they became aware of it, people started to search for some sort of overall meaning, or at least a direction. For the Hebrew prophets it was the approaching deliverance, the final act of divine intervention; for the Christians it was the coming of Judgement Day, the sorting out of the righteous from the unrighteous, while the Enlightenment contented itself with the overall tendency of growing rationality and the victory of reason over obscurantism and superstition. But then Hegel, and the Marxists after him, wanted to see the final goal – the realm of the Spirit, or a classless society, an end to the exploitation of man by man. For the historian, who sees the infinite intricacy of history from up close, so to speak, these are all gross simplifications – real history is never this straightforward. And as the Marxist concept of 'historical necessity' was abused as means of political argumentation, it is not only professional historians who nowadays have good reason to treat grand historical ideas with some suspicion.[*]

On the other hand, we also know that man can only gain an understanding of his situation when he has some understanding of his past – that is where our language and culture, cities and institutions stem from. Some form of historical awareness is a necessary part of general education, and it is more than just a handy topic for witty conversation. If we conceded that history was just a mass of life stories and events perpetually swarming in front of our eyes in a confusing manner, we would simply have to give up on this particular part of our cultural

---

[*] The French philosopher Jean-Francois Lyotard expressed this suspicion by coining the word *metanarration*, which is any attempt to give a global sense to history by a narrative.

tradition. But as that is not possible, history teachers must frequently reach for the outdated Marxist model of 'social orders', from the primitive community, to the slave system, the feudal system, and the capitalist system (it is better not to mention the socialist and communist systems any longer) – just to impart to their pupils some overview of history: not everyone can be a professional historian. Philosophy is then faced with the pressing problem of critiquing and expanding or amending this scheme, so that it provides us laymen with some sort of rough framework, within which the individual historical events can be placed and arranged. Let us attempt to do this.

The Marxist concept of the historical evolution of mankind was created over one hundred and fifty years ago, and it therefore shows all the limitations of its time. It views 'history' as the struggle of two antagonistic classes, the focus is on the political history of European civilisation, it is based only on written documents, and it sees material production as the fundamental driving force of history. Everything else is regarded as a derived 'superstructure', only a secondary by-product of the evolution of the forces and organisation of production. Nowadays, we consider it only natural to view human history as a certain extension of not just 'prehistory' and archaeology, but also of the evolution of organic nature and of the universe. With the evolution of speech and culture, human societies may have departed from biological evolution, but certain basic traits have been carried over from the primates and other mammals living in societies. European civilisation may have spread globally, but it has at the same time been significantly influenced by others, namely the civilisations of the Middle East, which cannot be scornfully dismissed with the mention of the 'Asian production method'. The techniques and methods employed to find and sustain livelihood have undoubtedly played an important role in every society, but nowhere did 'production' play such an important part as in the 19th century. Religion and culture have connections to the material culture of the given country, too, but they are not its mere reflection, rather they help shape it in a significant manner. And as human history is so rich and intricate, it cannot be reduced to a single cause as if it were theoretical mechanics.

A broader framework of the concept of the evolution of mankind was first introduced by sociologists (Herbert Spencer, Ferdinand Tönnies, Max Weber, Emile Durkheim, Lucien Lévy-Bruhl) and later incorporated by a number of historians, many of them influenced by Marxism, but not ideologically exclusive. In the mid 20th century, the Australian historian

V. Gordon Childe published a slim volume entitled *What Happened in History*, in which he briefly sums up the basic division of history according to 'way of life', that is according to the ways of obtaining a livelihood, and the ensuing social structure. Nowadays, we should extend Childe's starting point by what we know about the ethnology of primates, the ethnology of preliterate societies, from cultural anthropology, and linguistics. We know from philosophy that human life in this world does not amount only to obtaining food; it also includes some symbolic understanding of the world – especially in speech – of anxiety about the future, of morals and manners, values and hopes, which each society maintains and is governed by. We must, therefore, also take an interest in that which each particular society considers of utmost importance, what it tries to eschew, what it is guided by, the way it understands itself and the world, and what it prizes most highly.

Perhaps we would be talking about the way of 'existence' or 'dwelling', rather than the 'way of life', if these terms were not so closely connected to an analysis based purely on inner experience. It is definitely important for us that all the basic ways of life have left obvious traces in our behaviour – so that over the weekend, many city dwellers become ardent mushroom gatherers, keen hunters or fishers, or farmers on their allotments or at their weekend cottages. It is in large modern societies that different ways of life can be interchanged and exist side by side, but within each society, a certain way of life is prevalent and characteristic. It always emerges through historical circumstances, based on local conditions and previous cultural development. Various ways of life cannot be linked up with precise historical periods. For example, agriculture first appeared some ten thousand years ago in Asia Minor, in modern rich countries it became a way of life for the minority, while it only reached large parts of Africa through colonisation, if at all. Nevertheless, it is more or less possible to arrange the different ways of life – the hunter-gatherer needs several square kilometres to live, a square kilometre can sustain up to a few dozen farmers, and only the industrial and post-industrial way of city life can sustain hundreds of people per one square kilometre. The interdependence of culture and density of population probably goes both ways – that Western Europe has historically been culturally ahead of Eastern Europe very neatly correlates with demographic data.

Different ways of life are not just more or less a thing of distant past, a curiosity; their traces – similar to the traces of biological evolution - can be found in modern society, and even in ourselves. For example, smiling is a gesture which links us to primates. The value we attach to the upright figure, and which we partly relinquish when we bow or curtsey, goes back to the early people, for whom it was a feature setting them apart from all other animals. The importance of communal meals, or Europeans' attachment to horses and dogs, have similar roots. Many of us, at least once a week, become keen farmers whose relationship to the soil and property resembles that of the Neolithic people. Outbursts of xenophobia are a reminder of the homogenous tribal societies, and a rejection of the urban society. The death of a loved one brings us closer to Gilgamesh or St. Augustine, and the sight of the night sky closer to Thales of Miletus, or Johannes Kepler. Our language is a well of such reminiscences of the conditions and context of life long gone. We could just carry on piling up more examples – each of us carries within them a sort of 'memory of humankind', usually without being even aware of it.* But thanks to this memory, we can understand our history – for it is ours.

Man emerges from pre-human nature as an animal living in established groups, on which an individual's survival depends. The species is characterised by the care of their young, by upright walk, and certain universality, or perhaps a lack of specialisation. Man can adapt to various living conditions and discovers new ways of communal living – he does not consume the food where he found it, but brings it back to the group's camp, where the successful hunter shares it out. Man experiences sexuality much more intensively: it is the basis of lasting bonds. The family relationships within the group are intricately structured, and various meanings are attached to them. Binding behavioural patterns are formed, first rituals and rules. Fixed relationships, concern for the future, and intensive communication lead to the development of speech, the world of symbols, of thinking and tools. Quite early on, especially in attitudes towards the dead, man's religion begins to emerge, oriented in particular on conspicuous and unusual manifestations of the power of nature. As man lives from day to day, his worries focus mainly on the present moment. He soon achieves astonishing virtuosity in symbolic expression, especially in depicting animals. Prehistoric cave paintings are not just some primitive magic; they also serve the purpose of capturing a fleeting moment (drawings of dancers or of animals which man did not actually hunt etc.) Man's hunter-gatherer way of life enables him to live in the inhospitable north, but it does not allow for a great density of population, nor can it

---

* The Swiss psychologist C. G. Jung spoke about the 'collective unconscious'.

support permanent settlements – for a group of hunter-gatherers to find enough food, several square kilometres per head are necessary.

The discovery of farming and domestication of animals would radically change man's way of life. This happened in the early Neolithic Age (late Stone Age), probably under pressure of harsh conditions and the first instance of overpopulation; and this is the first great revolution in the history of mankind. A farmer may have to work harder than a hunter-gatherer, but his livelihood is more reliable and less dependent on the mercies of the weather. A group makes a permanent settlement, which enables it to build more substantial and lasting dwellings, and it consists of families, or 'houses', which are capable of self-sufficient survival. The time-span of man's concerns broadens significantly, for several months pass between the sowing and the harvest, and the resulting harvest must often be made to last throughout the whole year. The amassing and storing of supplies grows in significance, and with it the possibility of hoarding property, the need to safeguard it, and the question of legacy. The desire of the farming man is the steadiness of conditions, providing the future for his family and the whole group. This is reflected in his religious orientation, the focus on his deceased ancestors, and the perpetuation of the family. Just a hundred years ago, the majority of Europe's population lived by farming; it only began to dwindle in the course of the 20th century.

Prolonged periods of peace and prosperity led to supplies and surplus being amassed, which created the possibility of barter, trade, and the primitive division of labour. This created in turn a higher demand for tools, especially metal ones, something which not everybody was able to make for themselves. In very rich areas, the conditions became right for establishing large settlements, whose inhabitants would make their living at least partly out of crafts, barter, and trade. Such settlements then became the centre of larger areas, which require road networks to be constructed, and they accumulated a fair amount of wealth, which attracted various vagabonds, as well as hoards of raiders, and which therefore had to be defended. The greater concentration of people also increased the importance of communication, as well as the number of conflicts, giving rise to the need for justice and law. Within these larger communities, a great deal more effort must be expended to maintain safety, and it was therefore here that the need arose to concentrate and stabilise power. The desire to maintain stable and lasting conditions, and to ensure them for eternity, was again reflected in religion – the cult now focused on the sun, and the heavens as a paragon of stability. The internal stability of the urban situation, however, depended on the whole population following the same cult – no aberrations were tolerated. The organisation was hierarchical and each individual had his or her unique and unchangeable place, into which they were born. They did not belong, nor could they live, anywhere else. That too strengthened stability. Particularly successful cities would become the centres of large areas, to concentrate great power and wealth. Some would grow to become the centres of large empires. The oldest written document of this way of life is the Epic of Gilgamesh, but homogenous urban societies lived like this until not very long ago.

Old myths consider the time when man began to sail the seas as the end of the Golden Age. Seafaring, the first fast and effective form of transport over long distances, meant at first merely the advance of trade; soon, however, it became a means of migration, a permanent resettlement of people. As early as the last centuries BC, large and wealthy cities appear in the Mediterranean, which are largely populated by people who were not born there. They do not have any roots there, nor are their ancestors buried there. The traditional aristocracy dwindles, and with it the hereditary legitimacy of the ruler. The first open societies are created, where people speak different languages, worship different deities (or none at all), societies which are ruled by an assembly or a tyrant, and where it is nothing out of the ordinary for a person to travel around and move about the whole of the civilised world. No one holds any position by birthright, and if a man wishes to achieve something, he must compete with others and to make his own way up in the world. The ruling power does not wield any traditional legitimacy, and it must rely on the citizens' consent. Thus the first traits of democracy emerge in these urban societies. Livelihood in the open city societies is provided by crafts and trade, and religion, which slowly retreats from public life, is no longer supported by indisputable tradition. That is why in cities of this type – Athens, Alexandria, Ephesus, or Rome – universalistic and individual religions (in particular Christianity) take hold.

Another far-reaching change in ways of life was brought about by mediaeval urban Christianity and its emphasis on personal responsibility, individuality and – in contrast to the ancient urban societies – the rehabilitation of work, husbandry, and of activities to do with providing a livelihood in general. The Reformation and modern thought further developed specialisation, production and banking, and it prepared the ground for the fusion of science and production in the form of technology. Then, finally, the Industrial Revolution burst forth in the early 19th century, which meant the dismantling of the traditional institutions and structures, a thorough individualisation of life, the advancement of industrial production and exchange over the self-sufficient production of farmers, mass migration of population in search of livelihood, and a rather utilitarian and pragmatic worldview: 'Truth is what works,' William James says. The programme of societies is explicitly the largest amount of happiness for the largest number of people, who are seen as individuals. This corresponds to the advancement of personal freedoms, the weakening of familial and interpersonal ties, and the predominance of the economic aspects of life over all others – prosperity and profitability become the determining values of society, and of its individual atoms – human beings. The generalised market becomes the means of asserting and enforcing these values.

The changes of the 20th century are so profound and rapid that we can confidently speak of a new way of life. We surely lack the necessary distance to attempt a balanced description, so let us simply mention its most conspicuous aspects. The predominant means of making a livelihood in rich countries is no longer industrial production, but the 'tertiary sphere' – banking, communications, and services. 'Workers' are outnumbered by 'employees'. The importance of transport, travel, and communication is sharply increasing. This way of life spreads beyond national borders and erases differences between traditional cultures. While one or two hundred years ago almost all city dwellers would supplement their income by farming, nowadays millions of country people commute to the city to earn their living. Technological progress increases the energy demands of human life and man has definitively made himself at home in an artificial world, severing his ties with nature – with the obvious exception of his food provision (though even that is 'mediated' through industry and retail). Night and day, summer and winter, all of these factors play an ever-diminishing role in our lives. It would be no wonder if the majority of the urban population did not notice them at all. The whole world becomes one big market of finance, commodities, goods, and ideas, which force even the most hidebound governments to consider that their borders are ceasing to be functional and the world is becoming one. After all, the problems they face – such as economic dependency, energy, climate, hunger, migration, or terrorism – are of a truly global nature. Is this progress? Is it a disaster? In any case, should western civilisation fail, it can no longer be assumed that another civilisation would take over and carry the torch, as used to be the case. For there is no longer any other civilisation.

Questions:

- Try to briefly describe the predominant 'way of life' in our society. Would you be able to trace any trends within it?
- Have you ever encountered another way of life? Try to compare it to your own.
- Describe the traces of previous ways of life that remain in our own way of life, behaviour, and habits. Would it be desirable to get rid of them? Why? Or why not?
- Why do city people like to travel so much, go to their weekend houses or camping?
- Which human characteristics and abilities are most highly valued amongst hunters, farmers, traders? Which are valued in our society?
- An important aspect of our way of life is the way we understand our place in the world. Could there be a connection between majority religions and the way people live in Europe, the U.S., India, or China?

30. Civilisation, Culture, and Religion

In the previous chapter, we attempted to survey our past, the journey that led to where we find ourselves today. We did so with a brevity that would surely make any historian's hair stand on end; all we can say in our defence is that history was actually not what we were concerned with. What we were interested in was the journey itself, the footprints that the past has left in our present time. The social sciences speak of a *diachronic view*. Such a view is however not meaningful by itself, but as a sort of preliminary exercise, in order to help us take a better look at the present in which we all live.* This is sometimes called the synchronic view. It is not at all easy to take a good look at the present, even though we swim in it like fish in water – precisely because we are so 'submerged' in it. On the one hand, it continually bombards us with an abundance of events, news, trouble, and opportunity. On the other hand, it is natural, even boring, to us, we all know what it is – in short, it is nothing special. Today, tomorrow, next month, it will probably be almost the same as it is today. What is there to see?

To see – as we already know – means to distinguish. Let us try to take a similar attitude to the one we started out with, but with a greater distance. After all, we spend most of our time performing mundane, banal activities, which we mastered a long time ago. They do not require too much thinking or problem-solving; we carry them out routinely day after day, and we could easily listen to music while doing them. For simplicity's sake, I propose that we call this layer of our experience *civilisational layer*. Every now and then, something will disrupt this cosy routine – an unexpected experience, a grave decision to be made, a real problem, or a sudden idea. Suddenly, one has something to face up to

---

* A deep insight in these problems can be found in Nietzsche's *On the Use and Abuse of History for Life*.

and one must call upon abilities and resources which often lie idle in our everyday, run-of-the-mill routine. This layer of experience could perhaps be labelled as *cultural*. And finally, it may happen that we will have reason to pause and become more aware of ourselves – where did I come from and what am I? What am I doing here, and to what end? This experience is rare and many may never have it at all; or perhaps they had it, but forgot all about it. But for those who did glimpse it, it can be very formative, and once in a lifetime may be quite enough to have an impact. It tends to occur in our youth rather than in adulthood, or at traumatic moments, such as the death of a loved one; or on the contrary, in moments of great happiness. I will call this the *religious layer* of experience.

The term civilisation drives from the Latin *civis* (citizen) and *civitas* (city). Where does this connection stem from? Why the city, exactly? Because there, where people set up communities according to their wishes, a layer of fairly safe routine could be separated from life as a whole, in which one does not have to watch one's every step, but can confidently walk along the pavement while thinking of something else. Our ancient ancestors, who lived in forests and saw mysterious, unfathomable, dangerous or hostile beings in everything around them, could not afford this kind of luxury. We have defined the layer of civilisation as the sphere of run-of-the-mill everyday routine, within which we, without much deliberation, use the available options, imitate the behaviour of others, and operate machines which we do not even slightly understand, and for which we need instruction manuals. As with social custom (which in fact forms part of it) this civilisational layer involves constant reliance on the way things are done, without giving it much thought.

This can be best demonstrated by extreme examples. An elderly lady in a story by James Thurber is obsessed by the fixed idea that electricity might 'leak' out of an empty socket. And a certain Japanese firm is said to have manufactured a copy of an American fighter aircraft during the war, but with an extremely complicated crankshaft. It later transpired that the Japanese had copied a damaged craft, whose crankshaft had been painstakingly rebalanced with numerous weights after an accident.

This learned, automatic ability to operate things without any thought may lead to such extreme caricatures, but it also has indisputable advantages. It is immensely time- and energy efficient, the tried and tested patterns of behaviour tend to be fairly safe, and not at all bad; and if everybody adheres to them, there is less scope for conflict.

The greatest advantage, though, seems to lie in the fact that 'civilisational' stereotypes are so easy to master. That is why modern civilisation has spread so successfully over the world in recent decades, albeit only in the form of being able to operate things which we did not create ourselves, of which we have no clue as to how and why they work, because that is simply something we do not need to know. The civilisational layer and its ubiquitous companion, the instruction manual, have purposefully separated from the deeper layers, and made quite sure to become as independent of them as possible. We have spoken of the emergence of mass production, the industrial revolution, and global trade. We are now so far down that road that it is possible for (affluent) people to buy practically the same goods, the same appliances and gadgets, anywhere in the world, with the manufacturers' guarantee that they will be able to use them without knowing an iota about how they work. Despite a certain amount of superficial (and always belated) scientific education in school, European man, too, spends most of his days operating things which he does not have a clue about. When they stop working, they are likely to be thrown out and replaced with new ones, complete with a new instruction manual – for what else is one to do?

The separation of this layer (the layer of learned handling of things), however, also separates man from other things, such as responsibility for his own actions. It is difficult to reproach a person for using various chemicals which damage the environment in which people have to live. And the same goes for people who say, and eventually also think, what they have read in the papers or seen on TV – they did not come up with the idea. And can we even blame someone for joining a political party which everyone is joining, or someone who starts shooting at his neighbours, because 'everyone knows' them to be our sworn enemies? On the one hand, such a person is certainly a victim of the propaganda of others, but on the other hand, by laying the blame at their door, he forfeits his freedom, and, effectively, his true humanity. This person's 'opinions' are actually not his, and they therefore cannot have any significance; and whose actions are this person's actions if he cannot be held responsible for them? This aspect of modern existence, the mass world of procurement, general gossip, and that what 'is being done' (*das Man*), has already been described by Heidegger, although he failed to note its more agreeable features. After all, what would he have thought had he walked into a restaurant in Freiburg only to find the tables had not been correctly set?

The easy and convenient manipulation of things somewhat overshadows the obvious fact that the civilisational layer cannot exist independently. Car drivers know nothing about the ways in which the cars they drive differ from the cars of ten years ago; and this is only right, as they have no need to know. The technical specifications of cars have already disappeared from car advertising, because customers are not interested in these things. But before a car can be advertised, someone else has to design, develop, and test it. The creative layer of life and the world, the cultural layer, serves the civilisation, keeps it running and supplies it with new products, as well as new ideas, which creates trends and patterns of behaviour; but only a small number of people are engaged in it. Toynbee speaks of 'creative minorities', whom the majority then imitate. Nowadays, the inhabitants of 'developing countries' are practically excluded from it, as are the consumerist majority of the 'developed' countries. All those who decide to go down the convenient, tried-and-tested route of copying at school, aping the more successful, and borrowing templates, exclude themselves from it. But even those who participate in it only get to see a small fraction of it, within their own 'field of expertise', which each can only discuss with that small number of those who share it – whether it be moulding plastic, researching the human genome, educating optometrists, or writing orchestral arrangements. It is vitally important for the spiritual health of society for people to be aware of this, and to at least channel their creativity into their pastimes and hobbies as amateurs, or collectors, since the society's demand for creativity is so low that they have to go without it in their daily life.

The world 'culture', which we have used as a working label here, also comes from Latin and derives from the word *colere*, to cultivate (as in the cultivation of crops). Hence we have agriculture, we can talk of corn culture, or of bacterial cultures. Simply put, culture means anything which will not be made by itself, something which it is necessary to tend to, with perseverance and purpose – in the full knowledge that there will be no immediate gratification. The European obsession with organisation and clarity has compelled the cultural sphere to somehow 'demarcate' itself. That is why we nowadays use the word culture in a different, much narrower sense, to describe a certain domain. Culture nowadays denotes theatre, literature, museums and galleries, while medicine, engineering, or carpentry are excluded from it. We also have culture agencies, trusts and ministries. But culture is not just the concern of a particular field. It is to be found wherever a profession or a craft is 'cultivated', whether it be in a kitchen, a laboratory, a workshop, or a studio. It is to be found wherever people devote themselves to their field, whatever it may be, if they rack their brains to solve problems and feel joy at their success. And it is absent where activities are merely performed by rote – even if the activity is writing poetry, composing symphonies, or writing philosophical treatises – where it has become a routine, a mere employment, or a means to an end.

Unlike civilisation, which creates distinguishable, albeit superficial communities, culture is left to the individual. It is a sphere of great risk, requiring courage and responsibility. Creative people stand out from the crowd, and as a result often do not have it easy. They can become the object of derision, or envy, or naive imitation. As they differ from their surroundings, many may think that that is the whole point. Snobs will then try to make themselves stand out by whatever means they can, by an unusual haircut or by the make of their car – and they will be amazed that it does not work. Creative people, on the other hand, may often suffer from feeling undervalued and frustrated, and they may overcompensate for it through focusing on their own uniqueness.

However, it is nowadays quite clear that creativity is the greatest treasure of a society and the main prerequisite of material success as well. The perceived independence of the civilisational layer, which can easily be transplanted anywhere, may lead to the false belief that this superficial 'civilisation' is all that it is required. But wherever the civilisational layer is entirely imported, involving no indigenous effort, people will live in a schizophrenic condition, in which there is no connection between the various layers. This kind of environment is, moreover, highly unstable – just as the civilisational layer suddenly appeared one day, it can be gone the next, as it has no roots in the local environment. If it is not fulfilling its function properly, there is nobody to fix it or improve it, and so people will tend just to get rid of it altogether, and procure a new one, as they have learned that this can be done. This is why democracy is so unstable in countries where this layer has been imported, and can be swept aside by tin-pot dictators at the first sign of trouble.

Culture belongs to the creative sphere of our lives, and is also fully in our hands. However its motives, impulses, and aims stand apart, governed by no one. Who can explain why a fairly successful pub landlord from Stratford-upon-Avon took up writing theatre plays at the age of twenty-five, and then abandoned the theatre twenty years later? Where did his astonishing mastery of the English language come from, when his education went no further than the local grammar school?

Where did he gain his psychological insight, since he had probably never heard of psychology? How did he come up with such great artistic ideas, having had no tutor? This is why people who have attempted artistic creation have always said that their work does not come from them directly, hinting instead at muses, inspiration and the suchlike. And if culture is a sphere of individuality, its sources are supremely private. That is why sensible people choose not to speak about them, at least not out loud and not in public. Those observing the creative process from the outside can only guess whether the ideas come from within, from the depths of the unconscious, or from above; it is, however, worth asking whether really is such a huge difference between the two. The great Christian theologian and writer St. Augustine, in his best works, repeatedly turns to God, about whom he however says that he 'is closer to my heart than I myself'. The important thing is that it is not me.

If we stick to verifiable historical facts, we cannot deny that all typically cultural activity stems from the sphere of religion. Architecture, theatre, dance, music, poetry, science, law, history, and writing all have their beginnings in the sacred atmosphere of a celebration, later of the temple. And not only that – their original, and often most popular themes and subjects come from there too. For there was a time when religion formed a continuous layer in the fabric of human societies and shaped their identity. It was Christianity which led the way to the separation of religion and state. It pushed through the idea of the independent individual, guided by his own conscience and responsible for his actions. It is in a society made up of such individuals that the focus of religion shifts into the intimate sphere and becomes a unique intimate relationship. What is this relationship about?

If philosophy grows out of a sense of wonder at reality, at the fact that life and the world are anything but obvious, then the religious person takes one step further in understanding his or her life as a gift or inheritance and wants to let his or her appreciation of it be known. The precarious nature of human life was obvious to everyone in ancient societies. Each spring (indeed each morning) was, for those who had lived to see it, a cause for celebration and a collective feast. In the same way, the coming of winter (or night) filled them with anxiety and led them to pray for help. Modern urban societies provide people with a far greater level of overall security, and in times of danger, they place emphasis on those areas in which we can help ourselves. Religion, therefore, loses its natural appeal, and perhaps only after withstanding a natural disaster or a war does some sort of collective feeling of thankfulness rise up again.

Thus, religion naturally becomes a part of a person's inner life, rather than being openly public. That, however, presents new opportunities for it to be more profound, heartfelt and true; and also more free.

Its underlying motive, however, does not change. Even in modern societies, life, happiness, family and friends cannot be bought, and the more sensitive among us are fully aware that they do not in any way merit their happiness. Once we have seen through the veil of the seeming naturalness of life and the casual consumption of everything that life offers, there opens up to us the possibility of encountering the realm of the Other – the realm of religious experience. The image of that Other, which is not only far greater than man, but also shows him great generosity, was for the ancient peoples primarily the sun, whose return they could every morning and every spring collectively celebrate. The Greeks fused this with the ideas of Goodness and Beauty, while for the Jews, the Other became a personal being, whom they can not only speak to, but who hears them as well. Christianity, which has its roots in Judaism, signifies the belief that in Jesus of Nazareth, God Himself became a man. He took upon himself the fate of mortal man, causing the religious relationship to open out to others, to our fellow human beings. 'If a man say, I love God and hateth his brother, he is a liar.'

As culture and civilisation began to emerge from the originally undifferentiated whole of the tribal religious culture, religion began to lose its social importance and it became more and more a part of the inner life of free people. It can, however, never become purely private, for its mission is to influence and inspire and to mediate something which is common to all people. It is from this pressing and compelling aspect of religion that the danger of its misuse arises; something which religions have succumbed to many times. In modern societies, this danger is two-sided. The first side is the traditional seduction of power, when religion ceases to serve, and rather seeks to rule and enforce. If a modern state begins to lean on religion, the outcome cannot be good. The other, perhaps less conspicuous danger is presented by the 'rogue', uncultivated forms of religion. For many people, religion addresses an urgent need that they feel within themselves. And if this need is not fully met within society, it can turn into a blind and destructive force. The tragic and cautionary tales of 'religious' terrorists, fundamentalist sects and their leaders bear witness to that.

Despite all of this, it seems likely that no society can permanently dispense with religion as an expression of an unconditional communing of people before the Other, to whom they owe all that they have. Only religion can be the foundation of unconditional relationships which do not bring any immediate advantages, and which will last no matter how difficult circumstances become. The relationships of basic trust, the ability to feel remorse for what we have done – even to assume responsibility for what we have not done. The willingness and ability to forgive and to help people and causes that are seemingly lost. In moments of crisis, what can save a society is that such relationships are found within it. According to an old Rabbinical tradition, the world can only go on because so far, at least twelve just people can be found in it (although these twelve never know themselves to be such). On the other hand, in societies accustomed to long-term peace and prosperity, religion can help alleviate the feelings of futility and ennui which often assail people. It can open our eyes to the needs of others, to the beauty of bravery, purity, modesty, and selfless action, thus giving meaning to human freedom.

Questions:

- Characterise the layers of civilisation, culture, and religion. What are their typical features?
- Do you have any personal experience with them? When do you find yourself in each one? Do you notice any transition from one to the next?
- Try to explain the difference between a professional and an amateur (in art, science, sport, etc).
- Do you have a hobby? How do you relate to the professionals in that field?
- When does a chef find himself or herself in the cultural layer? Or a poet, a scientist, or an engineer?
- What is the role of routine (or 'going through the motions') in the arts, science and education? What form does it take? Can we do without it? What happens when the other two layers disappear and we are left with only routine?

31. Tolerance and Pluralism

The word tolerance is mentioned a lot these days, and many among us feel that tolerance is a precious and scarce thing. After years of extreme intolerance, it is, after all, hardly surprising, and tolerance is an important human characteristic. But this is not an area that can be entirely free of doubt. Is 'tolerance' not too vague a term? Tolerance of what? And to what extent? Is tolerance always appropriate? Surely there are some things which we must simply never tolerate. And is tolerance in important matters – matters of personal conviction – really anything more than an abnegation of truth, a demonstration of indifference, or even of cowardice?

Tolerance is the ability and willingness to put up with things that we do not like; I cannot say to my wife or girlfriend that I tolerate her – she would quite rightly take offence. We can stand, or tolerate, heat or hunger, an obnoxious boss, noisy neighbours, or talkative colleagues. Why do we actually put up with these things? Either because they does not bother us all that much, or simply because nothing can be done about them anyway. A friend of mine lives above a rock club; at first he tried to make them cut the noise down, at least late at night, but when he realised that this was not possible, he simply had to arrange his affairs so that he could put up with it as best as he could. Tolerance has a similar meaning in technology. Design engineers know that no component can be manufactured with absolute precision, so they make allowances for this by specifying a margin of error which will not hamper the functioning of the machine as a whole. This is called the *tolerance field*. If a crankshaft is to have a diameter of 20 millimetres, it can be some few hundredths less, and the hole in the bearing some few hundredths more, for the shaft to turn in the bearing with some (but not too much) give. If the shaft and the bearing are within the tolerance field, all is well; if they exceed it, they have to be scrapped. Similarly, a boss will tolerate his or her employees turning up maybe five minutes late for work, but no more than that, because that would not end well.

A negative attitude to what we tolerate is thus inherent in the term tolerance – we would never use it about a person or thing we value or are fond of. In addition, tolerance is always dependent on the particular level of annoyance which we tolerate, not exceeding a certain limit. Enough is enough. So to be very tolerant would mean to try to have as large a tolerance field as possible – ten minutes instead of five, ninety decibels instead of eighty. Is that the way to go? Surely not. Besides, there are some things which are so important that there can be no room for tolerance. The state and the police may tolerate petty crime up to a certain (small) amount; but the printing of fake banknotes cannot be tolerated under any circumstances. No margins can be set here, and those convicted will end up behind bars, even if they had only managed to print a single low-value note.

After all, the line between what annoys me and what does not is neither very distinct nor permanently fixed; the noise which does not bother us in the slightest one day can turn us red with fury the next. If things are going well and I am in a good mood, I can put up with a little annoying thing – I will shrug it off, then have a laugh at it. After all, I am a tolerant person, am I not? But if I have a bad day, have an argument with my wife, or if something has not gone to plan, or I am distracted by worry or anxiety – then, suddenly, things are different. Suddenly, everyone appears to be conspiring against me, deliberately trying to thwart me. That man who pushed me on the bus had a strange expression on his face, and the old nag at the shop – that was no coincidence. What I did not mind one bit yesterday suddenly turns into a full-blown tragedy. Ah, so that's the game you want to play? Well, just you wait. I will not leave it at that, you can be sure of that! What – I should be more tolerant? That'll be the day!

This is unfortunately not restricted to trivial everyday matters. The same applies between groups of people and between whole nations. From the Enlightenment until the rise of Hitler, Jews in Germany lived in peace, and were mostly treated as respected citizens. But then came defeat in World War I, hyperinflation and economic crisis – and suddenly, everything changed. All the certainties of a civilised society collapsed, and people started frantically looking around for someone to blame. Suddenly, there was a rich breeding ground for demagogy, which would destroy millions of human lives. In the former Yugoslavia, people lived in peace until recently, and still just one year before the conflict, nobody there could believe that something so terrible could happen. They managed quite nicely, smiling at each other, tolerating each other for their respective differences – it was no big deal. But then circumstances took a turn for the worse, inflation came along, stripping people of their assets, and everyone started looking round to find someone to blame. Someone to pour out their anger and frustration on. Suddenly people started noticing that their neighbours looked a bit strange – 'better keep an eye on them.' Well, those neighbours had exactly the same thoughts, and then, one day they may have seen each other bringing home a gun or an axe. And then the trouble would start. What used to be no big deal and could be tolerated suddenly became a mortal danger, and neighbours became enemies overnight. Thus, a human society cannot be built merely on people not minding each other; that would be pitifully little to build on.

But is there any more that we can do? How are we to behave towards those who are different from us? Could they perhaps be of some importance? Let us consider this question from a different angle. While there still are many people dying of hunger in the world, it is thanks to grain cultivators that the number is not double still. They have tried for centuries to grow wheat and corn with the highest yield possible, which could withstand drought, poor soil, and which would be resistant against parasites. They finally succeeded – they cultivated the best variety and started to grow it everywhere. But then, disaster struck – a new, unknown parasite appeared which thrived on this particular variety, and it decimated the entire crop. Previously, when the same variety of wheat did not grow everywhere, only a part of the overall crop would be destroyed. When the potato blight appeared in Ireland in 1845, over a million people died during the famine which ensued, because the entire country's crops had been decimated.

Thus the cultivators made an important discovery – no variety, not even the best one, is so good that we could rely on it alone. Even if it had the best properties, we can never test its resilience against every blight and parasite, because we do not even know them all. The blights, on the other hand, will try everything; after all, they have nothing else to do and as soon as they spot a window of opportunity, the will set to work. The disaster will be the greater, the more we grow the same variety of wheat all over the world. Therefore, there must always be a backup of other varieties, perhaps with a slightly lower yield, but resilient to unknown parasites. And since cultivators can only work with what they have found in the natural world, they began working on the preservation of as many varieties as possible – biodiversity, in other words. As early as two or three hundred years ago, they began to gather and collect seeds of cultivated and semi-cultivated plants all over the world, but not to put them in a museum or in a herbarium, but because we might well need them one day.

Successful cultivators of wheat naturally know that their new variety is better than all the previous ones, that it is the least demanding and the most high-yielding variety. But nowadays, they will also know that that alone is not enough and that it never will be. That is why modern-day biologists will travel to far-off parts of the world in order to persuade the local farmers not to give up on their traditional varieties, so that they do not completely disappear. Large countries have their own genetic banks, where seeds of thousands of varieties of plants are kept, which it is necessary from time to time to sow and to harvest new seeds, so that the seeds do not lose their germinative capacity.

People have experienced something similar within their own species. Modern societies and ways of life put subtle yet highly effective pressure on all of us to be the same. All over the world, we wear jeans, learn English, listen to similar music, live in high-rises, and hope to own a detached house. There are certain advantages to this – no matter which city we travel to, we will not be terribly conspicuous, we will have a fair idea of how to get around, we will be able to communicate. But there is also one big disadvantage, or danger, to be more precise. Where people are the same, they will fall prey to the same 'parasites'. Not just biological ones, either – we have doctors and medicines to deal with that – but above all ideological ones. And an ideological epidemic can prove more terrible than cholera. The events of the 20th century are testimony to that.

The Nazi epidemic focused primarily on Jews, but also on Roma and others. These victims most likely saw before everyone else that it was an epidemic, and they would perhaps have been able to put up some resistance, but they were in the minority, and the majority did not hear their warnings and did not come to their aid. Perhaps the majority felt it was a good riddance. The communist epidemic fell most heavily on farmers, religious people, and many others besides. How is it that such epidemics are possible in the modern world? Because people are too similar to each other, and are easily swayed by the same demagogy. There is therefore no other defence against ideological parasites than diversity and variety of options. That is why democratic societies nurture a variety of political parties, because we know very well that a society with only one party is no good. This is why it does not bother us today if people have the craziest opinions, as much as it would bother us if everybody thought exactly the same. Because a society where everybody is the same is a totalitarian regime in waiting. And the waiting will be over sooner rather than later.

When such a totalitarian regime has done its worst and when it is finally overturned, it is as if everyone wakes up, and feels a tiny bit ashamed of themselves – how could we have allowed ourselves to be so manipulated? We have to start afresh, from the beginning; and we shall go about it quite differently this time. But if everyone says that, it can easily happen that they will all fall into the same trap again. When World War II was over, too many people at once had the idea that communism would be the best defence against Nazism. And there it was again. Everyone the same, yet again.

This amazing discovery that people around us who are different and annoy us by being that way, are (or can be, in certain decisive moments) the only early warning mechanism against a collective 'dummification', in other words, against totalitarianism, is called pluralism. Note that this does not imply any sort of boundless tolerance. It means the ability to see in others, those who are not like us, merit and potential which we do not possess, or which we have at any rate not yet discovered in ourselves. It is important to notice that the advantage comes not from their being different as such,* but from the mutual ability and willingness to communicate, to keep up a dialogue. ('Four eyes see better than two' – or in other words, two people can benefit from sharing their views.) And it will be ascertained with finality once some ideological parasite attacks, who will try to gather us like sheep and wrap us round his little finger. Because if I can be fooled like that, all those who are like me can be fooled as well. There is even more to this though. Four eyes do not only mean greater security, but a greater chance to glimpse a better solution, to see opportunities.

Unlike tolerance, which views our neighbours who differ as an inconvenience which we should put up with, pluralism says that we should value their being different. Tolerance will lead us to keeping them within certain limits, that is, trying to diminish the gap between us and them – surely, they should assimilate to our ways a little too. Hence all the assimilation tendencies, which tend to be a springboard for conflicts,

---

* As the multiculturalists somewhat naively suppose.

nationalistic ones in particular. Pluralism certainly understands that *we* cannot be like *them* – and *they* cannot be like *us*. In short, we are different from each other. But pluralism does not see this as a mere inconvenience, but rather as a very useful quality or at least an opportunity. That is certainly a big difference. But is it even possible? Has anyone actually achieved it? We are aware of historical periods of tolerance (periods of prosperity tend to be like that) but has pluralism ever been achieved?

Pluralism is not some mass statistical feature of a society; it is the inner ability and conviction of individual people. There may have not been any pluralistic societies so far, but examples of marked pluralism can be traced very far back, and even where no one would think to look for them. One is to be found in the Bible. When, around 500 BC, after returning from captivity, anonymous Jewish scholars were putting together old documents and traditions, it struck them how different, and often contradictory, they were. But these scholars in their wisdom did not attempt to 'unify' them. They left them as they were and placed them alongside each other. At the very beginning of the Bible, the creation of the world is described. If you read the text carefully, you will find that it contains two different narratives (Genesis 1:1 – 2:3 and Genesis 2:4 – 3), which agree in one detail – that the world is God's creation. They differ in everything else. The first depicts the creation through the eyes of an impartial witness, who watches step by step the creation of the whole universe, and finally the creation of man. Everything is good and everything will turn out well in the end. The second is seen through the eyes of the first man, Adam, and sees the garden, trees, animals. He looks for a companion and finds one in woman. He hears for the first time that something is forbidden, only to go on to disobey the order. For that, the punishment and the curse follow. It is a drama which does not end well, and only a glimmer of hope remains. Despite that, both texts can hold such a prominent place side by side. Perhaps that is the reason why the Bible is still a living book. When Christian scholars were putting together the New Testament, they found themselves in a similar situation. Regarding the most important subject, the life and death of Jesus of Nazareth, they had four different accounts available to them, which we now know as the four Gospels. They resisted the temptation to rework them into one story, and kept them as they were. In the later history of Christianity, intolerance gained the upper hand. But there is something which can be traced right back to its roots, which enables us to overcome intolerance, and in a much better way than a bit of condescending, superficial tolerance.

The fact that we all differ from one another may sometimes be a hindrance in our everyday lives, and we can all get a bit upset about it from time to time. But those who want their children to live in a free society now know that these annoying people – the minorities, factions and parties, which they do not belong to or agree with – should not only be tolerated, but perhaps also valued. It could well happen that, one day, they will save us from something even worse than Nazism or communism.

Questions:

- Describe various situations when we speak of tolerance.
- What is tolerance determined by? What helps to expand or restrict it?
- In what way does tolerance differ from pluralism? Why do we value the diversity of people? Why is it important in nature?
- When do different groups of people tend to annoy each other most?
- When is it best for different groups to live 'together apart'? When is it necessary? Consider that, usually, one group is stronger than the other.
- What is the importance of being able to speak a foreign language (or more)?
- What makes cohabitation of different groups easier? Side by side, as neighbours?

32. Man and the World

A long time ago, at the dawn of history, humans not only lived in the world, they were also a natural part of it. As they gradually built up their cultural distance over millennia, and strengthened their position, they shed their dependence on the environment – and by so doing also excluded themselves from it. The giant Enkidu in the Epic of Gilgamesh lives in the woods with animals, but as soon as he moves to the city, animals begin to run away from him. This rift has been completed by modern science and philosophy. In the vision of modern rationalism, there is man as a thinking and ruling subject, pitted against the world, a jumble of dead objects, raw materials and resources, mechanical machines, all governed by the laws of physics. Incidentally, physics itself at the time forgot that it had ever started out as a natural science, with animate nature as its subject – the Greek *fysis* stems from the verb *fyó*, to be born, to grow, to propagate. On the other hand, philosophy rather overlooked that in order for man to think, he must first grow up and will always need to eat.

It is to the credit of the natural sciences that in the 19th century they started to bridge this terrible rift with reality. Perhaps only in part, hesitantly and against much resistance; but it did happen. Starting with Lamarck and Darwin, with the idea of evolution, there appeared the first tangible bridge between nature and the human race. It only went one way, however, and science could not have it otherwise. Man became for these sciences a part of this world, which until recently, was viewed as dead matter – and had been treated accordingly. Nowadays, science does not see the world as dead, but it is still constrained within the limits of exact measurements, necessary causes, and the possibility of reliable mastery of nature. It is owing to science that man is now included in this sphere. Man, too, can be measured, our bodies, too, are governed by the principle of causality. We can even measure human society, and find a number of regularities (perhaps even laws) within it.

Now it is the other party's turn. It is up to philosophy to demonstrate and establish that its point of view, the view from within, which does not seek to govern things but to understand them, can be applied to nature, technology, to the whole world. So far, science seems to be one step ahead in this role. For example, Konrad Lorenz's research into animal behaviour has clearly shown that we, as people, can understand animals, and that the anthropomorphisms we rely on when, say, describing the behaviour of wild geese, are in fact entirely justifiable. There are signs of similar shifts elsewhere, too. As the balance of power between man and nature has shifted, so, too, has our attitude towards nature. Passing by the office of a nature protection agency, I noticed in the window a stuffed eagle, which had been shot by a keen hunter in East Bohemia about a hundred years ago – and this man's great-grandchildren had gifted it to the nature protection people – what would their great-grandfather have said?

Typically, the modern person's attitude towards nature is certainly very inconsistent, sometimes cheap and sentimental, often aggressive and ruthless. But there are some perceptible changes. If they are somewhat superficial, based on impressions, unsystematic and inconsistent: well, philosophy is to blame for that. Who else is to lay the foundations of the bridge to lead man to nature? Science has only opened our eyes to the exact and measurable 'natural' aspects of man. What else but philosophy can point out the 'human' aspect of nature?

But when I talk now of philosophy and philosophers, I am in fact talking about us. You, bold reader, who have stuck with this book and reached these final pages, and me. We are now at the end of our whistle-stop tour of the terrain of philosophy – for sure, a very brief and superficial tour. But we have not undertaken it in order to receive definitive answers as to how exactly things stand. These kinds of answers to questions can be provided by science – and perhaps even by bureaucracy – but certainly not by philosophy. We have undertaken this tour through the world of ideas in order to remind ourselves of various areas of human life that are worth spending time thinking about. We did it in order to understand that philosophy does not always have to begin with the ever-popular questions about 'being' and so on; it can start anywhere. Or, to be more precise, anywhere where there is something for us to wonder at, something to be amazed by, or even just surprised by. All such things, however banal and mundane they may appear at first glance, contain within them some sort of mystery for a person who has learned to think and to see – whether it be a wet tarmac road in summer, the tune to Yellow Submarine, a scientific proof, time, money, or virtue.

These are all tasks, or rather opportunities for thought. Not just now, at school and during lectures, but afterwards. Especially afterwards. And it is the task of philosophy to maintain the awareness of the reality that wherever we turn, there are countless wondrous and amazing things, which beg to be pondered over. Why should anyone do that? The reason is twofold. Firstly, it can happen that by doing that, they will come up with a new idea, or they will discover or create something – an invention, a scientific discovery, a poem. Or they may simply learn to live surrounded by mysteries, which are, however, not at all 'mysterious', that is to say inaccessible, encoded and enigmatic, but profound and vital. They do not have to be conquered like Antarctica; but they wait for a person who will stop and wonder. People who have completely forgotten about them lose their own depth, and in the end their humanity. Philosophy should be here in order for us not to forget, not to lose our humanity.

But there is another, more immediate and pressing task. European civilisation once set itself the goal of ensuring the best living conditions for the greatest number of people. (Those who were talking about 'happiness' itself, probably did not know what they were saying.) This goal has now, at least in some parts of the world, been almost achieved. It has provided us with safety, comfort, and freedom to an extent which ordinary people throughout history could not have dreamed of. Now, it appears to be at a crossroads, not knowing which way to go. Besides, the realisation is beginning to sink in that it has only been successful in one part of the world, and that it may never succeed in the rest – our earth could not support such a load. And even the status quo is untenable – and those who have so far been short-changed want their share of the wealth, comfort and prosperity. It is becoming obvious to thinking people that the richer ones – and that means us, too – will have to curb their material demands. That means me, you, us. There are even some brave people who have started doing this of their own accord. They save energy and water, recycle their waste, cycle instead of driving, and they do not feel the need to have everything that money can buy.

But so far, the coherence of affluent modern societies, and their inner peace, has been founded on economic growth, on the hope that things will keep getting better forever. No politician can approach the electorate with a programme of perpetual self-restriction, and hope to stay in politics – the next election would see him or her ousted in no time. The more responsible among them at least try to convey the idea in a roundabout way, speaking of 'sustainable growth'. But it is only possible to sustain growth (in the long term or even the short term) which is not material and which makes no material demands. That was once the goal of Diogenes, of monks and hermits – individuals and small groups of devoted people. Today, mankind is faced with the task of devising and implementing such a civilisation for everyone. Naturally this must be done without the use of violence, for violence is not the way, and while maintaining freedom, because there would be no point in it otherwise. And that is a tall order. So far, we are just waiting for ideas, for brave and wise, and patient people who will – hopefully – take them up.

Jan Sokol

Thinking about Ordinary Things
A Short Invitation to Philosophy

Published by Charles University
Karolinum Press
Ovocný trh 560/5, 116 36 Prague 1, Czech Republic
Prague 2017
Translated by Markéta Pauzerová and Neil Cairns
Edited by Alena Jirsová
Cover and layout by Jan Šerých
Typeset by DTP Karolinum Press
Printed by Karolinum Press
First English Edition, First Reprint

ISBN 978-80-246-2229-3